"DEATH SEEM'D TO STARE":
The New Hampshire and Rhode Island Regiments at Valley Forge

Joseph Lee Boyle

Copyright © 2005 by Joseph Lee Boyle
All Rights Reserved.

Printed for
Clearfield Company, Inc. by
Genealogical Publishing Co., Inc.
Baltimore, Maryland
2005

International Standard Book Number: 0-8063-5267-1

Made in the United States of America

TABLE OF CONTENTS

Preface..iv

Introduction..vii

Glossary...xvi

Locations Mentioned...xxii

New Hampshire Name Index..1

Rhode Island Name Index...104

Bibliography..172

PREFACE

While the six-month encampment of the Continental Army at Valley Forge in 1777-1778 has been part of America's folklore for generations, most of the men who served there have remained anonymous. The names of over 30,000 men of all ranks appear on the surviving monthly muster and payroll records. This compilation is the third volume of an effort to recognize some of these heroes of the Revolutionary War.

The information in the Name Index has been abstracted from Record Group 93, M 246, "Revolutionary War Rolls, 1775-1783," at the National Archives in Washington, D.C. Microfilm copies can be found at the branches of the National Archives and at some larger libraries. Microfilm rolls 43-44 cover the First New Hampshire from 1777-1783; rolls 45-47 the Second; rolls 47-48 the Third; roll 85 the First Rhode Island; and rolls 85-87 the Second Rhode Island. This list does not include men in the cavalry and artillery regiments.

It must be noted that men were not required to enlist in a regiment from their home state. There was always competition for recruits, and as these regiments spent over a year in New York, New Jersey and Pennsylvania, it is likely that some men from these states joined the New Hampshire and Rhode Island ranks.

The information which follows in the Name Index has been taken from the muster and payrolls. The muster rolls were usually compiled in the early part of each month for the preceding month. Men are shown by company, with name and rank. Any alterations which happened during the month are shown, usually with the date it occurred. These include men joining and leaving the company for various causes and being promoted. Though the reports are for the preceding month, it cannot be assumed that a man who appears as "on command" for example, was in that status for an entire month. Such annotation indicates a soldier's status on the day a given roll was compiled.

The rolls were not compiled within consistent periods after the end of the month. Most of the rolls for December 1777 are dated January 2 and 4, 1778. However, the rolls for June 1778 are largely dated July 13 for the Rhode Island regiments and July 22 and 23 for those from New Hampshire. The latter can be accounted for by the fact that the Army had been on the move for several weeks after leaving Valley Forge and had fought in the Battle of Monmouth on June 28. As these were status reports, a man who appears as "sick absent" on a June roll may not have been sick at all in June, but become sick in July. The December New Hampshire rolls actually cover the period from September 1, 1777, through December 31, 1777.

The payrolls were derived from the muster rolls. These were also kept on a monthly basis and ideally, though rarely, the men were paid on a monthly basis for the preceding month. In practice, the pay was usually several months behind and the non-financial notations on payrolls may be less accurate. Where discrepancies are noted on the date a man enters or leaves the service, the payroll is probably more accurate than the muster roll, as the regimental paymaster was audited on his disbursements.

The companies are known by the name of the company captain. In some cases the captain had left the army, but his company continued to be listed for some months under his name, which sometimes causes confusion. Captain Frederick M. Bell of the Second New Hampshire died on October 9, 1777, from wounds received on September 17, but his company was known as "late Captain Bells" through June 1778. Captain Silas Talbot of the First Rhode Island was promoted to Major on December 24, and while his company continues under his name, he disappeared from the rolls.

For the most part the original rolls are reasonably legible. However, in some cases they are extremely poor. Brackets indicate illegible or questionable words. There is no June roll for the Field and Staff of the First New Hampshire, and the June roll for Bell's company of the Second New Hampshire is mostly illegible.

The reader should be very much aware that many of the names on the original lists have multiple spellings. For last and first names, the two most common spellings are shown. Some names appear with numerous variations such as those of Privates Charles Doritey/Dorrity/Dorithey/Dorathy/Derrity of the First New Hampshire and Jabez McBride/Bride/Bird/Bridee/McBrid/M'Bridez of the Second. There are probably other variations for the time periods before and after Valley Forge. In cases where no dominant spelling appears, the rolls have been checked forwards or backwards from the Valley Forge time period to find the most common variations. Additional variations can be found for some men on the rolls before and after the Valley Forge period. In these cases only the names shown on the rolls from December 1777 through June 1778 inclusive are used.

A common problem was that the record keeping was often months behind for men who had been sent to distant hospitals or were left behind on special duty. Lewis Billes of the First Rhode Island appears on the rolls for January-March 1778, but the April roll shows him as dead on January 20.

Some men were fortunate in being resurrected from the grave by the Army's paperwork. Gideon Dexter of the Second Rhode Island is shown dead on March 1, 1778, but reappears as sick at Princeton and Yellow Springs on the rolls of April-June. Uriel Wilber appears dead on February 30 [*sic*], but on the June

1778 payroll he received pay back to March 1 with the notation "taken prisoner 28th February."

A number of men appear as deserting and then returning. This may account for some of the gaps in the records for other men. Some may have deserted for a month or two, then returned, and the individual preparing the roll never noted the soldier's absence. Those who are interested in a particular individual before or after the Valley Forge Encampment should check the rolls for the months before or after Valley Forge or request a copy of the soldier's service record from the National Archives in Washington.

There are some men who appear on a single roll and then disappear without notation. They may have enlisted and then rapidly deserted or died. Some of these notations could be clerical errors or extreme errors in spelling, and some of these mysteries will never be clarified. George Ham appears as enlisting on May 1, 1777, in the Second New Hampshire but does not appear on a roll until June 1778. A Joseph Chace is shown to have deserted from the First Rhode Island on February 6, 1778, and a man of that name appears in the June roll of Second Rhode Island. It seems likely to be the same individual, but as two individuals named Trueworthy Dudley appear at the same time for seven months in two different New Hampshire regiments, assumptions about names can lead to errors.

Sergeant Jeremiah Greenman of Shaw's Company, Second Rhode Island, appears on the January 1778 roll as "recruiting" and on the rolls without comment through June. However, according to his published diary, he left for Rhode Island on January 10, 1778, and did not return to Valley Forge until May 29. Contemporary clerical error is the only explanation for such discrepancies.

The Rhode Island regiments show major changes for May and June. Cole's Dexter's, Flagg's and Lewis's Companies of the First have no rolls for May, and in June all the privates are different; Arnold's Company has rolls for May and June, but nearly all the privates are different. Clark's, Wallen's and Tolbut's Companies have no rolls after April. This is due to a major reorganization with the arrival of large numbers of African-American recruits from Rhode Island, which resulted in the movement of the white soldiers from the First to the Second Rhode Island, and African-Americans already in the Second moving to the First. These men are represented in this work by an entry for each regiment they are in due to frequent spelling discrepancies. Joseph Matthewson/ Mathewson, who appears in the First Rhode Island from December 1777 through April 1778 and Joseph Mattison who appears in the Second in May-June 1778 are likely the same individual, but no notation of a transfer confirms this.

INTRODUCTION

There are few regimental histories for units in the Revolutionary War. In several cases there are histories of the regulars, then called the Continental Line, of a given state. However, only one has been done for the regiments which served from the States of New Hampshire or Rhode Island. Frederick Kidder's *History of the First New Hampshire* is useful but was published in 1868. The best single source is Robert K. Wright's *The Continental Army*. This gives a short sketch of each regiment with an excellent bibliography for further reading.

In June 1775, the Continental Congress adopted the army of New Englanders besieging the British in Boston and appointed George Washington of Virginia as Commander in Chief of the Continental Army. Washington inherited what were essentially New England state forces with short terms of enlistment. Throughout the Fall of 1775 into the Spring of 1776, Congress authorized the formation of various regiments by the states in a piecemeal fashion while Washington and his officers strove to establish a coherent organization. These new units also had short term enlistments.

At the end of 1776, most of the enlistments for Continental troops expired. Congress had anticipated the problem of a disappearing army and had passed a resolve for eighty-eight battalions, or regiments, on September 16, 1776. This was intended to be an army for the duration of the war. However, efforts to recruit the new organization were ineffectual, and in January 1777 Washington was left with only a small cadre of veterans.

New Hampshire's quota for the new army in 1777 was three regiments, the core of which were three existing regiments; two others were allowed to disband, but some of these men probably joined the new units. Rhode Island dropped from four to two regiments, with the best officers and some of the men filling vacancies in the newly designated First and Second Rhode Island. The state legislatures reorganized their officer corps and made strenuous efforts to fill the regiments. However, most of the regiments did not achieve substantial numbers until April and May 1777.[1]

The British plan in 1777 was to cut the United States in half with a British army advancing south from Canada under General John Burgoyne. Burgoyne was to advance to Albany while other British troops moved up along the Hudson River from New York and down the Mohawk River Valley to meet him. After being defeated in two engagements against an American Army under Horatio Gates, Burgoyne was forced to surrender at Saratoga, which ended that threat.

---

[1]. Robert K. Wright, Jr., *The Continental Army*, (Washington: Government Printing Office, 1986), 110.

The second major British initiative of the year found General William Howe in late August with a British fleet at the head of the Chesapeake Bay. Howe landed in Cecil County, Maryland, and began to advance, defeated Washington at the Battle of Brandywine, and captured the American capital of Philadelphia.

Washington launched a surprise attack on the enemy positions on October 4, but he was defeated and forced to withdraw. After Germantown, the opposing armies licked their wounds. The British withdrew and fortified themselves in Philadelphia. They also began their "river assault" of nearly six weeks to clear the Delaware of obstructions and subdue the American strong points of Fort Mifflin south of Philadelphia and Fort Mercer on the New Jersey side of the river. This was critical for the British to be able to communicate with their fleet and bring up supplies and reinforcements.[2]

The actions of the British in New York kept both the New Hampshire and Rhode Island regiments on different courses until November 1777, when both joined Washington in Pennsylvania. In response to a summons from George Washington to the New Hampshire Committee of Safety, the three regiments of New Hampshire troops arrived at Ticonderoga, New York, in late May.

They remained there until the advance of John Burgoyne's army from Canada force forced the evacuation of that and the nearby posts. During the withdrawal, the British advance caught up to the Americans on July 7 at Hubbardton, Vermont, where the most of the New Hampshire men first tasted battle, and continued what proved to be a long and humiliating retreat.

Over two months later, the Continental Army in the north had been reinforced enough to stand and fight. On September 19, at the Battle of Freeman's Farm, the left wing of the army, including the New Hampshire men, fought three desperate hours under Major General Benedict Arnold against the best in the British Army, while the enemy held the field; the nearly 600 casualties they suffered crippled their advance.

Burgoyne waited eighteen days and sent out a reconnaissance in force to determine if an assault on left of the American position would be successful. The Continentals replied with three columns, one of which was Enoch Poor's Brigade with the New Hampshire troops, which fought against the elite British grenadiers who were "swept away by the ferocious charge."[3] This led to the Burgoyne's surrender at Saratoga on October 17, the biggest American victory to date.

---

[2]. John F. Reed, *Campaign to Valley Forge*, (Pioneer Press, 1965), 269-87.

[3]. For a description of this campaign see: Richard M. Ketchum, *Saratoga: Turning Point of the Revolutionary War*, New York: Henry Holt, 1997.

After his victory at Saratoga, Horatio Gates ordered four of his brigades, including the New Hampshire regiments, to march down the Hudson River Valley and join Israel Putnam. Washington in turn ordered them, as well as other brigades, to reinforce him in Pennsylvania.

Unfortunately, some of the New Hampshire men decided they had seen enough action without pay. On November 7, Major General Israel Putnam wrote to Washington from Fish Kill, New York, that "for want of pay, General Poor's brigade of Continental troops have refused to cross the North River. The troops mutinied, the officers endeavouring to suppress them, and they so determined to go home, that a Captain, in the execution of his duty, ran a soldier through the body, who soon expired, but not before he shot the Captain through, who is since dead." Putnam further reported that he was trying to obtain money to pay the men who were in the meantime "they are curing themselves of the itch." He remarked that paying the troops after a mutiny "is a bad precedent, but it is a worse one to keep troops ten months without pay."

Five days later Alexander Hamilton wrote Washington from New Windsor, New York, that Poor's Brigade was delayed again in marching as they were "under an operation for the itch, which made it impossible for them to proceed." Hamilton said that Poor informed him that he would march that morning. Poor's Brigade, which included two regiments of New York men, arrived at Washington's camp at White Marsh on November 22. Washington was happy to receive the reinforcements but was dismayed to discover that "many of them are very deficient in the Articles of Shoes, Stockings, Breeches and Blankets."[4]

The Rhode Island regiments had quietly spent the summer in the Hudson Highlands of New York as part of Israel Putnam's force. The British invasion of Pennsylvania, the American defeat at the Battle of Brandywine, and subsequent maneuvers prompted Washington to call for reinforcements. On September 10 Washington had ordered General Israel Putnam to send 1,500 troops from Peekskill to New Jersey to repel an expected British invasion there. Four days later, after the British had landed at Elizabeth Town and Second River, New Jersey, Washington asked Putnam for 1,000 more men. Learning that Putnam had delayed his response and only sent 900 men, Washington on September 23

---

[4]. Alexander Hamilton to Washington, 12 November 1777, Hamilton Papers, Library of Congress. Washington to Henry Laurens, 23 November 1777, *The Writings of George Washington from the Original Manuscript Sources, 1745-1799*, ed. John C. Fitzpatrick (Washington: Government Printing Office, 1933), *WGW*, 10:101.

peremptorily ordered the full 2,500 men be sent to join him and that, "No considerations are to prevent it."[5]

On October 7 Washington ordered General Varnum, who was marching to join the main army, to send the First and Second Rhode Island Regiments to "throw themselves into the Fort at Red Bank on the Jersey Shore....with the utmost dispatch...." The next day he wrote Colonel Christopher Greene "that the post with which you are intrusted is of the utmost importance to America....The whole defence of the Delaware absolutely depends upon it...."[6] The next day Washington reversed himself and ordered the Second Rhode Island to join the main army, but on October 16 he changed his mind and sent the Second to join the First at Fort Mercer, also known as Red Bank. The Second joined the First Rhode Island at Fort Mercer on 18 October. The Delaware River was blocked by rows of underwater obstacles. The strong points of Fort Mifflin on the Pennsylvania side and Fort Mercer on the New Jersey side, with a small American fleet above the obstacles, ensured no enemy naval force could remove them without opposition. This impeded British commander William Howe's freedom of action, for though he held the American capital of Philadelphia, he had no communication with the fleet, his main source of supply.

General Howe's frustration with the delays led him to send 2,000 Hessians under Colonel von Donop to take Fort Mercer by storm. The Hessian assault on 22 October against the Rhode Island regiments was a disaster, with 400 or more casualties. This was the biggest American victory of the campaign, and brightened hopes that the British army would suffer a logistical disaster. Washington commended Colonel Christopher Greene, who commanded the defense: "I heartily congratulate you upon this happy event, and beg you will accept my most particular thanks, and present the same to your whole garrison both officers and men."[7] While the forts eventually had to be abandoned in November, their prolonged defense meant that the lethargic Howe would not pursue Washington and that both armies would spend a relatively quiet winter in Philadelphia and Valley Forge, respectively.

On December 4, General Howe led his army out of Philadelphia to confront Washington. By this time the Americans were well fortified on the hills at White Marsh in present day Montgomery County. They had also been reinforced by three more brigades of men, fresh from victory over Burgoyne at Saratoga.

---

[5]. Washington to Israel Putnam, 10 September 1777, Washington to Putnam, 14 September 1777, Washington to Putnam, 23 September 1777, *WGW*, 9:201-202, 218-19, 253-54.

[6]. Washington to James Mitchell Varnum, 7 October 1777, *WGW*, 9:326; Washington to Christopher Greene, 8 October 1777, *WGW*, 9:335.

[7]. Washington to Christopher Greene, 24 October 1777, *WGW*, 9:424.

Howe looked things over for three days and tried to maneuver for an engagement, but Washington was too wise to leave his stronghold and engage the British in the open field.

After the British retired to Philadelphia, Washington remained at White Marsh until December 11. The army crossed the Schuylkill River to a place called the Gulph and remained there from December 12 until December 19. Exactly when it was decided to encamp the army at Valley Forge for the winter is not certain, but it was on December 17 that Washington told the men in General Orders that the army would take post in the neighborhood. On December 19 the Continental Army left the Gulph and marched into Valley Forge.

The tale of the Continental Army at Valley Forge has often been told. Recent books include John W. Jackson, *Valley Forge: Pinnacle of Courage* (1992), Herman O. Benninghoff III, *Valley Forge: A Genesis for Command and Control* (2001), and Dr. Wayne K. Bodle, *The Valley Forge Winter: Civilians and Soldiers in War* (2002). However, a body of folklore and myth has so encompassed the six-month encampment that the historical facts are sometimes difficult to discern.

The first few days of the Valley Forge Encampment and mid-February 1778 were the hardest times for the troops. Worn out after a hard campaign, they had to build log huts for their winter lodging. At the same time a food shortage so severe occurred that Washington wrote to the President of Congress on December 22 that if something was not done immediately "this Army must dissolve." Varnum, commanding a brigade of the two Rhode Island regiments and two from Connecticut, had written to Washington the same day that "Three Days successively, we have been destitute of Bread. Two Days we have been intirely without Meat."[8]

Washington General was forced to send details out from the camp to take food from the citizenry to feed his men. The citizens were not considered pleasant neighbors. Captain James Gray of the Third New Hampshire wrote to his wife Susan the day before Christmas that "In this State we find a people who are, (generally speaking), the most unfriendly of any we have passed through; insomuch that we are put to the disagreable necessity of taking our necessary support from them, by armed force—"[9] Gray was doubtless pleased to be on furlough for the months of January through June.

---

[8]. Washington to Henry Laurens, 22 December 1777, *WGW*, 10:183; Varnum to Washington, 22 December 1777, George Washington Papers, Library of Congress.

[9]. James Gray to Susan Gray, 24 December 1777, HM 22016, The Huntington Library, San Marino, California.

Thousands of troops were too ill-clad to be out of doors or participate in any work details. Many men left the Army in January 1778 as their terms of service were up. For the next few months few new enlistments appear. However, by April the number of recruits began to increase. Some historians have remarked that General Howe missed a golden opportunity to attack Washington at Valley Forge when the Continental Army was at a low ebb. This might be so, but if Washington could have kept a full complement of men at Valley Forge, there would have been no chance of feeding them. William Weeks, Paymaster of the Third New Hampshire mourned on February 16 that "The first thing I must enter upon is the *Scarcity* of *Provision* here. *Death* seem'd to stare the poor Soldiers in the Face; for this *five Days* the Soldiers have not drawn [the] Tenth Part of their Allowance...."[10]

There was much discontent among the officers at Valley Forge. Bethuel Curtis of the Second Rhode Island begged to be allowed to resign as he "have bin Obliged to spend a Considerable sum of money More than my Wages a mount too: My Private fund is Now almoste Exausted and my helth Grately impared; which renders me unfit to indure the Fatigues of the insuing Campaign."[11]

The men of both New Hampshire and Rhode Island suffered gravely from the disastrous supply situation. On January 21, Brigadier General wrote to the governor of New Hampshire that: "near one half of them destitute of any kind of shoes or stockings to their feet, and I may add many without either Breeches shirts or blankets exposed as they are unavoidably obliged to by all the inclemencies of the cold season living in log huts without doors or floors. Paint to yourself this their ragged suffering condition—At nearly the same time the Colonel of the Second Rhode Island was writing "at this Sevear Season of the year, are, the greatest part of them almost Stark naked, and Destitute of Every necessary of life...."[12]

Sergeant Isaac Gibbs of the First New Hampshire wrote on March 5 that "the Inhabitans are Chie[fly] what we Call quakers, & I Believe are the grater part of them. No friends to the Cause we are Engaged in but on th[e] Contorary which

---

[10]. William Weeks to Unknown, 16 February 1778, Hiram Bingham, Jr. *Five Straws Gathered from Revolutionary Fields* (Cambridge, Ma.: 1901), 23-25.

[11]. Bethuel Curtis to Washington, 2 May 1778, RG 93, M 859, Roll 49, Doc. 15641, National Archives.

[12]. Enoch Poor to Meshech Weare, 21 January 1778, Peter Force Mss, Ser. 7E, New Hampshire Council, Library of Congress. Israel Angell to Unidentified, undated but probably early February 1778, Louise Lewis Lovell, *Israel Angell, Colonel of the 2nd Rhode Island Regiment*, (The Knickerbocker Press, 1921), 121.

Causes us to suffer much on account of Provision that Sometimes we have ben Obliged to go our and take their Provision by Force...we also suffer much for want of Cloaths shoes &c which we Ought to had long agone from our own state which Causes great Uneasiness among our Troops—" Two days later General Varnum complained that "The Army have suffered very much the Winter past for want of Cloathing. This unfortunate Circumstance has prevented us from making those Advantages, wch have been frequently thrown in our Way by the Enemy's foraging Parties. Provisions also, at Times, have been far from us; but these Difficulties are submitted to with a degree of Patience and Fortitude, which will forever astonish the feeling part of Mankind.... the two Rhode Island Battalions have been sickly; They have lost a considerable Number. This is owing to their immense Fatigues in the Summer past." [13]

There were few opportunities for glory or excitement at Valley Forge. After the huts were constructed, many of the soldiers were given the opportunity to go home on furlough. Those who remained stood guard duty, cut firewood, drilled, and were sometimes sent out of camp "on command." This catchall term might mean guarding stores at an outlying post, collecting forage for the army's horses, or guarding prisoners. Throughout the six months the British were in Philadelphia and the Continental Army at Valley Forge, detachments were rotated to the "lines"–the area close to the British fortifications to stop civilians going into the city and harass enemy patrols. These assignments were probably a welcome break from the tedium of camp, but they were not without risk as men were killed, wounded, or captured in skirmishes.

A precedent breaking action at Valley Forge was the recruitment of a Black Regiment, the First Rhode Island. For most of the Revolutionary War, the United States faced a chronic shortage of manpower. Despite several short-lived bans early in the war, by 1778 African Americans were scattered in nearly all Continental regiments, particularly those from New England. An August 24, 1778 enumeration showed 755 African Americans with Washington's army, which did not include many regiments such as the two from Rhode Island.

For whatever reasons, Brigadier General Varnum wrote to Washington on January 2, 1778, suggesting that as the Rhode Island regiments were short men "The Field Officers have represented to me the Propriety of making one temporary Battalion from the two, so that one entire Core of Officers may repair to Rhode Island, in order to receive & prepare the Recruits for the Field. It is imagined that a Battalion of Negroes can be easily raised there." This apparently met Washington's

---

[13].Isaac Gibbs to his brother, 5 March 1778, RG 2, Box 31, Valley Forge National Historical Park Archives; Varnum to Nicholas Cooke, 7 March 1778, Letters, vol. 12, page 31, Rhode Island Archives.

approbation as he passed the suggestion on the Rhode Island's governor the same day.[14]

Troops were being raised in the state but at a slow rate. Despite some serious opposition, the legislature agreed to enroll slaves into the Continental Line. This act allowed any "able-bodied" male slave to enter the service and receive his freedom as well as the bounties and other "encouragements" offered by Congress to all who enlisted. The Assembly established a committee to evaluate these men and pay their owners "at a price not exceeding £120 for the most valuable slave; and in proportion for a slave of less value."

When the bill was passed, six members of the House of Deputies protested against it. Their reasons were that not enough negroes would enlist to constitute the desired regiment, that it would too expensive, and that many owners would not be content with the prices allowed. They also contended that many people throughout the world would look on this action with contempt as inconsistent with the principles of liberty and government they were contending for.

In May the Rhode Island legislature, in order to speed up recruiting, set June 10 as the final date for the enlistment of slaves. A nineteenth-century writer claimed this was evidence of the unpopularity of the original bill. He believed the May Assembly, which contained thirty-nine new members, repealed the February act in response to the wishes of the citizens. However this argument appears weak as three of the six protesters were not reelected to the new General Assembly. While the records are not complete, various researchers estimate that between 140 and 250 African Americans served in the First Rhode Island. It can be assumed that all the privates who appear on the rolls of that regiment, from May 1778 on are African Americans.[15]

In March 1778, the arrival of "Baron" Frederick von Steuben brought a new drill for the army. The Commander in Chief's guard was enlarged to serve as the model company. Some New Hampshire and Rhode Island men were transferred to the guard at this time. Steuben introduced a simple but highly efficient drill which was critical to the success of American arms.[16]

---

[14]. Varnum to Washington, 2 January 1778, George Washington Papers, Library of Congress; Washington to Nicholas Cooke, 2 January 1778, Ibid.

[15]. Joel Alden Cohen, "Rhode Island and the American Revolution: A Selective Socio-Political Analysis," Ph. D. Disseration, The University of Connecticut, (1967), 88-90; Lorenzo J. Greene, "Some Observations on the Black Regiment of Rhode Island in the American Revolution," *Journal of Negro History* 37 (April 1952), 164-65.

[16]. Wright, *Continental Army*, 141-42.

The high point of the Encampment was reached on May 6, 1778. Word of the American alliance with France was announced a few days before, and the entire army celebrated with an orchestrated *feude de joie*. Further good news arrived shortly after thes when it became certain that the British were preparing to evacuate Philadelphia. No one knew what the new British commander Henry Clinton was planning to do, but the simple fact that the American capital would be free was enough reason for joy.

Philadelphia was evacuated on June 18, and the Continental Army left Valley Forge in pursuit the next day. At the Battle of Monmouth, New Jersey, on June 28, Varnum's Brigade was at the left of the American line and held a hedgerow under heavy attack until outflanked. Poor's Brigade came up in the evening but was not engaged in the action.

The New Hampshire regiments were active participants in Sullivan's 1779 campaign against the Indians in Pennsylvania. At the Battle of Newtown on August 29, 1779, the Continental Army was engaged in battle with the British regulars, Loyalist rangers and 1000 Iroquois Indian warriors. The battle of Newtown was the decisive clash in one of the largest offensive campaigns of the American Revolution. The New Hampshire men under General Poor led the flanking movement which forced the enemy's precipitate withdrawal. This campaign proved to be the New Hampshire unit's last major action of the war.

After Monmouth, both Rhode Island Regiments returned to their home state as part of a failed attempt to push the British out of Newport. At the Battle of Rhode Island in August 1778, the First Rhode Island distinguished itself, and the bravery of the Black soldiers was praised by a number of officers. The Second Rhode Island participated in an action at Springfield, New Jersey, on June 23, 1780, where they held up a much larger enemy force for which Washington commended them on their "gallant behavior."[17]

The two Rhode Island New Jersey regiments in the Continental Line eventually consolidated into one on January 1, 1781, and became known at the Rhode Island Regiment. It was disbanded at Saratoga, New York, on December 25, 1783. After several reorganizations, the First and Second New Hampshire were consolidated into one unit on June 22, 1783, and became known as the New Hampshire Battalion. That unit was disbanded on January 1, 1784, at New Windsor, New York. The Third New Hampshire was disbanded on January 1, 1781, at Continental Village, New York.

---

[17]. Greene, "Some Observations," 170; Washington to William Heath, 29 June 1780, *WGW*, 19:93.

GLOSSARY

Absent Without Leave	Missing from his regiment without authorization.
After provisions	Sent out of camp to an unspecified location after food.
A. G.	The Adjutant General was responsible for directing and organizing the administrative paperwork of the Army.
Armorer's Shop	Armorers were responsible for repairing weapons and keeping them in service.
Artificer	Artificer was a generic term for skilled specialists such as blacksmiths, carpenters, and leather workers who made and repaired articles required by the army.
Assistant to the Forage Master	Forage refers to the grain and hay fed to the livestock. The forage master purchased and distributed the forage.
At the Lines	See on command at the lines.
Baggage	The clothes, tents, provisions, cooking equipment, and other stores and supplies.
Baker	A man detailed to bake bread for the Army.
Barren Hill/Barren Hill Church	This refers to the "Barren Hill Expedition" of May 18-22, in which Lafayette was sent out with several thousand men to scout towards Philadelphia. The enemy came out of the city with a much larger force and nearly caught the Marquis. Barren Hill Church still stands in Montgomery County, Pennsylvania.
B.G. Commissary Guard	On guard duty at the brigade level, guarding the food store of the brigade.
Brigade Commissary	The officer assigned to each brigade to obtain food from the army's commissary and deliver it to each regiment.
Brigade Hospital	In January 1778, each brigade was ordered to build a log hut to serve as a hospital for the men of the brigade.
Brigade Major	An officer in each brigade who was in charge of the unit's paperwork. This was a staff, not a command position.

Captivity	Captured by the enemy.
Cashiered	The term applied to an officer who was dismissed from the Army for incompetence or misconduct.
Clothier General	The official in charge of obtaining clothing for and delivering it to the army.
Commander-in-Chief's Guard	See General Washington's Guard.
Commissary Department	The department responsible for obtaining food and delivering it to the army.
Commissary Forage	The official in charge of obtaining and delivering hay and grain for the cavalry and draft animals.
Confined	Under arrest for one or more infractions of the army's regulations.
Corps of Invalids	See Invalids.
Deserter/Deserted	A man who left his regiment without authorization and may have gone over to the enemy or left for his home.
Discharged	Released from the army either due to a physical infirmity or completion of the required term of service.
Doing Brigade Major's duty to General Stark	On assigned with Brigadier General John Stark, who was not at Valley Forge.
Drum Major	The lead drummer in a regiment who teaches the other drummers the proper drum calls and their usage.
Enlisted	The man has joined the army as a private or non-commissioned officer.
Ensign	The lowest ranking officer, who carried the colors or ensign into battle.
Exchanged	An exchange was the trading of prisoners with the enemy for those of equal rank or a trade based on a mutually agreed on set of values by rank.
Fatigue/On Fatigue	Assigned to a work detail in camp such as building fortifications or cleaning the encampment.
Fife Major	The lead fifer in a regiment who teaches the other fifers the proper calls and their usage.

Furlough	See on furlough.
General Gates	Major General Horatio Gates commanded during the Saratoga Campaign.
His Excellency's Guard/General Washington's Guard	Washington's personal guard, usually called the Commander in Chief's guard. Originally all Virginians, in March 1778, one hundred men from the other ten states represented at Valley Forge were added. These men protected Washington's person, the official papers, and the army's cash.
Hubbarton Battle	On July 7, 1777, the American rearguard was attacked by the British advance at Hubbarton, Vermont.
Impressing	Out of camp on a detail seizing supplies from the civilian population
In/On Command Row Boat	In service in a small boat on the Schuylkill River, bringing food, forage, or other supplies to Valley Forge.
In his room/In place of	A man serving as a substitute for another.
In inoculation	Under inoculation for smallpox.
Invalids	A special unit of men who were physically unfit for field duty but who were capable enough to serve as guards for prisoners and supplies.
In General Washington's Guard	See His Excellency's Guard.
In the Train	On temporary service with an artillery unit.
Joined	The date the man reported to his regiment at camp.
Joined since last muster	The muster roll was usually done early in a given month. This means the man had joined in that month, after the muster roll was completed.
Left on the road	Unable to keep up with the line of march due to physical problems.
M. Gard	Probably the main guard, which was the daily guard detail for the encampment.
Not Joined	The soldier has not joined his regiment. This is usually noted when he has not reported when expected.

Oath	On February 3, 1778, Congress resolved that every officer who held a commission from Congress was required to take an oath of allegiance. Many of oaths do not survive. Details on the oaths can be found in Waldenmaier, *Some of the Earliest Oaths of Allegiance.*
On Clothier General guard	Serving as a guard for the man who headed the department that purchased and distributed clothing to the army.
On Command	On assignment outside the camp for periods of a day up to several months. Most of the time where, or what the assignment was, does not appear in the records.
On command at the Bridge	A few days after the army arrived at Valley Forge, work was started by the soldiers on a bridge across the Schuylkill River. The bridge was not completed until March 1778.
On command coaler	On detail outside the camp making charcoal for the use of the artificers.
On command Gen. Backhouse	Unidentified.
On command with Col. Hay	Serving with Colonel Udny Hay, a Deputy Quartermaster General.
On command with General McDougall	On assignment with Major General Alexander McDougall, who was not at Valley Forge.
On command with General Sullivan	On assignment with Major General John Sullivan who was at Valley Forge until March and then went to Rhode Island.
On command on the lines	On assignment with other soldiers close to the British line of fortifications at Philadelphia. Men on the lines were to harass British patrols and stop civilians from carrying supplies into Philadelphia for sale to the enemy.
On command thrashing	On assignment outside of camp threshing grain to be used as food by the army.
On command to the Adjutant General	On temporary assignment to the Adjutant General of the Army.
On court martial	An officer serving as one of the judges at a military trial.

On Detachment	A variable number of men sent out of camp on a particular task or assignment. Detachments could last for days or months.
On Genl. guard	Each general officer was entitled to a small personal guard detail, the men of which usually rotated.
On General Lee's Guard	On assignment in the personal guard of Major General Charles Lee.
On guard with the A.G.	On assignment in the personal guard of the Adjutant General.
On main guard	The regular daily guard detailed to protect the encampment. Several hundred men were assigned to this task each day.
On picquet/picquett	An advanced guard posted at various points outside the camp to keep watch for the approach of the enemy.
On present duty	In camp on some undifferentiated military assignment.
On quarter guard	On duty guarding the quarters of a unit.
Paymaster servant	Serving as the personal servant to the Paymaster General.
Picket	See on picquet/picquett.
P. M. G. Guard	Serving as a guard for the Paymaster General.
Prisoner	A soldier held captive by the enemy.
Prisoner in camp	A soldier under guard in camp for one or more violations of army regulations.
Q.M.G.	Quartermaster General
Quartermaster	The department responsible for setting up encampments, supplying wagons for transportation, and providing items such as tents, knapsacks, and tools for an army
Reduced	Lowered in rank due to incompetence or an infraction of regulations.
Redeemed from prison	Exchanged from captivity with the enemy.
Resigned	Officers could resign from the army without completing a specific term of service. However they could not do so without approval from their superiors.
Returned from captivity and joined since last muster	Refers to a man who had been taken prisoner by the enemy and returned to his unit at some time during the previous month.

Sick Absent	Sick at an unspecified location outside the camp.
Sick Present	Sick in a hut or tent at camp.
Sick Quarters	Sick in a hut or tent at camp.
Surgeon General	The doctor at the head of the army's medical department.
Under Guard	A man who faced charges for an infraction of army regulations.
Waggoner/Wagoner	Driving a wagon for the army.
With butchers	Detailed to slaughter and process the livestock brought to feed the army.

LOCATIONS MENTIONED

Counties listed are those which are on current maps. Many of the counties that existed in 1777-1778 are now much smaller, as they were broken up to form new counties. For example, all the land which forms the current Delaware County, Pennsylvania, was then part of Chester County. Some of the locations are not certain: Reading/Reding could be Reading, Massachusetts; Reading Township, New Jersey; Reading, Pennsylvania; or Redding, Connecticut.

Acworth/Ackworth	Sullivan County, New Hampshire.
Albany	Albany, New York.
Amwell	Amwell Township, Hunterdon County, New Jersey.
Barren Hill/Barren Hill Church	Montgomery County, Pennsylvania.
Bethleham	Northampton County, Pennsylvania.
Bickar	Not identified.
Billett	Crooked Billet, now Hatboro, Montgomery County, Pennsylvania.
Boscowen/Boscowin	Boscawen, Merrimack County, New Hampshire.
Bristol	Bucks County, Pennsylvania.
Brookline	Hillsborough, New Hampshire.
Brunswick	New Brunswick, New Jersey.
Cakeatt/Cakoatt	Now New Hempstead, Rockland County, New York.
Chesterfield	Cheshire County, New Hampshire.
Cochenmouth/Cockermouth	Cockermouth, Grafton County, New Hampshire.
Corryell's Ferry	This ferry crossed the Delaware River between what is now New Hope, Bucks County, Pennsylvania and Lambertville, Hunterdon County, New Jersey.
Cransburytown	Cranbury, Middlesex County, New Jersey.
Cross Road	Now Hartsville, Bucks County, Pennsylvania Chester County, Pennsylvania.
Crumpond	Now Yorktown, New York.
Cuckoldstown	Now Berwyn, Chester County, Pennsylvania
Derefield	Derryfield, Hillsborough County, New Hampshire.
Downingtown	Chester County, Pennsylvania.

Dunkers Town	Now Ephrata, Lancaster County, Pennsylvania.
Dunstable	Now Nashua, Hillsborough County, New Hampshire.
D. W. River	Not identified.
Englishtown	Monmouth County, New Jersey.
Fish Kill	Dutchess County, New York.
French Creek/French Creek Hospital	East Vincent and East Whiteland Townships, Chester County, Pennsylvania.
Gilson	Probably Gilsum in Cheshire County, New Hampshire.
Gulph	Montgomery County, Pennsylvania.
Hillsborough	Hillsborough County, New Hampshire.
Hopewell	Mercer County or Cumberland County, New Jersey.
Jersey/Jerseys	New Jersey had been divided into the colonies of East and West Jersey. Well before of the Revolution it had been unified into one colony, but was still frequently called the "Jersies" or "Jerseys."
Killen Mill	Not identified.
Kings Ferry	Kings Ferry was a major crossing point on the Hudson River. It connected Verplanck's Point on the east side of the Hudson with Stony Point on the west side.
Lancaster	Lancaster County, Pennsylvania.
Lebanon	Grafton County, New Hampshire.
Lidice	Lititz, Lancaster County, Pennsylvania.
Morristown	Morris County, New Jersey,
New Brunswick	New Brunswick, New Jersey.
New City/N. City	New City was probably Newtown, now Half Moon, New York,
New Hampstead	Possibly Hampstead, Rockingham County, New Hampshire.
New Ipswich	Hillsborough County, New Hampshire.
Newtown	Bucks County, Pennsylvania.
New Providence New Jersey	Essex County, New Jersey.
Peekskill	Westchester County, New Jersey.
Portsmouth	Rockingham County, New Hampshire.
Potts Grove	Now Pottstown, Montgomery County, Pennsylvania.
Poughkeepsie	Poughkeepsie, New York.
Princeton/Princetown	Mercer County, New Jersey.

Providence	Providence, Rhode Island.
Radnor	Delaware County, New Jersey.
Reading/Reding	Probably Reading, Berks County, Pennsylvania.
Red Lion	Now Uwchlan, Chester County, Pennsylvania.
Rednigh	Possibly Red Lion, see above.
Rocky Hill	Middlesex County, New Jersey.
Sanahday/Sanahedy/Sanakdey	Probably Schenectady, New York.
Slaughter[sdam]	Slawterdam, Sloterdam or Slaterdam stood on the east bank of the Passaisc River near the present site of Dundee Dam in Bergen County, New Jersey.
Swedes Ford/Sweds Fort	Swede's Ford crossed the Schuylkill River at what is now Norristown, Montgomery County, Pennsylvania.
Ware	Probably Weare, Hillsborough County, New Hampshire.
Westminster	Westminster, Massachusetts.
White Marsh	Montgomery County, Pennsylvania.
Wilmington	Wilmington, Delaware.
Yellow Springs	Now Chester Springs, Chester County, Pennsylvania.

New Hampshire

Name/ Rank	Enlistment or Commission Date/Term of Enlistment	Regiment/ Company	Remarks
Abbot/Abbott, Ebenezer Private	April 23, 1777, Three Years	Third, Frye	Dec 1777; Jan 1778 on command; Feb-March 1778; April-May 1778 sick in camp; June 1778 sick in General Hospital.
Abbot, George Private	March 27, 1777, Duration of War	Second, Bell	Dec 1777-May 1778 on furlough.
Abbot, Solomon Private	Dec 27, 1776, Duration of War	Second, Bell	Dec 1777-May 1778 on furlough.
Abbott/Abbot, Beriah Private	March 22, 1777, Three Years	Third, Livermore	Sept 5, 1777 Missing since Hubbarton Battle July 7, 1777; Dec 1777 joined since last muster; Jan 1778 on command; Feb-May 1778; June 1778 sick absent.
Abbott/Abbot, Peter, Private	Jan 25, 1777, Three Years	Third, Beal	Dec 1777-June 1778.
Abbott/Abbot, Stephen Drummer	Feb 15, 1777, Duration of War	First, Scott	Dec 1777 on command at the lines; Jan 1778; Feb 1778 sick absent; March 1778 on command at the lines; April-June 1778.
Abraham, David Private	Nov 15, 1776, Duration of War	First, Farwell	Dec 1777-June 1778.
Adams, Aaron Private	March 12, 1778, Three Years	First, Farwell	June 1778.
Adams/ Addams, David Private	May 18, 1777, Duration of War	First, Scott	Dec 1777-March 1778 sick at Albany; April 1778; May 1778 sick at Albany; June 1778 sick at Gilson.
Adams, Isaac Private	March 10, 1778, Three Years	First, Scott	June 1778.
Adams, Jonas Private	Feb 1, 1777, Three Years	First, Farwell	Dec 1777 wounded absent; Jan-May 1778 wounded at Albany; June 1778.
Adams/Adam, Levi Sergeant	Feb 1, 1777, Three Years	First, Farwell	Dec 1777-Feb 1778; March 1778 sick present; April-June 1778.
Adams, Samuel Ensign	Nov 8, 1776	Second, Bell	Dec 1777-May 1778 sick absent.

Name	Enlisted	Company	Notes
Aiken, James Corporal	April 1, 1777. Three Years	First, Emerson	Dec 1777-Jan 1778; Feb 1778 sick in camp; March-April 1778; May 18, 1778 deserted.
Aikon/Aiken, Samuel Private	April 3, 1777, Three Years	First, Emerson	Dec 1777-Jan 1778; Feb 1778 on command; March 1778; April-May 1778 sick at French Creek Hospital; June 1778 sick in Pennsylvania.
Akerman/Ackerman, Peter Private	April 9, 1777. Three Years	Third, Beal	Sept 5, 1777; wounded at Albany; Dec 1777-May 1778 wounded at Albany; June 2, 1778 transferred to the Corps of Invalids.
Aldrich, Caleb Corporal	March 19, 1778	Third, Ellis	June 1778.
Allard/Allord, James Private	April 9, 1777, Duration of War	Third, Weare	Dec 1777; Jan 1778 after provisions; Feb 1778 sick in camp; March 1778; April 1778 sick in camp; May-June 1778.
Allard, Noah Private	Dec 26, 1776, Duration of War	First, Bell	Dec 1777; Jan 1778 on command; Feb 1778; March 1778 on guard; April-May 1778.
Allds, John Private	March 1, 1778, Two Years	First, Scott	June 1778.
Allen/Alen, John Private	April 5, 1777, Duration of War	First, Scott	Dec 1777-Jan 1778; Feb 1778 sick in camp; March-June 1778.
Allen/Alen, Samuel Private	Nov 25, 1776, Duration of War	First, Wait	Dec 1777-Jan 1778 wounded September 19 and at Schenectady; Feb 1778 wounded on furlough; March 1778 wounded in hospital; April-June 1778.
Alley/Ally, Daniel Corporal/Sergeant	Nov 11, 1776, Duration of War	Second, Blodget	Dec 1777 sick absent; Jan 1778 promoted to Sergeant; Jan-March 1778 sick absent; April-June 1778.
Alls/Allds, Isaac Private	April 21, 1777, Three Years	First, Scott	Dec 1777 sick in camp; Jan 1778 on command at ye lines; Feb-March 1778; May 1778 sick in camp; June 1778 sick at Valley Forge.
Ames, Francis Private	March 21, 1778	First, Frye	June 1778 joined since last muster, on command with General McDougall.
Amy/Amey, Heman Private	May 30, 1777, Three Years	Third, Gray	Dec 1777-April 1778; May 1778 sick present; June 1778.

Name	Enlistment	Company	Service Record
Andrews/ Andris, Amy/Ammi Private	Three Years	Third, Gray/ McClary	Dec 1777 on command; Jan 1778; Feb-March 1778. April 1778 transferred to McClary's Company; April 1778; May 1778 sick in camp; June 1778.
Andrews, Joel Private	Jan 1, 1778, Three Years	First, Farwell	April-June 1778.
Andrews, Nathaniel Private	May 15, 1777, Three Years	First, House	Dec 1777-Jan 1778; Feb 1778 sick in camp; March-April 1778; May 1778 on guard; June 1778.
Arms/Arme, Edward Private	April 9, 1778	Third, Livermore	May-June 1778.
Ash, John Private	March 8, 1777, Duration of War	First, Morrill	Dec 1777; Jan 1778 on command; Feb 1778; March 1778 on guard; April-June 1778.
Ashton, Thomas Blanshard Private	Nov 15, 1776, Three Years	Second, Norris	Dec 1777-Jan 1778; Feb-March 1778 on command with General; April 1778; May 1778 on command at Genl. Poor's; June 1778.
Atkisson, Stephen Private	Feb 3, 1777, Three Years	Third, Weare	Dec 1777; Jan 1778 after provisions; Feb-May 1778; June 1778 sick General Hospital.
Atwood/ Attwood, Benjamin Private	Feb 27, 1777, Three Years	Third, Weare	Dec 1777; Jan 1778 sick in General Hospital; Feb 1778 sick in camp; March-June 1778.
Aubare/Aubert, Etenna/Etnna Private	April 1, 1778, Three Years	Third, McClary	May-June, 1778 missing at Barren Hill. July 1778 muster roll dated August 5, 1778 shows him dead on May 13, 1778.
Averill see Everill			
Ayres see Eyers			
Ayres, Samuel Private	March 14, 1778, Three Years	First, Scott	June 1778.
Bachelder, Mark Private	May 2, 1777, Eight Months	Third, Gray	Dec 1777 sick absent; Jan 10, 1778 discharged.
Bachelder/ Batcheldor, James Private	Feb 21, 1777 Three Years	Third, McClary	Dec 1777-May 1778 sick at Albany; June 1778.
Bachelder/ Batcheldor, Nathaniel Sergeant	Feb 10, 1777, Three Years	Third, McClary	Dec 1777-Jan 1778; Feb 1778 on command; March 20, 1778 died.
Bacheldor/ Bacheloor, William Private	Jan 10, 1777, Three Years	First, Hutchins	Dec 1777-Jan 1778 sick present; Feb-March 1778; April 1778 sick present; May 1778 sick at Yellow Springs; June 1778.

Name	Enlisted	Company	Service
Bailey, Andrew Private	May 6, 1777, Eight months	Third, Frye	Dec 1777; Jan 10, 1778 discharged.
Bailey, Joel Private	May 6, 1777, Eight months	Third, Frye	Dec 1777; Jan 10, 1778 discharged.
Baily/Bailey, William Private	April 13, 1777, Three Years	Third, Gray	Dec 1777-Feb 1778 sick absent; March 20, 1778 died.
Baker, Cato Private	May 1, 1777, Three Years	Second, Drew	Dec 1777 sick present; Jan 1778; Feb-March 1778 sick present; April 1778: May 1778 on guard; June 1778.
Balch, Hart Private	April 1, 1778, One Year	Second, Robinson	June 1778.
Balch, John Private	May 9, 1777, Three Years	Third, Ellis	Dec 1777; Jan-March 1778 on command; April-June 1778.
Baldwin, John Private	Dec 23, 1776, Duration of War	First, Farwell	Dec 1777-Feb 1778 sick at Albany; March 1778 sick present; April 1778; May 1778 sick in camp; June 1778.
Ballard, Uriah Drummer	May 8, 1777, Three Years	Third, Frye	Dec 1777-June 1778.
Barker, Josiah Private	June 17, 1777, Eight Months	Second, Robinson	Dec 1777; Jan 10, 1778 discharged.
Barker, Samuel Private	June 25, 1777, Three Years	Third, Weare	Dec 1777 on command with General Poor, Jan-April 1778; May 1778 on guard; June 1778 on command with Forage Master.
Barnes/Barns, Amos Private/Sergeant	Jan 20, 1778, Three Years	First, Hutchins	April 1778 joined since last muster; May-June 1778; June 1778 promoted to Sergeant.
Barnes/Barns, Ceasor/Ceser Private	Nov 10, 1776, Duration of War	First, Morrill	Dec 1777-Feb 1778; March 1778 sick in camp; April-May 1778; June 1778 on duty at Valley Forge.
Barnes/Barns, James Private	March 4, 1777, Duration of War	Third, Stone	Nov 5, 1777 deserted. May-June, 1778 on guard.
Barnett, Benjamin Private/Corporal	Feb 17, 1777, Three Years	First, House	Dec 1777-Feb 1778; Feb 24, 1778 promoted to Corporal; March 1778 sick in camp; April 1778; May 1778 sick in camp; June 1778 sick at Downingtown.
Barron, John Private		First, Emerson	June 1778 joined June 1st in Room of Asa Boutwell discharged. See Boutwell.
Barrus/Barrows, Nathan Private	May 9, 1777, Eight Months	Third, Ellis	Dec 1777; Jan 10, 1778 discharged.

Name	Enlistment	Company	Notes
Barter, Henry Private	Jan 1, 1777, Duration of War	Second, Robinson	April 1778 muster roll shows he deserted on Nov 15, 1777 and rejoined April 25, 1778; May 1778; June 1778 sick Valley Forge.
Barter/Bartor, John Private	Nov 11, 1776, Duration of War	Second, Blodget	Dec 1777 wounded absent; Jan-March 1778 on furlough; April 1778 on furlough New Hampshire; May-June 1778.
Barter, Peter, Private	Jan 7, 1777, Duration of War	Second, Bell	April-May 1778.
Bartlet, Nathaniel Private	May 1, 1777, Three Years	First, Scott	Dec 1777; Jan 1778 on duty; Feb 1778; March 1778 sick in camp; April-June 1778.
Batchelder, James Private	Feb 21, 1777, Three Years	Third, McClary	Dec 1777-May 1778 sick at Albany; June 1778.
Batchelder/Bachelder, Nathaniel Corporal	March 20, 1777, Three Years	First, Emerson	Dec 1777-Jan 1778; Feb 1778 sick in camp; March-June 1778.
Batcheldorn, David Corporal		Second, Rowell	Only record is the June 1778 muster roll which shows he deserted on April 20, 1778.
Bates, Samuel Private	May 1, 1777, Three Years	First, Scott	Dec 1777 sick at the Billet; Jan-June 1778.
Bates, Thomas Private		First, Scott	April-June 1778.
Batlama/Bartleme, Joseph Jon Private	April 1, 1778, Three Years	Third, McClary	May 1778; June 1778 sick at Valley Forge.
Batterson/Betterson, Naboth Private	April 20, 1777, Duration of War	Third, Ellis	Dec 1777; Jan 1778 sick in camp; Feb-June 1778.
Baxter, Thomas Private	April 28, 1777, Three Years	First, House	Dec 1777 sick at Albany; Dec 31, 1777 dead.
Beal/Beeal, James Private	Jan 1, 1777, Duration of War	Second, Robinson	March 1778 muster roll shows he was taken prisoner on July 7, 1777 and rejoined on March 8, 1778; March-May 1778; June 29, 1778 died.
Beal, Thomas Sergeant	May 30, 1777, Three Years	Third, Gray	Dec 1777 on command; Jan 1778 sick present; Feb 1778; March 1778 on command; April-May 1778 on command in the Armorer's Shop; June 1778.
Beal, Zachariah Captain	Nov 8, 1776	Third, Beal	Killed by a mutinous soldier in New York on Nov 6, 1777.
Bean, Ebenzer Private	Nov 15, 1776, Three Years	Second, Norris	Dec 1777-March 1778 on furlough; April-June 1778.

Name	Date	Regiment	Notes
Bean, John Corporal	April 15, 1777, Three Years	Third, McClary	Dec 1777-June 1778.
Bean, Jonathan/John Private	April 20, 1777, Three Years	Third, Gray	Dec 1777-June 1778 on furlough.
Bean, Josiah Private	Jan 28, 1777, Three Years	Third, McClary	Dec 1777-May 1778 on furlough; June 1778.
Bebee, Peter Private	April 9, 1778, Three Years	Third, Ellis	June 1778.
Belding/Bilding, Moses 1st. Lt.	Nov 8, 1776	Third, Ellis	Dec 1777; Jan-June 1778 on furlough.
Bell, Joshua Private	Feb 19, 1777, Duration of War	Third, Livermore	Dec 1777-March 1778; April-May 1778 sick in camp; June 1778 sick absent.
Bell, William Private	March 1, 1777, Three Years	Second, Robinson	Dec 1777-March 1778 Surgeon General Clerk Albany.
Bell, William H. Ensign	Nov 8, 1776	Second, Drew	Dec 1777-June 1778.
Bent, William Private	April 15, 1778	Second, Rowell	June 1778 muster roll shows he deserted on April 16, 1778.
Berrey/Barrey, Ebenezor Private	April 3, 1777, Three Years	First, Emerson	Dec 1777-May 1778 sick at Albany; June 1778 sick at Chester, New Hampshire.
Berry, Benjamin Private	Jan 20, 1777, Duration of War	Second, Drew	Dec 1777 muster roll shows he deserted on July 15, 1777 and joined on October 5; Jan 1778; Feb-March 1778 sick present; April 1778 on guard; May 1778; June 1778 sick at Peekskill.
Beverly, James Private	Twelve Months	First, Morrill	Dec 1777; Jan 1778; Feb 12, 1778 died.
Bevins/Bevens, Benjamin Private	Feb 1, 1777, Three Years	First, Scott	Dec 1777-Jan 1778 on General Poor's Guard; Feb 1778 on generals Guard; March-June 1778.
Bickford, Aaron Private	Feb 5, 1777, Duration of War	Second, Bell	Dec 1777-May 1778.
Bickford, Abner/Abenr Private	Feb 13, 1777, Three Years	Second, Drew	Dec 1777 on furlough; Jan 1778; Feb-March 1778 on furlough; April 1778; May-June 1778 on furlough.
Bickford/Bicford, Dennis Private	Feb 1, 1777, Duration of War	Second, Robinson	Dec 1777-May 1778 sick absent; June 1778.
Bickford, Samuel Private	Jan 22, 1778	Second, Rowell	June 1778.

Name	Enlisted	Company	Service Record
Bigford, Joseph Private	March 31, 1777, Three Years	Third, Livermore	Dec 1777; Jan 1778 on command; Feb 1778; March 1778 on command; April 1778; May 1778 sick in camp; June 1778 sick absent. July 1778 muster roll shows he died on June 29.
Bingham, Abner Private	March 10, 1777, Three Years	First, Wait	Dec 1777-May 1778; June 1778 sick at Valley Forge.
Bingham, Gustavus Private	June 10, 1777, Eight Months	Third, Ellis	Dec 1777; Jan 10, 1778 discharged.
Bingham, Ripley/Repeley Private/Sergeant	Nov 13, 1776, Three Years	First, Wait	Dec 1777 wounded Sept 19 and on furlough; Jan 1778 wounded on furlough per Genl. Gates; Feb 1778 wounded & on furlough; March 1778 on furlough; April 1778; May 1778 on duty; May 1, 1778 promoted to Sergeant; June 1778 sick at Wards [ ].
Bishop, Enos Private	Nov 17, 1776, Duration of War	First, Wait	Dec 1777 missing since July 7, 1777, joined Jan 22, 1778; Jan-June 1778.
Bishop, John Private	Nov 16, 1777, Three Years	First, Wait	Dec 1777; Jan 1778 on command at the lines; Feb 1778; March 1778 on command; April-June 1778.
Bixby, Asa Private	April 23, 1777, Three Years	Second, Robinson	Dec 1777; Jan 1778 on guard; Feb-April 1778; May 20, 1778 dead.
Blake, Joshua Fifer	April 20, 1777, Three Years	Third, McClary	Dec 1777; Jan 1778 on command with ye Colonel; Feb 1778; March 15, 1778 died.
Blake, Moses Private	April 4, 1777, Three Years	Second, Robinson	Dec 1777-June 1778.
Blake, Thomas Ensign	Jan 8, 1776	First, House	Dec 1777; Jan-Feb 1778 on command; March-June 1778.
Blake, William Private	Feb 20, 1777, Three Years	Third, McClary	Dec 1777; Jan-Feb 1778 on command; March 1778 sick in camp; April 1778.
Blanchard/ Blanchad, Jacob Private	April 2, 1777, Three Years	Third, Frye	Dec 1777 sick absent; Jan 1778 on command; Feb-April 1778; May 1778 sick in camp; June 1778 sick in General Hospital.
Blanchard, James Quartermaster	Nov 8, 1776	Third	Dec 1777 on command at Albany; Jan-June 1778.
Blasdal/Blazedel, Thomas Private	Nov 21, 1776, Three Years	Second, Bell	Dec 1777 waggoner; Jan 1778; f7 on command; March-April 1778; May 1778 waggoner.

Name	Enlistment	Company	Service
Blasdall/Blasdel, John Private	Jan 30, 1777, Duration of War	Second, Weare	Dec 1777-May 1778; June 1778 sick in General Hospital.
Blasdel/Blasdell, Philip Private	Nov 15, 1776, Duration of War	Second, Rowell	Dec 1777; Jan 1778 on command; Feb-March 1778; April 1778 on command coaler; May-June 1778.
Blodget/Blodgit, Caleb Sergeant	April 1, 1777, Three Years	Second, Blodget	Dec 1777-March 1778 on furlough; April 1778 on furlough New Hampshire; May 1778; June 1778 sick in camp.
Blodget/Blodgett, Joshua Private	March 4, 1777, Three Years	First, Morrill	Dec 1777; Jan 1778 on command; Feb-June 1778.
Blodget, Samuel Captain	Nov 8, 1776	Second, Blodget	Dec 1777 sick on furlough; Dec 22, 1777 resigned.
Blood/Bloode, Daniel	April 10, 1777, Three Years	First, House	Dec 1777-June 1778.
Blood, Reuben Private	Three Years	First, House	June 1778.
Blood, Simeon Private	Three Years	First, House	June 1778.
Blood, Thomas Private	April 28, 1777, Three Years	Third, Frye	Dec 1777 sick absent; Jan-May 1778 on furlough; June 1778.
Bloys, Walter Private	March 10, 1778, One Year	Second, Clayes	June 20, 1778 joined; June 1778.
Bonney, Jacob Private	May 10, 1777, Three Years	First, Farwell	Dec 1777-Jan 1778; Feb 1778 on present duty; March 1778 on guard; April-May 1778; June 1778 sick at Amwell.
Boutwell/Bowtell, Asa Private	May 12, 1777, Three Years	First, Emerson	Dec 1777-May 1778; June 1, 1778 discharged, John Barron in his room. See Barron.
Bowles/Boales, Charles Private	April 14, 1777, Three Years	First, Hutchins	Dec 1777-Jan 1778 sick present; Feb 1778 sick in camp; March 1778; April 1778 sick in hospital at French Creek; May-June 1778.
Bowls, Charls Private	Feb 2, 1778, Two Years	First, Emerson	June 1778.
Boyd, Samuel Private		First, Scott	April-May 1778; June 1778 sick at Hopewell.
Boyes/Boys, James Private	Jan 2, 1777, Three Years	Second, Carr	Dec 1777; Jan-March 1778 sick in camp; April 1778; May 1778 sick in camp; June 1778.
Boyes/Boys, John Private	April 6, 1777, Three Years	Third Livermore	Dec 1777-April 1778; May 1778 sick in camp; June 1778.
Boynton/ Boyington, Amos Sergeant	Jan 25, 1777, Three Years	Second, Clayes	Dec 1777; Jan-May 1778 on furlough; June 1778.

Name	Enlistment	Company	Service Record
Boynton, Isaac Private	April 10, 1777, Three Years	First, House	Dec 1777-Jan 1778; Feb 1778 sick in camp; March 1778 on command; April 1778 on command at the lines; May-June 1778.
Boynton, John Private	April 10, 1777, Eight Months	First, House	Dec 1777 at Albany wounded; Jan 6, 1778 discharged.
Boynton/Boyndon, Joseph Ensign	Nov 8, 1776	Third, Beal	Dec 1777-Jan 1778; Feb 1778 sick in camp; March-June 1778.
Boynton/ Boyington, Snow Drummer	March 10, 1778, Two Years	Second, Clayes	June 20, 1778 joined; June 1778.
Boyse/Boyes, James Private	Nov 14, 1776, Three Years	First, Frye	Dec 1777; Jan 1778 on command on picquet; Feb-June 1778.
Bradbury, Sanders Sergeant	April 10, 1777, Three Years	First, Emerson	Dec 1777-May 1778 sick at Albany; June 1778.
Bradford, Samuel 1st. Lt.	Nov 8, 1776	Second, Clayes	Dec 1777; Jan 1778 on command Albany; Feb 1778 on command at Albany; March 1778 on command; April 1778 on command at Albany; May 1778 sick at Hillsborough; June 1778 sick absent.
Bradford, William 2nd. Lt.	Nov 8, 1776	First, Wait	Dec 1777 missing Aug. 3d. 1777 redeemed from prison; Jan 1778; Feb 1778 at home redeemed from prison; March 1778 returned home from prison; April 1778 returned home from prison & on his march to Camp; May-June 1778.
Bradshars, John Private	Three Years	Third, Stone	Only record is the June 1778 muster roll which shows he deserted.
Bragdon, James Private	Feb 16, 1778	Second, Rowell	Only record is the June 1778 muster roll which shows he deserted on March 20, 1778.
Bragg, Robert Private	Jan 30, 1777, Three Years	Third, Weare	Dec 1777; Jan 1778 after provisions; Feb-March 1778; April 1778 on a weeks Command at the Lines; May-June 1778.
Brasbee, John Private	Jan 22, 1778	Second, Rowell	June 1778.
Bride see McBride			
Brinlnall, George Private	April 1, 1778, One Year	Third, Stone	June 1778.

Name	Enlisted	Company	Service
Britton, Samuel Private	March 7, 1778, Three Years	Third, Ellis	June 1778.
Brooks, David Private	March 10, 1778, Two Years	Second, Clayes	June 20, 1778 joined; June 1778.
Brooks, John Private	April 10, 1777, Eight Months	First, House	Dec 1777 on furlough by General Gates; Jan 6, 1778 discharged.
Brown, Edward Private	Jan 20, 1777, Three Years	Second, Drew	Dec 1777-Jan 1778; Feb 1778 sick present; March 1778; April 1778 sick present; May 1778; June 1778 on Genl. Guard.
Brown, Elijah/Elisha Private	Dec 1, 1776, Duration of War	Second, Drew	Dec 1777-Jan 1778; Feb-March 1778 sick present; April 1778; May 28, 1778 dead.
Brown, James Private	April 1, 1777, Three Years	First, Frye	Dec 1777 "Returned from Captivity & Joyn'd Since Last muster"; Jan 1778; Feb 1778 sick in camp; March 1778; April 1778 on guard; May 1778; June 1778 on guard.
Brown, John Private	March 10, 1777, Duration of War	First, Scott	Dec 1777; Jan 1778 sick in camp; Feb-March 1778 sick in hospital; April 1778; May 1778 sick in camp; June 1778 sick at Valley Forge.
Brown, Nathaniel Drummer	Sept 2, 1777, Three Years	Third, Beal	Dec 1777-Feb 1778; March 1778 sick absent; April 1778; May 1778 sick in camp; June 1778 sick Valley Forge.
Brown, Oliver Private	May 12, 1777, Eight Months	Third, Livermore	Dec 1777; Jan 10, 1778 discharged.
Brown, Richard Quartermaster	Nov 8, 1776	Second	Dec 1777-Jan 1778; Feb-March 1778 sick in camp; April 1778; May 1778 sick in camp; June 1778.
Brown, Silas Private	March 4, 1777, Duration of War	Third, Stone	Dec 1777 sick General Hospital Albany; Jan 1778 muster roll shows he died on Dec 31, 1777.
Brown, Sipio/Scipio Private	March 10, 1777, Three Years	First, Emerson	Dec 1777-March 1778 sick at New City; April-June 1778 sick at Albany New City.
Brown/Browne, William Private	Nov 21, 1776, Three Years	First, Wait	Dec 1777-Feb 1778; March-April 1778 sick in camp; May-June 1778.
Bryant/Bryent, David Private	Nov 12, 1776, Three Years	First, Frye	Dec 1777-Jan 1778; Feb 1778 on guard; March-June 1778.

Name	Enlisted	Company	Service Record
Bryer/Brier, Peter Private	April 28, 1777, Three Years	First, Emerson	Dec 1777-Jan 1778 sick at Albany; Feb 1778 sick at New City; March-April 1778 sick at Albany; June 1778 muster roll shows he died on April 1, but the April 1778 payroll shows he died on April 30.
Bugby/Bugbey, Nathaniel Private	April 22, 1777, Three Years	First, House	Dec 1777 sick at Albany; Jan-March 1778 on furlough; April-May 1778 sick at Lebanon; June 1778 sick at New Hampshire.
Bumford, Charles Sergeant	May 1, 1777, Three Years	Second, Drew	Dec 1777-Jan 1778; Feb 1778 sick present; March 1778; April 1778 sick present; May-June 1778.
Burbee/Burby, Peter Private	March 10, 1777, Three Years	Second, Blodget	Dec 1777 deserted July 7 returned and pardoned; Jan-April 1778; May 1778 sick in camp; June 12, 1778 died.
Burbee/Burby, Peter, Jr. Fifer/Private	March 18, 1777, Three Years	Second, Blodget	Dec 1777; Jan 1778 reduced to Private; Jan 1778 on command; Feb-May 1778; June 1778 left sick at Valley Forge.
Burjett/Burgett, Charles Private	Three Years	Third, McClary	Dec 1777; Jan 1778 on command; Feb 1778; March 1778 on guard; April 1778 on a week's command at the Lines; May 1778; June 1778 driving wagon.
Burk, Joseph Private	Feb 9, 1777, Three Years	First, Farwell	Dec 1777 sick at Reding; Jan 1778 sick absent Reding; Feb-June 1778.
Burkheart, Jacob Private	April 12, 1778	Third, McClary	June 1778.
Burley, Stephen Private	May 30, 1777, Eight Months	Third, Gray	Dec 1777; Jan 10, 1778 discharged.
Burley, William Private	April 20, 1777, Three Years	Third, Gray	Dec 1777; Jan 1778 on command; Feb-May 1778; June 1778 on command at Valley Forge.
Burnham, Enoch Private	Feb 1, 1777, Three Years	Second, Rowell	June 1778 muster roll shows him as missing on July 7, 1777, June 7, 1778, joined, June 1778 sick at Valley Forge.
Burnham, George Sergeant	March 18, 1777, Duration of War	Second, Bell	Dec 1777-May 1778.
Burnham, Joseph Private	Jan 14, 1777, Duration of War	Second, Bell	Dec 1777-May 1778 on furlough.

Name	Enlisted	Company	Service Record
Burns, Philip Corporal	June 26, 1777	Third, Weare	Dec 1777-March 1778 left wounded at Albany; April 1778 died April 1, 1778.
Burrows, Jonathan Sergeant	Jan 1, 1777, Three Years	First, Emerson	Dec 1777-March 1778 sick at Dunstable; April-June 1778.
Burton, Josiah Sergeant	Aug 8, 1777, Three Years	First, Wait	Dec 1777-Jan 1778 sick at "Skynekity"; Feb-March 1778 wounded in hospital; April 1778 wounded & in hospital Albany; May-June 1778.
Burton, William Fifer	April 8, 1777, Three Years	Third, Frye	Dec 1777-March 1778; April 1778 sick in camp; May 1778; June-July 1778 sick at Valley Forge; August 1, 1778 died.
Burts, Robert Private	April 28, 1777, Three Years	First, House	Dec 1777-Jan 1778; Feb 1778 sick in camp; March 1778; April 1778 on command at Radnor; May 1778 on guard; June 1778.
Busell/Buswell, Noah Private	Jan 31, 1777, Three Years	First, Emerson	Dec 1777; Jan 1778 on command after provisions; Feb-June 1778.
Buss, John Private		Second, Blodget	Dec 1777 missing July 7 returned Oct 19; Jan 1778 on duty; Feb 1778 on command; March-May 1778; June 1778 left sick at Valley Forge.
Butler, Aseph Private	April 1, 1778, Two Years	First, Wait	June 1778 sick at Valley Forge.
Butler/Butlor, Benjamin Private	March 10, 1777, Three Years	First, Morrill	Dec 1777; Jan-Feb 1778 sick in camp; March-June 1778.
Butler, Levi Private	March 10, 1777, Three Years	Third, Ellis	Dec 1777; Jan 1778 on command; Feb-March 1778; April 1778 sick in camp; May 5, 1778 died.
Butterfield, Simon/Simeon Private	March 1, 1777, Three Years	First, Emerson	Dec 1777-March 1778 nurse in General Hospital; April-June 1778.
Buzzell, Elijah Sergeant	Nov 10, 1776, Three Years	Second, Carr	July 7, 1777 prisoner; May 16, 1778 joined; May-June 1778.
Buzzell, Jonathan Private	March 16, 1778, Three Years	Second, Carr	June 1778.
Cady, Curtis Private	Feb 13, 1777, Three Years	First, House	Dec 1777 at Albany wounded; Jan-April 1778 on furlough wounded; April 11, 1778 died.
Cain, Francis Private	Three Years	Third, Stone	Only record is the June 1778 muster roll which shows he deserted.

Name	Enlisted	Company	Service
Caldwell, John Private	June 7, 1777, Eight Months	First, Hutchins	Dec 1777; Jan 1778 discharged.
Caldwell, Samuel Sergeant	July 3, 1777, Eight Months	First, Hutchins	Dec 1777; Jan 1778 on command with waggons; Feb-April 1778 assistant to the Waggon Master; May-June 1778 on command with Waggon Master.
Calkins/Colkins, John Private	Nov 11, 1776, Duration of War	Second, Blodget	Dec 1777; Jan 1778 on command; Feb-April 1778; May 1778 on guard.
Calley, John Private	March 22, 1777, Three Years	Second, Norris	Dec 1777-May 1778 sick at Albany; June 1778 sick at Pennsylvania.
Calley, Josiah Corporal	March 15, 1777, Three Years	Second, Norris	Dec 1777-May 1778; June 1778 sick at Pennsylvania.
Cambwell, Duncan Private	Nov 13, 1776, Duration of War	Second, Blodget	Dec 1777-Jan 1778 sick absent; Feb 1778 sick at Albany; March 1, 1778 deserted.
Cammet, Samuel Private	March 1, 1777, Three Years	First, Hutchins	Dec 1777-May 1778; June 1778 tending sick at Valley Forge.
Cammet/Cammot, Thomas Private	March 13, 1777, Three Years	First, Hutchins	Dec 1777 sick present; Jan 1778; Feb 1778 sick in camp; March-June 1778.
Camp see Kemp			
Campbell/Cammell, Archibald Private	March 30, 1778, Three Years	Second, Drew	May 1778 sick present; June 1778 at Princeton.
Campbell, James Drum Major	March 4, 1777, Three Years	First	Jan-June 1778.
Campbell/Campbel, James Private	April 26, 1777, Three Years	First, Frye	Dec 1777 wounded absent; Jan-May 1778 wounded & on furlough; June 1778.
Campbell/Camwell, Jese/Jesse Private	April 7, 1777, Three Years	Second, Clayes	Dec 1777; Jan 1778 on command foraging; Feb-June 1778.
Canney/Conney, Ames/Amos Private	Feb 5, 1777, Duration of War	Second, Bell	Dec 1777-May 1778.
Canney/Conney, John Private	Nov 21, 1776, Duration of War	Second, Bell	Dec 1777-Jan 1778; Feb-March 1778 on command; April-May 1778.
Cant, John Private	Feb 2, 1778, Three Years	First, Emerson	June 1778.
Caprin, Otis Private	May 9, 1777, Eight Months	Third, Ellis	Dec 1777; Jan 10, 1778 discharged.
Capron, Thomas Private	April 11, 1778, Three Years	First, Scott	June 1778.

Name/Rank	Enlistment	Company	Service Record
Card, Samuel Corporal	Jan 7, 1777, Duration of War	Second, Bell	Dec 1777-May 1778.
Carlton/Carleton, Ebenezer Private	March 21, 1777, Duration of War	Third, Frye	Dec 1777 on furlough; Jan-March 1778 on command; April 1778 on command at his Excellency's Guard. March 19, 1778 transferred to the Commander-in-Chief's Guard.
Carr, Daniel Private	Jan 22, 1777, Three Years	Third, Weare	Dec 1777 sick hospital; January 1, 1778 died.
Carr, Elias Private	April 18, 1777, Three Years	Third, Gray	Dec 1777; Jan 1778 on command; Feb 1778; March 20, 1778 died.
Carr, James Captain	Nov 8, 1776	Second, Carr	May 1778 muster roll shows he was taken prisoner July 7, 1777, joined May 25, 1778; June 1778 on duty.
Carter, Edward Private	Feb 1, 1777, Three Years	First, House	Dec 1777 on duty; Jan 1778; Feb 1778 sick in camp; March-May 1778; June 1778 sick at Downingtown.
Carter/Cartor, Henry Private	May 9, 1777, Three Years	Third, Ellis	Dec 1777; Jan 1778 on command; Feb-June 1778.
Carter, Hubbard/Hubart Sergeant	Nov 13, 1776, Duration of War	First, Morrill	Dec 1777-June 1778.
Carter, Jacob Private	June 17, 1777, Eight Months	Second, Robinson	Dec 1777; Jan 10, 1778 discharged.
Cass, Daniel Sergeant	March 8, 1777, Three Years	Third, Gray	Dec 1777; Jan 1778 on fatigue; Feb 1778 on command; March-May 1778; June 1778 on General Poor's Guard.
Cass, Jonathan Ensign	Nov 8, 1776	Third, Gray	Dec 1777-Jan 1778; Feb 1778 sick with the small pox; March-June 1778.
Cass, Moses Private	March 8, 1777, Three Years	Third, Gray	Dec 1777-Feb 1778; March 1778 sick in camp; April 1778; May 1778 sick present; June 1778.
Cass, Theopholis/Theophilus Private	Nov 12, 1777, Duration of War	First, Morrill	Dec 1777; Jan-March 1778 wounded and on furlough; April 1778 on guard; May 1778; June 1778 sick at Princeton.
Casson/Cason, Robert Private	Nov 12, 1776, Duration of War	Second, Blodget	Dec 1777; Jan-March 1778 on command; April 1778 on command Newtown; May 7, 1778 deserted.
Caswell, Gilbert Sergeant	April 8, 1777, Three Years	First, Hutchins	Dec 1777-Feb 1778; March 1778 sick present; April-June 1778.

Name	Enlisted	Company	Service
Cate, Benjamin Private/Corporal	March 13, 1777, Three Years	Third, Weare	Dec 1777-May 1778; May 3, 1778 promoted to Corporal; June-July 1778 sick at Valley Forge.
Cater, Edward Private	Nov 25, 1776	Second, Drew	June 1778.
Chadwick, Edmund Surgeon's Mate/ Surgeon	Nov 8, 1777	Third	Dec 1777-March 1778; April 1, 1778 promoted to Surgeon; April-June 1778.
Chadwick/ Shadock, John Corporal	April 6, 1777, Three Years	First, Hutchins	Dec 1777; Jan 1778 on command thrashing; Feb-June 1778.
Challes/Chelles, Thomas Sergeant	Jan 1, 1777, Duration of War	Second, Robinson	Dec 1777-June 1778.
Chamberlain/ Chamberlin, Thomas Private	May 10, 1777, Three Years	Second, Rowell	Dec 1777-March 1778; April 1778 sick in camp; May 1778; June 1778 sick Fish Kill.
Chamberlin/ Chamberling, Calvin Private	June 4, 1777, Eight Months	Third, Ellis	Dec 1777-May 1778 on furlough; June 1778.
Chandler, Daniel Private	May 10, 1777, Three Years	Third, Livermore	Dec 1777-June 1778 on furlough.
Chandler, Peter Private	June 4, 1777, Three Years	Third, Frye	Dec 1777 on furlough; Jan-Feb 1778 on command; March 1778 sick in camp; April 1778; May 1778 sick in camp; June 1778 sick at Valley Forge.
Chandonel/ Chandonet, Francis Ensign	Nov 8, 1776	First, Scott	He appears on the muster rolls for Dec 1777-March 1778 as on command with the Quartermaster General in Albany, but does not appear on the payrolls after January.
Chapman, Benjamin Private	May 18, 1777, Eight Months	First, Scott	Dec 1777; Jan 10, 1778 discharged.
Chapman/Chapon, Solomon Private	Feb 1, 1777, Duration of War	First, Morrill	Dec 1777-May 1778; June 1778 sick at Princeton.
Chase/Chace, Benjamin Private	May 23, 1777, Three Years	Third, Gray	Dec 1777-March 1778 sick absent; April 1778 on furlough to [New] City; May-June 1778 on furlough.

Name	Enlisted	Regiment	Remarks
Chase, Dudley L. Ensign	Nov 8, 1776	Third, McClary	Dec 1777-March 1778 doing Quarter Master's duty for General Poor's Brigade; May-June 1778 doing Brigade Quarter Master's duty.
Chase, Enoch 1st. Lt.	Nov 8, 1776	Second, Rowell	Dec 1777-June 1778.
Chase, Jonathan Sergeant	June 26, 1777, Three Years	Third, Weare	Dec 1777-June 1778 on furlough.
Chase, Joseph Private	Feb 13, 1777, Three Years	Third, Stone	Dec 1777; Jan 1778 on command, Feb 1778; March 1778 sick in camp; April-May 1778; June 1778 on command.
Chase, Josiah Private	Jan 20, 1777, Three Years	Third, McClary	Dec 1777-Jan 1778; Feb 1778 sick in camp; March 1778; April 1778 sick present; May-June 1778.
Chase, Moses Private	May 1, 1777, Three Years	First, Scott	Dec 1777 sick in camp; Jan-May 1778; June 1778 sick at Princeton.
Chase, Nathaniel Private	Feb 3, 1777, Three Years	Third, Stone	July 7, 1777 deserted; May 1778; June 1778 on command.
Chase, Nehemeiah Private	May 9, 1777, Eight Months	Third, Ellis	Dec 1777 on command Albany.
Chautard/Chautad, Joseph Private	April 1, 1778, Three Years	Third, McClary	May-June 1778 missing at Barren Hill.
Chelis/Chelise, Enos Private	May 7, 1777, Three Years	First, Hutchins	Dec 1777; Jan 1778 absent with leave; Feb-May 1778; June 1778 sick Yellow Springs.
Chellis, Christopher Private	April 27, 1777	Second, Robinson	April 25, 1778 joined; April 1778 on guard; May-June 1778.
Cheney, Elias Private	April 17, 1777, Three Years	Second, Clayes	Dec 1777-May 1778 sick in hospital at Albany; June 1778.
Cherry/Cherrey, Samuel 1st. Lt.	Nov 8, 1776	Second, Carr	Dec 1777-March 1778; April 1778 on weeks command; May-June 1778.
Chesley, Corydon Private	May 1, 1778, Three Years	Second, Drew	May 1778 sick present; June 1778.
Child/Childs, Cyrel Sergeant Major	Feb 1, 1777, Three Years	First, Scott	Dec 1777-Jan 1778 wounded on furlough; Feb 1778 promoted to Sergeant Major; Feb-March 1778 wounded & on furlough; April-June 1778.
Christopher, George Private	March 13, 1778, Three Years	Third, Stone	June 1778.

Name	Enlisted	Company	Notes
Church, Joshua Private	May 18, 1777, Three Years	First, Hutchins	Dec 1777-March 1778; April 1778 on main guard; May-June 1778.
Church, Thomas Sergeant	Jan 1, 1777, Duration of War	First, Scott	Dec 1777; Jan 1778 impressing waggons; Feb 1778; March 1778 sick in camp; April-May 1778; June 21, 1778 died.
Cilley/Seeley, Jonathan Private	Nov 12, 1776, Three Years	First, Morrill	Dec 1777; Jan-March 1778 on furlough; April-June 1778.
Cilley, Joseph Colonel	April 2, 1777	First	Jan-March 1778 on furlough; April-June 1778.
Clapp/Clap, Daniel 2nd. Lt.	Jan 8, 1776	First, House	Dec 1777-May 1778; June 1778 sick at Amwell.
Clark, Bunker Private	Feb 1, 1777, Three Years	First, Farwell	Dec 1777 missing in Retreat July 7, 1777; Jan 1778 sick at N. Ipswich prisoner retaken; Feb-May 1778 sick at New Ipswich; June 1778 taken prisoner July 7, 1777, joined June 2, 1778; June 1778.
Clark, Caleb Sergeant/ Corporal	Nov 15, 1776, Three Years	Second, Norris	Dec 1777-April 1778; May 1, 1778 reduced to Private; May-June 1778.
Clark, Daniel Private	Nov 18, 1776, Duration of War	Third, Beal	Dec 1777-Jan 1778; Feb-April 1778 on command; May 1778; June 1778 sick Valley Forge.
Clark, Ebenezer Private	March 27, 1777, Three Years	Third, Gray	Dec 1777 on command; Jan 10, 1778 discharged.
Clark/Clarke, Hezekiah Drummer	April 21, 1777, Three Years	First, Wait	Dec 1777; Jan 1778 on command; Feb-June 1778.
Clark, John Private	Feb 3, 1777, Three Years	First, Farwell	Dec 1777 sick in camp; Jan-June 1778.
Clark, John Private	May 1, 1777, Three Years	First, Scott	Dec 1777; Jan 1778 on command; Feb-April 1778; May 1778 on guard; June 1778.
Clark, Nathaniel Private	Nov 15, 1776, Three Years	Second, Norris	April 1778 muster roll shows him as taken prisoner on July 7, 1777, joined April 23, 1778; April-June 1778.
Clark, Thomas Private	April 14, 1777, Duration of War	First, House	Dec 1777 at Albany wounded; Jan-June 1778 on furlough wounded.
Clark, Ward/Word Private	May 27, 1777, Three Years	Third, Stone	Dec 1777-June 1778.

Name	Enlisted	Company	Notes
Clayes/Clays, Elijah Captain	Nov 8, 1776	Second, Clayes	Dec 1777-April 1778; May-June 1778 on furlough.
Clement, Richard Drummer/Private	April 23, 1777, Three Years	Second, Robinson	Dec 1777-March 1778; March 12, 1778 reduced to Private; April-May 1778; June 1778 on guard.
Clifford, Abraham Private		Second, Blodget	May 1778 muster roll shows he was taken prisoner July 7, 1777, joined May 16, 1778; May 1778; June 1778 left sick at Valley Forge.
Clifford, David Private	June 30, 1777, Three Years	Third, Gray	Dec 1777-March 1778; April 1778 sick in camp; May 1778; June 1778 on command to Lancaster.
Clifford/Clafford, William	Nov 22, 1776, Duration of War	Second, Bell	Dec 1777-April 1778; May 1778 sick in camp.
Clough, Cesar Private	Feb 9, 1778, Three Years	Second, Robinson	June 1778 sick Brunswick.
Clough/Cluff, John Private	April 1, 1777, Three Years	Third, McClary	Dec 1777-May 1778; June 1778 sick at Valley Forge.
Cobby/Colba, Bartlene/Bartlema Private	April 1, 1778, Three Years	Third, McClary	May-June 1778 missing at Barren Hill.
Cochran, James Private	April 5, 1777, Three Years	First, Scott	Dec 1777-April 1778; May 1778 sick in camp; June 1778.
Cochran, Jonath Private	April 5, 1777, Three Years	First, Scott	Dec 1777-Feb 1778; March 24, 1778 died.
Coffin, Primus Private		Second, Norris	Dec 1777-June 1778.
Cogan, Patrick Quartermaster	Nov 8, 1776	First	Jan-June 1778.
Colbath/Coalbath, Benjamin Corporal	Three Years	Second, Rowell	Dec 1777; Jan-Feb 1778 on command; March 20, 1778 died.
Colbath/Colboth, Dependence/ Independence Private	Feb 1, 1777, Three Years	Second, Bell	Dec 1777-Feb 1778; March 1778 on furlough; April 1778; May 1778 on guard.
Colbath/Colboth, Downing/Dowen Private	Feb 1, 1777, Three Years	Second, Bell	Dec 1777-May 1778 on furlough.
Colbey/Clobey, Zebulon Private	Jan 10, 1777, Three Years	First, Frye	Dec 1777; Jan 1778 sick out of Camp; Feb-May 1778; June 1778 on guard.

Name	Enlisted	Company	Service
Colburn, Amos 2nd. Lt.	Nov 8, 1776	Third, Livermore	Dec 1777; Jan 1778 on command; Feb-April 1778; May 1778 sick in camp; June 1778.
Colburn, James Private	April 10, 1777, Eight Months	First, House	Dec 1777; Jan 6, 1778 discharged.
Colburn/Colman, John Sergeant	April 22, 1777, Three Years	First, House	Dec 1777; Jan-June 1778 on furlough.
Colburn/Colban, Thomas Private	Jan 15, 1777, Three Years	First, Frye	Dec 1777-Feb 1778; March 1778 on command; April 1778; May 1778 on guard; June 1778.
Colby, David Private	Jan 1, 1777, Duration of War	Second, Robinson	Dec 1777-March 1778; April 1778 on command coaling; May-June 1778.
Colby, John Private	April 8, 1777, Three Years	Second, Robinson	Dec 1777-Jan 1778; Feb 1778 sick in camp; March-April 1778; May 1778 sick in camp; June 27, 1778 died.
Colby/Colbey, Moses Private	April 4, 1777, Three Years	First, Hutchins	Dec 1777; Jan 1778 on command with waggons; Feb 1778; March 1778 a waggoner; April 1778 waggoner for General Poor's Brigade; May 1778; June 1778 sick Valley Forge.
Colby, Theophilus Quartermaster Sergeant	Three Years	Second	Dec 1777-June 1778.
Colby/Colbey, William Private	Nov 16, 1776, Three Years	Second, Carr	Dec 1777-May 1778; June 1778 left on the road.
Cole, Solomon Private	April 18, 1777, Three Years	Second, Robinson	Dec 1777-June 1778 wounded and at Albany.
Colin, William Private	March 1, 1778, Two Years	First, Scott	June 1778.
Collins, Benjamin Private	Jan 18, 1778	First, Hutchins	June 1778 sick Valley Forge.
Collins, John Private	Feb 1, 1777, Three Years	Second, Bell	Dec 1777-March 1778 on furlough; April-May 1778.
Collumbo/ Cloumbe, Glaud Private	April 1, 1778, Three Years	Third, McClary	May 1778; June 1778 sick at Brunswick.
Colomy/Colony, Richard Private	March 30, 1777, Duration of War	Second, Bell	Dec 1777 sick in hospital Albany; Jan-Feb 1778 sick in hospital; March-May 1778 on furlough.
Colton, William Private	Three Years	Third, Weare	June 8, 1778 joined; June 1778 sick at Valley Forge.

Name	Date/Term	Company	Notes
Combs, John Private	April 21, 1777, Three Years	First, Scott	Dec 1777 sick at White Marsh; Jan-April 1778; May 1778 on guard; June 1778 sick at Princeton.
Comstock, Josiah Private	April 20, 1778, Three Years	Third, Ellis	June 1778 sick at Fishkill.
Conant, Jonathan Private	Feb 22, 1777, Three Years	First, House	Dec 1777-April 1778; May 1778 on guard; June 1778.
Connick, William Private	Feb 1, 1777, Three Years	First, House	Dec 1777 on duty; Jan 1778 sick in camp; Feb-April 1778; May 1778 on guard; June 1778.
Connor, Johnthing/ John Thing Corporal	April 8, 1777, Three Years	First, Hutchins	Dec 1777-June 1778.
Connor, Joseph/Josiph Private	May 1, 1777, Three Years	Second, Drew	Dec 1777-April 1778; May 1778 sick present; June 1778.
Conrary, John Private		First, House	June 1778.
Conrary, Stephen Private		First, House	June 1778.
Cook, Daniel Private	May 10, 1777, Three Years	Second, Rowell	Dec 1777-Feb 1778; March 1778 [ ]; March 19, 1778 transferred to the Commander-in-Chief's Guard.
Cook, Ebenezer Private	Feb 5, 1777, Duration of War	Second, Rowell	Dec 1777; Jan 1778 on duty; Feb 1778; March 1778 sick in camp; April-June 1778.
Cook, John Private	Nov 15, 1776, Duration of War	Second, Bell	Dec 1777-March 1778; April 1778 on guard; May 1778.
Cook, Thomas Private	Jan 28, 1777, Duration of War	Second, Rowell	Dec 1777-March 1778 on furlough; April-May 1778 on furlough to New Hampshire; June 1778.
Cooks/Coock, William Private	Three Years	First, Morrill	May 1778 missing July 1, 1777, now joined; May 1778; June 1778 sick Princeton.
Coolidge/ Cooledge, Silas Sergeant	Jan 1, 1777, Three Years	Second, Clayes	Dec 1777-Jan 1778; Feb 1778 on command; March-April 1778; May 1778 sick in camp; June 1778.
Cooper, George Sergeant	Feb 3, 1777 Duration of War	Third, Livermore	Dec 1777; Jan 1778 on command; Feb 1778 sick in camp; March 1778; April 1778 on guard; May-June 1778.
Cooper, John Private	April 27, 1778	First, Hutchins	June 1778 joined since last muster; June 1778.

Name	Enlistment	Regiment, Company	Service Record
Cooper, Philip Private	Jan 13, 1777, Three Years	Third, Beal	Dec 1777-May 1778 sick at Fishkill; June 1778 sick Valley Forge.
Copp, Aaron Sergeant	Feb 27, 1777, Three Years	Third, Stone	Dec 1777 sick in General Hospital Albany; Jan 1778 sick General Hospital; Feb-April 1778 sick at Albany; May 1778 on furlough; June 1778 at Boston with the invalids.
Copp, Joseph Corporal	Jan 27, 1777, Three Years	Third, Stone	Dec 1777; Jan 1778 on command; Feb-June 1778.
Copps, David Sergeant	Nov 27, 1776, Duration of War	Second, Drew	Dec 1777-May 1778 on furlough; June 1778.
Coster, Bishop Private	April 9, 1777, Three Years	First, Frye	Dec 1777; Jan 1778 on command; Feb-March 1778; April 1778 on command at the lines; May-June 1778.
Costo/Coste, Joseph Private	April 1, 1778, Three Years	Third, McClary	May 1778; June 1778 sick at Valley Forge.
Cotton, Benjamin Corporal/ Sergeant	Nov 12, 1776, Duration of War	First, Morrill	Dec 1777; Jan 1778 on present duty; Feb 1778 on command at the lines; March 1778; March 7, 1778 promoted to Sergeant; April 1778; May 1778 sick in camp; June 1778 sick at Valley Forge.
Cowdry/Cowdery, John Private	April 21, 1777, Three Years	First, Scott	August 2, 1777 taken prisoner; Dec 1777 returned from prison; Jan-March 1778 at home; April 1778; May 1778 on his march from New Hampshire; June 1778
Craig/Craigg, James Private	April 18, 1777, Three Years	Third, Livermore	Dec 1777-April 1778; May 1778 sick in camp; June 1778.
Craig/Craigg, John Private	April 18, 1777, Three Years	Third, Livermore	Dec 1777 on command as waggoner; Jan-March 1778 on command; April-June 1778 on command in the waggons.
Craig/Craige, Robert Private	Nov 12, 1776, Duration of War	Second, Blodget	Dec 1777 missing June 7, 1777 returned Oct 19, sick absent; Jan-March 1778 sick absent; April 1778; May 1778 sick in camp; June 1778 left sick at Valley Forge.
Cram, Humphrey/ Humphery Private	June 16, 1777, Three Years	Third, Frye	Dec 1777 sick absent; Jan 1778 on command; Feb 1778; March 1778 on guard; April-May 1778; June-July 1778 sick at Valley Forge.

Name	Date/Term	Company	Notes
Craton/Creighton, James, Private	Nov 15, 1776, Duration of War	Second, Rowell	Dec 1777 wounded at Albany; Jan-April 1778 wounded absent; June 30, 1778 died.
Crawford/Craford, Robert, Private	Nov 11, 1776, Three Years	First, Morrill	Dec 1777-Feb 1778; March 1778 on the General's Guard; April-June 1778.
Creasey/Cresy, Daniel, Musician	April 10, 1777, Three Years	First, Hutchins	Dec 1777-Feb 1778; March 1778 on command at the lines; April-May 1778; June 1778 sick Valley Forge.
Crison/Criston, Nathan, Private	May 9, 1777, Eight Months	Third, Ellis	Dec 1777; Jan 10, 1778 discharged.
Critchet/Chritchet, Benjamin, Private	Feb 18, 1777, Three Years	First, Farwell	Dec 1777-June 1778 on furlough by General Poor.
Critchett, Jonathan/Johnathan, Private	May 1, 1777, Three Years	Second, Drew	Dec 1777-May 1778 on furlough; June 1778 sick present.
Crombie/Crombee, James, 1st. Lt.	Nov 8, 1776	Second, Blodget	Dec 1777 sick on furlough; Jan-March 1778 on furlough; April-May 1778 on furlough New Hampshire.
Cromwel/Cromet, James, Private	Feb 2, 1777, Three Years	Second, Bell	Dec 1777-Feb 1778; March 1778 sick in camp; April-May 1778.
Cromwell, Ebenezer, Private	Feb 13, 1777, Three Years	Second, Drew	Dec 1777 muster roll shows he deserted on July 15 and joined Oct 5; Dec 1777-Feb 1778; March-April 1778 on command; May 1778; June 1778 on command.
Crosby, Jonathan, Private	April 6, 1777, Three Years	Third, Weare	Dec 1777-June 1778 left wounded at Albany.
Crosfield, Timothy, Corporal	May 9, 1777, Three Years	Third, Ellis	Dec 1777-April 1778; May 1778 sick in camp; June 1778.
Cross, Benjamin, Private	Feb 17, 1777, Three Years	Third, Beal	June 1778 "taken prisoner July 7th (evacuation of Fort Ticonderoga) now joined."
Cross, Daniel, Private	April 4, 1778, Two Years	Third, Stone	June 1778 sick General Hospital.
Cross, Ephraim, Private	April 16, 1777, Three Years	First, Hutchins	Dec 1777-Feb 1778 on the General's Guard; March 1778; April 1778 on command in the country; May-June 1778.
Cross, John, Private	Jan 1, 1778, Three Years	First, Farwell	April-June 1778.

Name	Enlistment	Company	Notes
Cummins/ Cummings, Ebenezer Private	Feb 20, 1777, Three Years	Third, McClary	Dec 1777; Jan 1778 on command; Feb 1778 muster roll shows he died on March 7, 1778.
Cuningham/ Coningham, Robert Private	April 18, 1777, Three Years	First, Morrill	Dec 1777 sick General Hospital; Jan-March 1778 sick at Albany; April-June 1778. Note this man and the man below appear to be father and son as the notation "Junr." appears in April 1778 and later rolls. It is not certain which comments go with which man for the earlier months.
Cuningham/ Coningham, Robert Private	April 18, 1777, Three Years	First, Morrill	Dec 1777 on command Artillery; Jan 1778 on command; Feb 1778; March 1778 sick in camp; Albany; April-June 1778.
Cunningham/ Cunninham, John Private	Feb 10, 1777, Three Years	Third, McClary	Dec 1777; Jan 1778 on command; Feb 1778; March 1778 on command; April-June 1778.
Currier/Curier, Jonathan Sergeant	Aug 26, 1777, Three Years	First, Emerson	Dec 1777-Jan 1778; Feb 1778 sick present; March 15, 1778 died.
Currier, Serjeant/Sargent Private	May 24, 1777, Three Years	Third, Gray	Dec 1777; Jan 1778 on command; Feb 1778; March 1778 on command; April 1778 on command a wagoner; May 1778 wagoner; June 1778 "On Command Drivg Comissy Waggon."
Currier/Curryer, Thomas Private	April 2, 1777, Three Years	Second, Bell	Dec 1777-Jan 1778; Feb 1778 sick in camp; March 1778 on command; April 1778; May 1778 on guard.
Currier, Thomas Private	April 23, 1777, Three Years	Second, Robinson	June 1778 muster roll shows him taken prisoner on July 7, 1777, and joined June 8, 1778; June 1778.
Curtis, John Sergeant	May 9, 1777, Eight Months	Third, Ellis	Dec 1777 on furlough; Jan 10, 1778 discharged.
Curtis, Nathaniel Private	Jan 11, 1777, Duration of War	First, Wait	Dec 1777-Feb 1778 sick in General Hospital; March-June 1778 sick at Albany.
Curtis, Timothy Private	Nov 14, 1776, Three Years	First, Farwell	Dec 1777-April 1778; May 1778 sick in camp; June 1778 sick at Valley Forge.
Cutler/Cutlar, William Private	Duration of War	Second, Blodget	Dec 1777-Jan 1778 sick absent; Feb-April 1778 sick at Albany; May-June 1778.

Cutting, Jonas Corporal	Nov 14, 1776, Three Years	First, Frye	Dec 1777 sick absent; Jan 1778 wounded at Albany; Feb 1778 wounded & on furlough; March-April 1778 wounded at Albany; May 1778 wounded on furlough; June 1778.	
Dalton/Dolton, Samuel Private	Feb 1, 1777, Three Years	First, Frye	Dec 1777-June 1778.	
Danford, Samuel Private	April 27, 1778, Three Years	First, Frye	June 1778 joined since last muster; June 1778.	
Danforth/Danford, Joshua Private	Nov 12, 1776, Duration of War	First, Morrill	Dec 1777; Jan 1778 sick in camp; Feb-March 1778; April 1778 on command at the lines; April 23, 1778 taken prisoner.	
Daniels, John Private	June 11, 1777, Eight Months	Third, Ellis	Dec 1777; Jan 10, 1778 discharged.	
Daniels, Nathaniel Corporal	April 21, 1777, Three Years	Third, Gray	Dec 1777-March 1778; March 31, 1778 died.	
Daniels, Samuel Private	Feb 14, 1777, Three Years	Second, Norris	Dec 1777; Jan 1778 on command; Feb-June 1778.	
Davis, Aquilla Private	May 10, 1777, Three Years	Third, Livermore	Dec 1777; Jan 1778 on command; Feb 1778 sick in camp; March-May 1778; June 1778 sick absent.	
Davis, Edmund Private	June 1, 1777, Eight Months	First, Hutchins	Dec 1777 sick at Albany; Jan 1778 discharged.	
Davis, Ephraim Private	March 2, 1777, Three Years	Second, Drew	Dec 1777-June 1778.	
Davis/Davise, Ezekiel Private	Dec 15, 1776, Three Years	First, Scott	Dec 1777-May 1778; June 26, 1778 died.	
Davis/Davies, John Private	Nov 10, 1776, Duration of War	First, Morrill	Dec 1777-Feb 1778; March 1778 sick at hospital; April 15, 1778 died.	
Davis, Jonathan/ Johnathan Private	Nov 25, 1776, Duration of War	Second, Drew	Dec 1777-May 1778; June 1778 sick at Yellow Springs.	
Davis/Davise, Joseph Private	Dec 16, 1776, Duration of War	First, Scott	Dec 1777-June 1778.	
Davis/Daves, Moses Private	Nov 22, 1776, Duration of War	Second, Bell	Dec 1777-March 1778 on furlough; April-May 1778.	
Davis, Nathan Private	March 17, 1778, Three Years	First, House	June 1778.	
Davis/Daves, Samuel Private	April 14, 1777, Three Years	Second, Bell	Dec 1777 on duty; Jan-May 1778.	

Name	Enlistment	Company	Service Record
Davis, Samuel Private	Nov 13, 1776, Duration of War	Third, Beal	Dec 1777-Jan 1778; Feb-March 1778 on command; April 1778 on command making shoes; May 1778 sick at Cuckoldstown; June 1778 sick Valley Forge.
Davis/Davise, Thomas Private	April 21, 1777, Three Years	First, Scott	Dec 1777-June 1778.
Day, Daniel Private	May 9, 1777, Eight Months	Third, Ellis	Dec 1777 on command in hospital; Jan 10, 1778 discharged.
Dayen/Dawing, Jacob Private	Jan 20, 1777, Three Years	First, Frye	Dec 1777-June 1778.
Dean, Lemuel Private	March 3, 1777, Three Years	First, House	Dec 1777-Jan 1778; Feb 1778 on command; March-April 1778; May 1778 on guard; June 1778 sick at Princeton.
Dearborn, Edward Private	Jan 20, 1777, Three Years	Second, Drew	Dec 1777-April 1778 on furlough; May-June 1778 wounded at Albany.
Dearborn, Henry Lieutenant Colonel	Sept 20, 1777	Third	Dec 1777; Jan-April 1778 on furlough; May-June 1778.
Dearborn, John Private	April 23, 1777, One Year	Third, Weare	Dec 1777; Jan 1778 on command; Feb 1778; March 1778 on duty; April 26, 1778 discharged.
Dearborn, John Jr. Private	Jan 24, 1777, Three Years	Third, Weare	Dec 1777-June 1778.
Dearborn, Samuel Sergeant	Jan 20, 1777, Three Years	Third, Weare	Dec 1777-Feb 1778; March-May 1778 sick in camp; June 1778 sick Valley Forge.
Dearborn, Simon Private	Feb 13, 1777, Duration of War	Third, McClary	Dec 1777; Jan-May 1778 on furlough; June 1778.
Dedois/Dedos, Joseph Private	April 1, 1778, Three Years	Third, McClary	May-June 1778 missing at Barren Hill. July 1778 muster roll dated August 5, 1778 shows him dead on May 13, 1778.
Demeritt/ Demmerit, Jonathan/ Johnathan Sergeant	Feb 1, 1777, Three Years	Second, Drew	Dec 1777-Feb 1778; March 1778 sick present; April-June 1778.
Demery/Domery, Ezekiel Private	Nov 10, 1776, Duration of War	Second, Carr	Dec 1777-June 1778.
Dennett, John 2nd. Lt.	Nov 8, 1776	Third, Beal	Dec 1777-June 1778.

Name	Enlisted	Company	Service Record
Dickey, David, Private	April 11, 1777, Three Years	First, Frye	Dec 1777-June 1778 sick at Albany.
Dickey, James, Private	March 4, 1777, Three Years	First, Morrill	Dec 1777-March 1778; April 1778 sick in camp; May-June 1778.
Dickey, William, Corporal/Private	April 9, 1777, Three Years	First, Frye	Dec 1777-May 1778; May [29], 1778 reduced to Private; June 1778.
Dickey, William, Private	Dec 19, 1776, Three Years	Second, Carr	Dec 1777-April 1778; May 1778 sick in camp; June 19, 1778 died.
Dimon, John, Private	Feb 9, 1778, Three Years	Second, Robinson	June 1778.
Dixon, John, Private		Second, Blodget	June [30], 1778 joined.
Dockham, Enoch, Private	Nov 14, 1777, Duration of War	Second, Drew	Dec 1777-Jan 1778; Feb-March 1778 sick present; April-May 1778; June 1778 with Brigade Major.
Dodge/Dodg, Benjamin, Corporal	Nov 14, 1776, Duration of War	Second, Rowell	Dec 1777-Jan 1778; Feb 1778 on duty; March 1778; April 1778 on weeks command; May-June 1778.
Dodge, John, Private	Feb 2, 1777, Three Years	Second, Clayes	Dec 1777-March 1778; April 1778 sick in camp; May 1778; June 1778 sick Valley Forge.
Dodge/Dodg, Shadrick, Private	June 6, 1777, Eight Months	Third, Ellis	Dec 1777; Jan 10, 1778 discharged.
Dodge, Thomas, Fifer	May 14, 1777, Three Years	First, Farwell	Dec 1777; Jan 1778 on command with General Greene; Feb 1778 sick in camp; March-June 1778.
Dodge, Zadock/Dedock, Corporal	Jan 1, 1777, Three Years	Second, Clayes	Dec 1777; Jan-Feb 1778 on command with Genl. Poor; March 1778; April-May 1778 on command with Genl. Poor; June 1778.
Doe, Jonathan, Private	March 30, 1777, Duration of War	Second, Bell	Dec 1777-Feb 1778 on furlough; March 1778 on command; April 1778; May 1778 on command in hospital.
Dole, John, Private	May 18, 1777, Three Years	First, Scott	Dec 1777-Jan 1778; Feb 1778 on duty; March-May 1778; June 1778 sick at Valley Forge.
Dollar/Doller, Thomas, Private	May 24, 1777, Three Years	Third, Gray	Dec 1777; Jan 1778 on command; Feb-April 1778; May 1778 sick present; June 1778.
Doritey/Dorrity, Charles, Private	Nov 14, 1776, Duration of War	First, Wait	Dec 1777-April 1778; May 1778 on guard; June 1778.

Name	Date	Company	Notes
Dormon, John Private	Jan 20, 1778, Three Years	First, Hutchins	April 1778 joined since last muster; April-May 1778; June 1778 waggoner.
Dorrah/Darrah, William Private	Dec 31, 1777, Three Years	First, Scott	Dec 1777; Jan-Feb 1778 sick absent; April 1778; May 1778 sick at Bristol; June 1778.
Doud/Doude, James Private	April 10, 1778, Duration of War	First, Hutchins	April 1778 joined since last muster; May 1778; June 1778 on General's guard.
Douglass, John Private	April 19, 1778, Three Years	First, Frye	June 1778 joined since last muster.
Dove/Doe, David Private	Nov 11, 1776, Duration of War	Second, Blodget	Dec 1777 on command in hospital; Jan-March 1778 on command at Albany; April 1778; March 1778 sick in camp; June 1778 left at Valley Forge sick.
Dow, Benjamin Private	Nov 12, 1776, Duration of War	First, Morrill	Dec 1777; Jan-Feb 1778 on command; March-June 1778.
Dow, Jabez/Javis Private	Dec 25, 1776, Three Years	Second, Drew	Dec 1777 muster roll shows he deserted from hospital on October 5, 1777; April 25, 1778 joined; April-June 1778.
Downing, George Private	Nov 15, 1776, Duration of War	Second, Rowell	Dec 1777-May 1778; June 1778 on guard.
Downing, Jonathan Sergeant	Nov 15, 1776, Duration of War	Second, Rowell	Dec 1777-Feb 1778; March 1778 on duty; April 1778 sick in camp; May 1778; June 1778 sick at Valley Forge.
Downs, Noah Private	March 1, 1778, Duration of War	Second, Clayes	June 1, 1778 joined; June 1778.
Downs/Dohns, Robert Private	Nov 14, 1776, Duration of War	Second, Blodget	Dec 1777; Jan-April 1778; May 1778 sick in camp; June 1778 left sick at Valley Forge.
Drew, Francis Fifer	April 6, 1777, Three Years	Second, Bell	Dec 1777-Jan 1778; Feb 1778 sick in camp; March-April 1778; May 1778 sick in hospital; June 1778.
Drew, Jonathan/ Johnathan Captain	Nov 8, 1776	Second, Drew	Dec 1777-March 1778 sick absent; April 1778 sick at Fish Kill; May 1778 sick absent; June 1778.
Drury, Ebenezer Private	March 13, 1777, Three Years	Third, Frye	Dec 1777 taken prisoner Sept 19, 1777; April 1778 "Joined since last Muster"; April 1778; May 1778 sick in camp; June 1778 sick in General Hospital.
Drury, John Private	April 2, 1777, Three Years	Third, Frye	Dec 1777-May 1778 on furlough; June 28, 1778 killed.

Name	Enlistment	Regiment/Company	Service Record
Dudey/Dudy, Obadiah Private	April 20, 1777, Duration of War	Third, Livermore	Dec 1777-June 1778 on furlough.
Dudley/Dudly, Ephraim Private	April 1, 1777, Three Years	Third, Gray	Dec 1777-June 1778.
Dudley, Jonathan Stone, Private	Duration of War	Second, Robinson	June 30, 1778 joined.
Dudley, Trueworthy/Worthy Private	Feb 14, 1777, Three Years	Second, Norris	Dec 1777-May 1778; June 1778 sick present.
Dudley, True/Trueworthy Private	April 1, 1777, Three Years	Third, Gray	Dec 1777-June 1778.
Dudy/Doody, Lemuel/Limuel Private	March 1, 1777, Duration of War	Second, Rowell	Dec 1777-March 1778 on command artillery; April-May 1778 on command Albany; June 1778.
Dudy/Duty, Moses Private	Feb 17, 1777, Three Years	Third, Weare	Dec 1777-Feb 1778 sick in General Hospital; March 1778 absent; April 1778 on guard; May-June 1778.
Duncan, David Corporal	Jan 2, 1777, Duration of War	Third, Beal	Dec 1777-April 1778; May 1778 sick in camp; June-October 1778 sick at Valley Forge.
Duncan/Dunkin, Thomas Private	May 2, 1777, Three Years	First, House	Dec 1777-May 1778; June 1778 sick at Princeton.
Dunnel/Dunnal, Reubin Private	Three Years	First, Emerson	Dec 1777-April 1778 sick at Albany; April 1778 payroll shows he died on April 25, 1778, but the June 1778 muster roll shows he died on April 15.
Durgan/Durgin, John Private	April 20, 1777, Three Years	Third, Gray	Dec 1777-April 1778; May 1778 sick present; June 1778 sick at Yellow Springs.
Durgin, Benjamin Private	Nov 13, 1776, Duration of War	Third, Beal	Dec 1777-Feb 1778; March 7, 1778 died.
Durgin/Dergin, Henry Private	May 10, 1777, Three Years	Second, Rowell	Dec 1777; Jan 1778 sick in camp; Feb-April 1778; May 1778 sick in camp; June 1778 sick at Yellow Springs.
Duset/Dusett, Philemon Private	Jan 1, 1777, Duration of War	First, Scott	Dec 1777-Jan 1778; Feb 1778 on duty; March-May 1778; June 1778 sick in camp.
Dust, Stephen Private	April 12, 1778	First, Hutchins	June 1778 joined since last muster; June 1778.

Dustin/Durstin, Zaicheus/Zach Private	Nov 14, 1776, Three Years	Second, Carr	Dec 1777 guard; Jan 1778; Feb 1778 sick in camp; March 1778; April 1778 on command; May-June 1778.
Duston, Moody 1st. Lt.	Nov 8, 1776	First, Scott	Dec 1777-June 1778.
Dutton/Dutten, Joshua Private	Nov 14, 1776, Three Years	Second, Carr	Dec 1777-Jan 1778; Feb 1778 on guard; March 1778 on command; April 1778; May 1778 sick in camp; June 1778 sick Valley Forge.
Easmon, Joseph Private	April 10, 1777, Three Years	First, Hutchins	Dec 1777 dead.
Eastman, Ebenezer Corporal	April 23, 1777, Three Years	Second, Robinson	Dec 1777-May 1778; June 1778 on guard.
Eastman/Eastam, Edward Private	March 21, 1777, Three Years	Second, Robinson	Dec 1777; Jan 1778 sick absent; Feb-March 1778 on command; April 1778 on command at Adjutant Generals; May 1778; June 1778 sick in camp.
Eastman, Jacob Private	April 12, 1777, Three Years	Third, Livermore	Dec 1777-Jan 1778; Feb 1778 sick in camp; March 1778; April 1778 on guard; May 1778 sick in camp; June 1778 sick absent.
Eastman/Estman, James Private	April 16, 1777, Three Years	Second, Bell	Dec 1777-April 1778; May 1778 on Qr. guard.
Eastman/ Eastmand, Jonathan Private	Feb 21, 1777, Three Years	First, Wait	Dec 1777; Jan 1778 on command; Feb-April 1778; May 11, 1778 died.
Eastman, Samuel Private	March 16, 1778, Two Years	First, Wait	Payroll shows enlistment date as March 15, 1778, muster roll shows March 16; April 1778-May 1778; June 1778 sick at Kings Ferry.
Eastman/Easmon, Thomas Private	April 10, 1777, Three Years	First, Hutchins	Dec 1777-March 1778 on furlough by General Gates; April 1778; May 1778 on guard; June 1778.
Eastman, William Private	April 9, 1777, Three Years	Third, Livermore	Dec 1777; Jan 1778 on command; Feb 1778; March 1778 on command; April 1778 sick in camp; May 1778; June 1778 sick absent.
Eaton/Eatton, John Ensign	Nov 8, 1776	Third, Stone	Dec 1777; Jan-May 1778 on furlough; June 1778.
Eaton, Jonathan Private	March 14, 1778, Two Years	Third, Weare	June 12, 1778 joined; June 1778.

Name	Date	Company	Notes
Eddy/Eadey, James Private	Feb 12, 1777, Three Years	Third, Ellis	Dec 1777 on command at Albany; Jan 1778 tending the sick; Feb-March 1778 on command at Albany; April-June 1778.
Edgerly/Edgely, James Private	April 4, 1777, Three Years	First, Hutchins	Dec 1777-June 1778.
Edgerly/Edgley, James Private	Jan 24, 1777, Three Years	Third, Beal	Dec 1777-May 1778 sick at Fishkill; June 1778.
Edgerly/Edgely, Joshua Private	Nov 9, 1776, Three Years	Second, Carr	Dec 1777-Feb 1778 on furlough; March 27, 1778 joined; March-June 1778.
Edwards, John Private	Nov 12, 1776, Duration of War	Second, Blodget	Dec 1777-Jan 1778; Feb 1778 sick present; March-June 1778.
Elkins, Joseph Private	April 21, 1777, Three Years	First, Hutchins	Dec 1777; Jan 1778 on command; Feb-April 1778; May 17, 1778 discharged. See Greenfield, Charles
Ellinwood, Ralph Private	April 3, 1778, Three Years	First, Scott	June 1778.
Elliott/Eliot, John Private	Nov 12, 1776, Duration of War	First, Hutchins	Dec 1777-April 1778; May 20, 1778 died.
Ellis, Benjamin 2nd. Lt.	Nov 8, 1776	Third, Ellis	Dec 1777; Jan-March 1778 on command; April-June 1778.
Ellis, William Captain	Nov 8, 1776	Third, Ellis	Dec 1777; Jan-April 1778 on furlough; May 1778 sick in camp; June 1778.
Emerson, Amos Captain	Nov 8, 1776	First, Emerson	Dec 1777-Jan 1778; Feb 1778 on command; March-June 1778.
Emerson, Jonathan 1st. Lt.	Nov 8, 1776	First, Emerson	Dec 1777-June 1778 wounded and on furlough.
Emerson, Ralph Private	April 10, 1777, Three Years	First, House	Dec 1777-June 1778.
Emory, Noah Private	April 10, 1777, Three Years	First, Frye	Dec 1777; Jan 1778 on command; Feb-June 1778.
English see Inglish			
Esquire/Esquier, Daniel Private	Nov 14, 1777, Three Years	Second, Clayes	Dec 1777; Jan 1778 on command foraging; Feb-March 1778 on command; April-May 1778; June 1778 sick Valley Forge.
Evens, Edward Private	Feb 1, 1777, Three Years	First, House	Dec 1777-Jan 1778; Feb 1778 on duty; March-June 1778.
Evens/Evans, Ira/Ire Corporal	Nov 16, 1776, Three Years	First, Farwell	Dec 1777-April 1778; May 1778 sick in camp; June 1778 sick at Valley Forge.

Name	Enlistment	Company	Service Record
Everill/Averill, Elijah Private	April 9, 1777, Three Years	First, Wait	Dec 1777-April 1778; May 1778 sick in camp; June 1778 sick Valley Forge.
Everill, George Drummer	March 20, 1778, Two Years	Third, Stone	May-June 1778.
Eyers/Eyars, Samuel Private	April 28, 1777, Three Years	First, Frye	Dec 1777 on command after leather; Jan 1778; Feb 1778 sick in camp; March-June 1778.
Fairfield/Farefield, Elijah Private	April 17, 1777, Three Years	First, Hutchins	Dec 1777-Feb 1778; March 1778 on P.M.G. Guard; April 1778 on the Paymaster Guard; May 1778 on command at Paymaster Generals; June 1778 on command Paymaster General.
Fairfield, Jeremiah Private	April 8, 1777, Three Years	Third, Livermore	Dec 1777; Jan-Feb 1778 on command; March 1778 on guard; April 1778 sick in camp; May 1778 on command in the wagons; June 1778 sick absent.
Fall, George Private	Nov 10, 1776, Duration of War	Second, Carr	Dec 1777-Jan 1778; Feb 1778 on command; March 1778 sick in camp; April-June 1778.
Farley/Ferley, William Private	May 25, 1777, Three Years	Third, Ellis	Dec 1777; Jan 1778 on command; Feb-May 1778; June 1778 sick at General Hospital; July-Aug 1778 sick at Valley Forge.
Farnsworth/Fawnsworth, Moses Private	Feb 1, 1777, Three Years	First, Farwell	Dec 1777 wounded and at Sanahday; Jan-May 1778 sick at Sanahday/Sanakdey; June 1778.
Farnum/Varnum, Ebenezer Private	March 4, 1777, Three Years	Third, Livermore	Dec 1777 "missing since Hubbarton Battle, July 7, 1777"; June 15, 1778 joined; June 1778.
Farr, Thomas Private	May 12, 1777, Eight Months	Third, Livermore	Dec 1777; Jan 10, 1778 discharged.
Farwell, Isaac Captain	Nov 8, 1776	First, Farwell	Dec 1777-June 1778.
Fay, Joseph Fifer	March 1, 1777, Three Years	Third, Ellis	Dec 1777-June 1778 on furlough.
Felch, Daniel Private	April 13, 1777, Three Years	Third, Gray	Dec 1777; Jan 1778 on command; Feb-June 1778.
Fellows, Moses Corporal	April 13, 1777, Three Years	Third, Gray	Dec 1777; Jan 1778 on command; Feb-June 1778.
Ferguson, Eleazer Private	March 7, 1778, Two Years	Second, Robinson	June 1778.

Name	Date/Term	Regiment	Notes
Fering/Fearing, Jonathan, Private	May 5, 1777, Eight Months	Third, Stone	Dec 1777 sick General Hospital Albany; Jan 1778 muster roll shows he was discharged on Feb 19, 1778.
Ferrin/Firrin, Moses, Private	Jan 1, 1777, Three Years	Second, Robinson	Dec 1777-Jan 1778.
Ferwell, Levi, Corporal	June 6, 1777, Eight Months	Third, Ellis	Dec 1777; Jan 10, 1778 discharged.
Fish, Nathan, Private	April 1, 1778, One Year	Second, Robinson	June 1778.
Fish, Nathan, Private	May 19, 1777, Three Years	Third, Frye	Dec 1777-June 1778 on furlough.
Fishley, George, Private	Three Years	Third, Weare	June 12, 1778 joined; June 1778.
Fisk, Cato, Private	March 1, 1778, Three Years	Second, Rowell	June 1778.
Fisk, Solomon, Private	March 22, 1777, Three Years	Third, Livermore	Dec 1777-March 1778; April 1778 on guard; May 1778 sick in camp; June 1778 sick absent.
Flanders, Jacob, Private	Feb 20, 1777, Three Years	First, Hutchins	Dec 1777; Jan 1778 on command with General Greene; Feb 1778 sick in camp; March-May 1778; June 1778 sick at Valley Forge.
Flanders, John, Private	Feb 10, 1777, Three Years	First, Hutchins	Dec 1777; Jan 1778 on command at Lancaster; Feb 1778; March 1778 on present duty; April-June 1778.
Flanders/Flanders, Philip, Private	Nov 12, 1776, Duration of War	First, Morrill	Dec 1777-March 1778; April 1778 sick in camp; May-June 1778.
Fletcher, Ebenezer, Fifer	March 5, 1777, Three Years	Second, Carr	Feb 1778 muster roll shows he was taken prisoner July 7, 1777 and joined on Feb 23; Feb-May 1778; June 1778 sick Valley Forge.
Fling/Flyng, Patrick, Sergeant	April 1, 1777, Three Years	Third, Beal	Dec 1777; Jan-March 1778 on command; April 1778; May 1778 in waggons; June 1778 with the waggons.
Flood/Flod, Amos, Private	April 1, 1777, Three Years	Third, Livermore	Dec 1777 joined since last muster; Jan-Feb 1778; March 1778 on guard; April 1778; May 1778 sick in camp; June 1778.
Flood, Daniel, Private	June 2, 1777, Eight Months	First, Hutchins	Dec 1777; Jan 1778 discharged.
Flood/Flud, Jonathan, Private	Jan 22, 1777, Duration of War	Third, McClary	Dec 1777; Jan 1778 sick in camp; Feb-March 1778 sick in General Hospital; April-June 1778.

Name	Enlisted	Company	Service Record
Flood, Joseph Private	June 6, 1777, Eight Months	First, Hutchins	Dec 1777; Jan 1778 discharged.
Floyd, James Musician	Three Years	Third, Weare	June 24, 1778 joined; June 1778.
Fogg, Jeremiah Paymaster	Nov 8, 1776	Second	Dec 1777; Jan 1778 on furlough by Genl. Poor; Feb-March 1778 on furlough; May-June 1778.
Folsom, John Private	Nov 14, 1776, Duration of War	Second, Drew	Dec 1777-Jan 1778; Feb 1778 with butchers; March 1778 sick present; April 5, 1778 died.
Folsom, Johnathan/ Jonathan Private	March 3, 1777, Duration of War	Second, Drew	Dec 1777-May 1778; June 1778 on guard.
Folsom, Jonathan Private	March 29, 1777, Three Years	Third, Gray	Dec 1777-June 1778 on furlough.
Forrest, Robert Private	March 16, 1778, Three Years	First, Frye	May 1778 joined; May-June 1778.
Forsythe/Forsyth, David Ensign	Nov 8, 1776	Second, Blodget	Dec 1777 sick absent; Jan-March 1778 on furlough; April 1778 sick at Chester, New Hampshire; May 10, 1778 discharged.
Fosgate/Fosgett, Ebenizor/Ebenezer Private	Jan 27, 1777, Duration of War	First, Wait	Dec 1777 sick in camp; Jan 1778 on fatigue; Feb-March 1778 on command; April 1778 sick in camp; May 1778; June 1778 on guard.
Foss, Samuel Private	June 4, 1777, Three Years	Second, Rowell	Dec 1777; Jan 1778 on guard; Feb-May 1778; June 1778 sick at Yellow Springs.
Foster, Daniel Musician	March 1, 1777, Three Years	Second, Carr	Dec 1777; Jan-March 1778 on command; April 1778; May 1778 on weeks command; June 1778.
Foster, Daniel Private	March 16, 1778, Three Years	Third, Ellis	June 1778.
Foster, Ephraim Corporal/ Sergeant	Feb 1, 1777, Three Years	First, Farwell	Dec 1777-Feb 1778; March 1778 sick present; April-May 1778; May 1, 1778 promoted to Sergeant; June 1778.
Foster, Jonathan Private	April 30, 1777, Three Years	Third, Frye	Dec 1777 missing July 7th 1777; June 1778.
Foster, Samuel Private	March 1, 1777, Three Years	Second, Bell	Dec 1777-Jan 1778 on furlough; Feb-May 1778; June 1778 sick Valley Forge.
Fowler, Abner Private	May 28, 1777, Three Years	Third, Gray	Dec 1777; Jan-Feb 1778 on command; March 1778; April 1778 on a weeks command at the Lines; May 1778 sick present; June 1778.

Name	Date	Company	Notes
Fowler, Philip Sergeant Major	Three Years	Second	Dec 1777-June 1778.
Fowler, Philip Private	March 2, 1778	Second, Drew	June 9, 1778 joined; June 1778 sick at Princeton.
Fox, Silas Private	Feb 12, 1777, Duration of War	Third, Stone	Dec 1777-May 1778; June 1778 sick at General Hospital.
Fremon/Freeman, Ezra Private	May 9, 1777, Eight Months	Third, Ellis	Dec 1777 on furlough; Jan 10, 1778 discharged.
French, Moses Private		Second, Norris	Dec 1777 never joined.
French, Winthrop/Wintrop Private	Jan 28, 1778, Three Years	Third, McClary	June-July 1778 sick at Valley Forge; Aug 15, 1778 died.
Frost, George Pepperell, Ensign	Nov 8, 1776	Second, Carr	Dec 1777-March 1778; April 1778 on guard; May-June 1778.
Frost, Nathaniel Private		Second, Bell	May 1778 muster roll shows he deserted July 7, 1777; April 17, 1778 joined and pardoned; May 1778.
Frye, Ebenezer, Captain	Nov 8, 1776	First, Frye	Dec 1777 now returning from captivity; Jan 1778 exchanged from being a prisoner; Feb 1778 exchanged from captivity; March 1778 at New England; April-June 1778.
Frye, Isaac Captain	Nov 8, 1776	Third, Frye	Dec 1777-May 1778; June 1778 sick at Valley Forge.
Fugard, Samuel Private	Nov 13, 1776, Three Years	First, Frye	Dec 1777-Jan 1778; Feb 1778 on the advance picquet; March-April 1778; May 1778 on guard; June 1778.
Fuller, Amos Private	March 25, 1777, Three Years	Third, Frye	Dec 1777-May 1778 on furlough; June 1778 sick at Amwell.
Fuller, Daniel Private	July 1, 1777, Three Years	First, House	Dec 1777 at Albany wounded; Jan-March 1778 on furlough wounded; April-June 1778.
Fuller, Ezra Private	May 1, 1777, Three Years	Third, Frye	Dec 1777-March 1778 on furlough; April-May 1778 sick in camp; June 1778 sick in General Hospital. July muster roll dated August 5, 1778 shows he died on July 14, 1778, but rolls of Aug 1778 through March 1779 show him as sick at Valley Forge.
Fuller/Fuler, Levi Private	April 15, 1777, Three Years	Third, Ellis	Aug 10, 1777 deserted; Feb-April 1778 sick at Albany; May-June 1778 on furlough.

Name	Enlistment	Company	Service Record
Fuller/Fullar, Thomas Private	April 3, 1777, Three Years	First, Emerson	Dec 1777-Feb 1778; March 1778 sick present; April 1778 sick in camp; May 1778; June 1778 sick at Brunswick.
Fullerton/ Fullonton, Jonathan Private	May 13, 1777, Three Years	Second, Rowell	Dec 1777-May 1778 wounded at Albany; June 2, 1778 died.
Fullerton/ Fullonton, Joseph Private	May 13, 1777, Three Years	Second, Rowell	Dec 1777-March 1778 on furlough; April-May 1778 on furlough to New Hampshire; June 1778 sick at Albany.
Furnald/Funnell, William Private	Feb 25, 1777, Three Years	Third, McClary	Dec 1777-May 1778 sick at Fishkill; June 1778 sick at Valley Forge.
Gage, Andrew Private/Corporal	May 30, 1777, Three Years	Third, Gray	Dec 1777-Jan 1778; Feb 1778 on command; March 1778; April 1, 1778 promoted to Corporal; April-May 1778; June 1778 on command at Yellow Springs; July 1, 1778 died.
Gale, William Sergeant	Feb 5, 1777, Three Years	Third, Beal	Dec 1777-May 1778; June 1778 sick at Fishkill.
Gansey/Gansay, John Private	May 9, 1777, Eight Months	Third, Ellis	Dec 1777; Jan 10, 1778 discharged.
Gant/Gatt, George Private	Nov 14, 1776, Three Years	First, Frye	Dec 1777-Feb 1778; March 1778 absent; April-June 1778.
Gardner/Gardiner, Thomas Private	Jan 1, 1777, Duration of War	Second, Drew	Dec 1777 on furlough; Jan 1778; Feb-June 1778 on furlough.
Garland/Garlon, John Private	May 10, 1777, Three Years	Second, Rowell	Dec 1777-Feb 1778 sick in Fish Kill; March 1778; April 1778 sick in camp; May-June 1778.
Garland, John Private	April 28, 1777, Three Years	Third, Livermore	Dec 1777; Jan-Feb 1778 on command; March 1778; April 1778 sick in camp; May 10, 1778 died.
Garland, John Private	April 23, 1777, One Year	Third, Weare	Dec 1777; Jan 1778 on command; Feb-March 1778; April 26, 1778 discharged.
Garrill/Garrett, Anthoney/Antoni Private	April 1, 1778, Three Years	Third, McClary	May 1778 missing at Barren Hill; June 1778 on command with Baron Steuben.
Gay, Isaac Private	Three Years	Third, Stone	Only record is the June 1778 muster roll which shows he deserted.

Name	Date	Company	Notes
Geer/Gears, Charles Private	Feb 19, 1778, Two Years	First, Wait	June 1778.
Geer/Gears, Walter Private	March 16, 1778, Two Years	First, Wait	June 1778.
George, Austin/Austain Private	June 10, 1777, Three Years	Third, Stone	Dec 1777; Jan-March 1778 on command; April-May 1778; June 1778 sick at General Hospital.
George, Benjamin Private	March 1, 1777, Three Years	First, Morrill	Dec 1777-June 1778.
George, David Sergeant	April 7, 1777, Three Years	Second, Carr	Dec 1777-April 1778; May 1778 sick in camp; June 1778.
George/Gorge, Isaac Private	March 1, 1777, Three Years	First, Morrill	Dec 1777; Jan-March 1778 sick at Albany; April 1778 on command in camp; May-June 1778.
George, Jonathan Private	Nov 14, 1776, Three Years	Second, Carr	Dec 1777-May 1778; June 1778 sick D. W. River.
George/Gorg, Josiah Private	May 7, 1777, Three Years	Third, Weare	Dec 1777-June 1778 on furlough.
George, Michael Private	Nov 23, 1776, Three Years	Second, Carr	Dec 1777-June 1778.
George, Moses Swet/Sweet Private	April 10, 1777, Three Years	Second, Clayes	Dec 1777 wounded in hospital Bennington; Jan-April 1778 wounded in hospital Bennington; May 1778 wounded at Bennington; June 1778 sick at Valley Forge.
George, Thomas Private	April 17, 1777, Three Years	First, Hutchins	Dec 1777-May 1778; June 1778 sick Valley Forge.
George, Thomas Private	March 1, 1777, Three Years	First, Morrill	Dec 1777-April 1778; May 1778 on guard; June 1778.
Gibbs, David Private	March 10, 1777, Three Years	First, House	Dec 1777-March 1778 wounded returned home; April-May 1778 sick at Chesterfield.
Gibbs, Isaac Sergeant	March 10, 1777, Three Years	First, House	Dec 1777-June 1778.
Gibbs, Joshua Private	March 10, 1777, Three Years	First, House	Dec 1777-Feb 1778; March 1778 on command; April 1778 sick in camp; May 1778; June 1778 sick at Downingtown.
Gill, Silas Private	Feb 1, 1777, Three Years	First, Farwell	Dec 1777 wounded absent; Jan-May 1778; wounded and at Albany; June 1778 wounded and at New England.
Gillman, Samuel Private	June 17, 1777, Eight Months	Second, Robinson	Dec 1777; Jan 10, 1778 discharged.

Name	Enlisted	Company	Service Record
Gilman/Gilmon, Anthony Private	Jan 1, 1777, Three Years	First, Hutchins	Dec 1777-Jan 1778; Feb 1778 sick in camp; March 1778 on command; April 1778; May 1778 on command; June 1778.
Gilman, Caleb Private	May 28, 1777, Eight Months	Third, Gray	Dec 1777; Jan 10, 1778 discharged.
Gilman, Carter/Cater Private	Nov 14, 1776	Second, Drew	April 1778 muster roll shows him as a prisoner on July 7, 1777, April 25, 1778 joined; May 1778; June 1778 sick at Valley Forge.
Gilman, Carter Private	May 27, 1777, Eight Months	Third, Gray	Dec 1777 on furlough; Jan 10, 1778 discharged.
Gilman/Gillman, David 2nd. Lt.	Nov 8, 1776	Second, Drew	Dec 1777; Jan 1778 on command; Feb-March 1778; April-June 1778.
Gilman/Gillman, Ezekiel Private	Jan 1, 1777, Duration of War	Second, Robinson	Dec 1777-April 1778; May 1778 on guard; June 1778.
Gilman, Jeremiah Major	April 2, 1777	First	Jan 1778; Feb 1778 sick absent; March 1778 sick present; April 1778; May 1778 sick present; June 1778.
Gilman, John Private	Feb 10, 1777, Three Years	Third, McClary	Dec 1777-Feb 1778; March 15, 1778 died.
Gilman, Joseph Private	April 25, 1778, One Year	Second, Robinson	June 1778.
Gilman, Nathaniel 1st. Lt.	Nov 8, 1776	Third, Beal	Dec 1777-Jan 1778; Feb 1778 sick with small pox; March-April 1778; May 1, 1778 discharged.
Gilman, Nicholas Adjutant	Nov 8, 1776	Third	Dec 1777; Jan 15, 1778 appointed assistant to Adjutant General.
Gilman, Simon Private	Jan 15, 1777	Second, Drew	Missing on July 7, 1777; June 1778.
Gilmore/Gillmore, James Private	April 24, 1777, Three Years	First, Frye	Dec 1777; Feb 1778 on command on picquett; Feb 1778 sick in camp; March-April 1778; May 1778 on command at Downingtown; June 1778 sick at Hopewell.
Gilmore/Gillmore, Thomas Private	Nov 14, 1776, Three Years	First, Farwell	Dec 1777-April 1778; May 1778 on command with ye waggons; June 1778.
Glidden/Gliden, Gideon Private	Feb 12, 1777, Duration of War	Second, Drew	Dec 1777-Jan 1778; Feb 1778 on duty; March 1778 on command; April-May 1778; June 1778 at [ ] sick.

Name	Enlisted	Company	Service Record
Glines/Glins, Nathaniel Private	June 9, 1777, Three Years	First, Frye	Dec 1777 sick absent by order the doctor; Jan 1778 on fatigue; Feb 1778 sick in camp; March 1778 on guard; April-June 1778.
Goatham/Gotem, Edward Musician	Jan 1, 1777, Three Years	Second, Blodget	Dec 1777-Jan 1778; Feb 1778 sick present; March-May 1778.
Goatham/Gotem, Samuel Fifer/Private	Nov 28, 1777, Three Years	Second, Rowell	Dec 1777-Feb 1778; March 1778 sick in camp; April-May 1778; June 1, 1778 reduced to Private; June 1778 sick Valley Forge.
Gob see Job			
Godfrey/Godfree, John Corporal	April 20, 1777, Three Years	Third, Frye	Dec 1777-April 1778; May 1778 sick in camp; June 1778 sick at Valley Forge.
Godfrey, Jonathan Private	March 22, 1778, Three Years	Second, Carr	June 1778.
Goodale, Ezekiel 2nd. Lt.	Nov 8, 1776	Third, Frye	Dec 1777-Feb 1778 sick absent; March 1778 on furlough; April 1778 muster roll shows he was discharged on May 1, 1778.
Goodenough/ Goodnough, Adine/Addino Sergeant Major	Dec 1, 1776	Third	Jan 1778 prisoner; April 1, 1778 joined; April 1778; May 1778 sick in camp; June 1778.
Goodman, Richard Corporal/Private	March 18, 1777, Three Years	Third, Frye	Dec 1777; Jan 1778 on command; Feb 1, 1778 reduced to Private; Feb 1778; March 1778 on command; April 1778 on command after leather; May 1778 sick in camp; June 1778 sick in General Hospital; June 27, 1778 died.
Gookin/Gooking, Daniel Sergeant Major	Three Years	Second	Dec 1777-May 1778.
Goold, James 1st. Lt.	Jan 8, 1776	First, House	Dec 1777 wounded and on furlough; Jan-June 1778 on furlough wounded.
Goold/Gould, Moses Private	April 29, 1777, Three Years	First, Wait	Dec 1777 wounded September 19th, on furlough by General Gates; Jan-Feb 1778 wounded and on furlough; March 1778 on furlough; April-May 1778 wounded and on furlough; June 1778 sick at Albany.

Name	Enlistment	Company	Service Notes
Goold/Gould, Nehemiah, Private	April 29, 1777, Three Years	First, Wait	Dec 1777-Feb 1778; March 1778 on command; April 1778; May 1778 sick in camp; June 1778 sick at Valley Forge.
Goold, Simeon, Private	Feb 1, 1777, Three Years	First, House	Dec 1777 sick at Fish Kill; Jan-Feb 1778; March 1778 on command; April-May 1778; June 1778 sick at Downingtown.
Gorden, Ithiel/Ithial, Private	May 13, 1777, Three Years	Second, Rowell	April 1778 muster roll shows him captured on July 7, 1777, April 24, 1778 joined; May 1778 on guard; June 1778.
Gorden/Gordon, Joseph, Private	Jan 1, 1777, Duration of War	Second, Robinson	Dec 1777-March 1778; April 1778 on command detachment; May-June 1778.
Gordon/Gorden, Eliphlet/Eliphalet, Private	May 13, 1777, Three Years	Second, Rowell	Dec 1777-Feb 1778; March 1778 on command; April 1778; May 1778 on guard; June 1778.
Gordon, James, Private	Jan 15, 1777, Three Years	Third, Livermore	Dec 1777-March 1778; April-May 1778 sick in camp; June 1778 sick absent.
Gordon/Godding, Samuel, Private	March 20, 1777, Three Years	Second, Blodget	Dec 1777 on guard; Jan 1778 on command; Feb 1778; March 1778 on duty; April-May 1778; June 1778 sick at Corryell's Ferry.
Gotey/Goley, Mathew, Private	April 1, 1778, Three Years	Third, McClary	June-Aug 1778 sick on the road from Valley Forge.
Gould/Guld, Elijah/Eliger, Private	April 16, 1777, Three Years	Second, Bell	Dec 1777-May 1778.
Grandey, John, Private	June 15, 1777, Eight Months	Third, Ellis	Dec 1777 sick present; Jan 10, 1778 discharged.
Grant, Duncan/Dunkan, Private	April 4, 1777, Three Years	First, Emerson	Dec 1777-Jan 1778 on duty; Feb 1778 on command; March-April 1778; May 1778 sick at Yellow Springs; June 1778 sick in Jersey.
Grant, Edward, Private	March 2, 1777, Duration of War	Second, Carr	Dec 1777-April 1778 sick absent; May-June 1778.
Grant, Joseph, Private	March 5, 1778	First, Morrill	June 1778 sick at Valley Forge.
Grant, Samuel, Private	March 11, 1778, Three Years	Second, Carr	June 1778.
Grant, William, Private	Nov 13, 1776, Three Years	Second, Carr	Dec 1777-Jan 1778 wounded and in Albany; Feb-March 1778 wounded; April-May 1778 wounded Albany; June 1778 left at Albany.

Gray, James Captain	Nov 8, 1776	Third, Gray	Dec 1777; Jan-June 1778 on furlough.
Gray, Joseph Private	March 30, 1777, Three Years	Third, Frye	Dec 1777; Jan 1778 on command; Feb 1778; March 1778 on command; April 1778 on guard; May 1778 sick in camp; June 1778 sick at Valley Forge.
Grear, John Private	June 1, 1778	Third, McClary	June 1778 "On command Genl Sullivan."
Greeley/Grealy, Matthew Private	April 13, 1777, Three Years	Third, Gray	Dec 1777-Jan 1778 sick absent; Feb-June 1778.
Greely/Grealy, Reuben, Privatep	April 13, 1777, Three Years	Third, Gray	Dec 1777-March 1778 sick absent; April 1, 1778 died.
Green, Bradbury Drummer	Nov 14, 1776, Three Years	Second, Carr	April 1778 muster roll shows he was missing on July 7, 1777, joined on April 30, 1778; April 1778; May 1778 sick in camp; June 1778 sick in Valley Forge.
Green, Jonathan Private	April 25, 1777, Three Years	Second, Robinson	Dec 1777-Jan 1778; Feb 1778 sick in camp; March-June 1778.
Green, Richard Private	March 7, 1778	Third, Weare	June 8, 1778 joined; June 1778 sick at Valley Forge.
Greenaway, Abraham Corporal	Nov 14, 1776, Three Years	Second, Rowell	Dec 1777-Feb 1778; March 1778 on command; April-May 1778; June 1778 with armorers.
Greenfield, Charles Private	April 21, 1778, Three Years	First, Hutchins	May 1778 "in place of Joseph Elkins"; June 1778. See Elkins, Joseph.
Greenleaf/ Grondlaf, Nathan Private	May 15, 1777, Three Years	Third, Weare	Dec 1777; Jan 1778 after provisions; Feb-May 1778; June 1778 tending sick at Hospital.
Greer/Grear, John Private	April 1 1778, Three Years	Third, McClary	May-June 1778 on command with General Sullivan.
Greer, Mathew Private	March 16, 1778, Three Years	First, Farwell	June 1778.
GriffinGriffen, Joseph Private	Jan 30, 1777, Three Years	Third, McClary	Dec 1777; Jan-Feb 1778 sick in camp; March 1778 sick General Hospital; April-June 1778.
Griffin, Minicus/ Dominicus Corporal	Feb 14, 1777, Three Years	Third, McClary	Dec 1777-March 1778 sick at Fishkill; April 1778 sick in camp; May 15, 1778 died.
Griffin, Richard Private	March 20, 1778, Three Years	Third, Stone	July 1778 sick at Pennsylvania.
Grimes, Nathaniel Private	Jan 9, 1778	First, Morrill	June 1778 sick at Valley Forge.

Name	Enlisted	Company	Notes
Groutt/Groute, John Private	May 1, 1778, Three Years	First, Farwell	June 1778.
Gruss/Grush, Thomas Private	March 23, 1777, Three Years	First, Emerson	Dec 1777-Feb 1778 sick at White Marsh; March 1778 sick present; April-June 1778.
Gun, Samuel Private	May 9, 1777, Eight Months	Third, Ellis	Dec 1777 on furlough.
Hackety/Hakety, Barnabas/ Barnabee Private	Dec 15, 1776, Duration of War	First, Wait	Dec 1777-June 1778.
Haines, Simeon Private	Nov 15, 1776, Three Years	Second, Norris	Dec 1777; Jan 1778 on guard; Feb-June 1778.
Haines/Heains, Walter, Private	May 15, 1777, Three Years	First, Frye	Dec 1777 sick absent Albany; Jan-June 1778 sick at Albany.
Haines, William Private	Feb 10, 1777, Three Years	Second, Norris	Dec 1777 on command armourer at Albany; Jan-May 1778 on command Albany; June 1778 on command at Albany armourer
Hains/Heains, Thomas Private	April 15, 1777, Three Years	First, Frye	Dec 1777 wounded absent; Jan-May 1778 wounded and on furlough; June 1778 sick at Albany.
Hale, Aaron Private	Jan 1, 1777, Three Years	Second, Blodget	Dec 1777-April 1778; May sick in camp; June 1778.
Hale, John Surgeon	July 2, 1777	First	Jan-April 1778 on furlough; May-June 1778.
Hale, William Private	April 10, 1777, Three Years	First, House	Dec 1777-April 1778 on furlough; May-June 1778.
Hall, Benjamin Private	Jan 28, 1777, Three Years	Third, McClary	Dec 1777; Jan 1778 sick in camp; Feb 1778 sick in General Hospital; March 12, 1778 died.
Hall, David Sergeant	April 29, 1777, Three Years	Third, Frye	Dec 1777 sick in camp; Jan 1778 on command Feb 1778 on guard; March-April 1778 sick in camp; May-June 1778.
Hall, Ephraim Private	Nov 13, 1776, Duration of War	Second, Blodget	Dec 1777; Jan 1778 on command; Feb 1778; March 1, 1778 deserted; March 9, 1778 joined; April-May 1778; June 1778 left sick at Valley Forge.
Hall, James Private	April 4, 1777, Duration of War	Third, McClary	Dec 1777; Jan 1778 sick in camp; Feb 1778 sick in General Hospital; March 8, 1778 died.
Hall, James Jr. Private	Feb 3, 1777, Three Years	Third, McClary	Dec 1777-Jan 1778; Feb 1778 tending ye sick; March 10, 1778 died.

Name	Enlistment	Company	Service
Hall, John Private	March 12, 1778, Three Years	First, Frye	June 1778.
Hall, Jude Private	Nov 14, 1776, Three Years	Second, Clayes	Dec 1777 on command with Colo. Hay at Albany; Jan 1778 on command with Q.M.G. at Albany; Feb-May 1778 on command at Albany; June 1778 on command with Col. Hay.
Hall, Laban Private	March 10, 1778, One Year	Second, Clayes	June 20, 1778 joined; June 1778.
Hall, Reuben Private	March 14, 1777, Three Years	First, Emerson	Dec 1777-May 1778 retaken and sick at Albany; June 1778 sick in camp.
Hall, Thomas Private	Jan 1, 1777, Duration of War	Second, Robinson	Dec 1777-Jan 1778; Feb 1778 sick in camp; March-April 1778; May 1778 sick in camp; June 1778.
Hall, Ziba/Zibe Corporal	May 1, 1777, Three Years	Third, Ellis	Dec 1777 sick at Whitemarsh; Jan 1778 sick in hospital; Feb-March 1778 sick absent; April 1778 muster roll shows he died on Jan 30, 1778.
Hamblet, Reubin/Rubin Private	April 14, 1777, Three Years	Second, Bell	Dec 1777; Jan 1778 on command; Feb 1778; March 1778 on guard; April-May 1778.
Ham, George Private	May 1, 1777, Three Years	Second Drew	June 1778.
Hamm/Ham, Ephraim Private	May 1, 1777, Duration of War	Second, Bell	Dec 1777-May 1778.
Hamm/Ham, John Private	May 1, 1777, Three Years	Second, Bell	Dec 1777; Jan 1778 on command; Feb 1778; March 1778 on command; April-May 1778.
Hanscom/ Hunscomb, Thomas Private	Jan 29, 1777, Duration of War	Second, Bell	Dec 1777 sick in camp; Jan-Feb 1778 on command; March 23, 1778 dead.
Hanson, Anthony Sergeant	Feb 11, 1777, Three Years	Second, Carr	July 7, 1777 missing; May 1778; June 1778 on guard.
Hanson, Charles Private	Jan 1, 1777, Three Years	First, Emerson	Dec 1777-June 1778.
Hardy, Cyrus/Syrus Private	April 14, 1777, Three Years	Second, Bell	Dec 1777-Jan 1778 on furlough; Feb 1778 muster roll shows him dead on Jan 29, 1778.
Hardy, James Private	Feb 13, 1777, Three Years	First, House	Dec 1777 sick present; Jan 1778; Feb 1778 sick in camp; March 1778 on guard; April-May 1778 sick in camp; June 1778 sick at Valley Forge.

Name	Enlistment	Company	Notes
Hardy/Hardey, Nathaniel Private	Three Years	First, Emerson	Dec 1777-Feb 1778; March 5, 1778 dead.
Hardy, Thomas Private	April 20, 1778, One Year	First, House	June 1778.
Harmon, Stephen Private	April 1, 1777, Three Years	Third, Weare	Dec 1777 on command with Doctor H[arv]y; Jan 1778 comment illegible; Feb-May 1778; June 1778 on command as Waggoner.
Harper, John Private	Jan 23, 1777, Three Years	First, Farwell	Dec 1777 sick absent; Jan-May 1778 sick at Ackworth/Acworth; June 1778 "Returnd from Desartion & Joind a Contl officer March 1st 1778."
Harper, Samuel Private	Nov 31, 1776, Three Years	First, Farwell	Dec 1777 sick absent on furlough; Jan-May 1778 sick on furlough; June 1778 "Returnd from Desartion & Joind a Contl officer March 1st 1778."
Harrington/ Herrinton, Timothy Private	Nov 14, 1776, Three Years	First, Frye	Dec 1777; Jan 1778 on command making Clous; Feb-June 1778.
Harris/Herrice, Salomon Private	March 22, 1778, Two Years	First, Wait	May 1778 on main guard; June 1778.
Harriss/Herrice, Henry Private	April 9, 1777, Three Years	First, Wait	Dec 1777; Jan 1778 on command; Feb 1778 on guard; March 1778; April 1778 on guard; May 1778 sick in camp; June 1778 sick Valley Forge.
Harsey, Petter/Peter Private	April 8, 1777, Three Years	First, Hutchins	Dec 1777; Jan 18, 1778 dead.
Harvey, John Sergeant	Feb 22, 1777, Three Years	Third, Gray	Dec 1777-May 1778; June 1778 sick Crumpond.
Harvey, Kimber Private/Sergeant	May 9, 1777, Three Years	Third, Ellis	Dec 1777; Jan 10, 1778 promoted to Sergeant; Jan 1778 on command; Feb-June 1778.
Haselton/ Haseltine, David Private	June 16, 1777, Three Years	Third, Frye	Dec 1777 on furlough; Jan-March 1778; April 1778 on guard; May 1778 sick in camp; June 1778 sick at Valley Forge.
Haselton/Heselton, Jeremiah Private	Nov 14, 1776, Duration of War	First, Morrill	Dec 1777; Jan 1778 on command; Feb-April 1778; May 12, 1778 dead.

Name	Enlisted	Company	Service Record
Haselton/Heselton, Jonathan Private	Nov 10, 1776, Duration of War	First, Morrill	Dec 1777-Jan 1778; Feb 1778 on command in the country; March 1778 on command at Potts Grove; April-June 1778.
Haselton/Heselton, Joseph Private	Feb 12, 1777, Three Years	First, Morrill	Dec 1777; Jan 1778 on duty; Feb-March 1778 on command at the Bridge; April 1778; May 1778 on guard; June 1778.
Haskel/Haskell, Abijah Private	March 20, 1777, Three Years	Second, Blodget	Dec 1777-May 1778; June 1778 sick at Englishtown.
Hastings/Haistings, Robert Private	Feb 10, 1777, Duration of War	Third, Stone	Dec 1777-May 1778; June 1778 sick at General Hospital.
Hastings, Silvanus Private	Jan 1, 1778, Three Years	First, Farwell	April-June 1778.
Hawkins, William Adrian 1st. Lt.	Nov 8, 1776	Third, Frye	Dec 1777-Feb 1778 on command at Albany; March 1778 on furlough; April-June 1778.
Hawkley, James Private	March 1, 1777, Three Years	First, Farwell	Dec 1777 wounded absent on furlough; Jan-March 1778 wounded on furlough; April-June 1778.
Hayes/Hayse, Nathaniel Private	Feb 1, 1777, Three Years	First, Farwell	Dec 1777-Jan 1778; Feb 1778 on Genl Guard; March-June 1778.
Haywood/Howard, Samuel Private	April 14, 1777, Three Years	Second, Bell	Dec 1777; Jan-April 1778 on furlough; May 1778.
Hazelton, John Private	Feb 1, 1777, Three Years	First, House	Dec 1777 sick at Albany; Jan-March 1778 on furlough; April-May 1778 sick at Cochenmouth/Cockermouth; June 1778 sick at New Hampshire.
Hazelton, Nathaniel Private	April 1, 1778	Second, Bell	June 1778.
Head, John Private	Nov 13, 1776, Three Years	First, Frye	Dec 1777; Jan-March 1778 on command with Colo. Reid; April-May 1778; June 1778 on command in the country.
Heath, Asa Private	May 8, 1778, Nine Months	First, Hutchins	June 1778 joined since last muster; June 1778.
Heath, David Private	May 6, 1777, Eight Months	First, Hutchins	Dec 1777 dead.
Heath, Enoch Private	June 1, 1777, Eight Months	Third, Stone	Dec 1777 sick at Fish Kill; Jan 1778 muster roll shows he was discharged on Feb 19, 1778.

45

Name	Enlistment	Regiment/Co.	Notes
Heath, Enoch, Jr. Private	May 8, 1777, Eight Months	Third, Stone	Dec 1777; Jan 10, 1778 discharged.
Heath, Ephraim/Ephiriam Corporal	Three Years	Third, Gray	Dec 1777; Jan 1778 sick in quarters; Feb 1778; March 26, 1778 died.
Heath, Jesse Private	April 25, 1777, Three Years	First, Emerson	Dec 1777-Feb 1778; March 1778 on guard; April 1778; May 1778 on guard; June 1778 sick in Pennsylvania.
Heath, Jonathan, Private	May 8, 1777, Eight Months	Third, Stone	Dec 1777; Jan 10, 1778 discharged.
Heath, Richard Private	Feb 7, 1777, Three Years	Third, Stone	Dec 1777; Jan 1778 sick in camp; Feb-April 1778 sick in General Hospital; May 1778 sick in camp; June 1778 sick at General Hospital; July 6, 1778 died.
Heath, Starling Private	Feb 27, 1777, Duration of War	Third, Stone	May 1778; June 1778 muster roll shows he was "Taken July 7th 1777 Joind"; June 1778.
Heath, William Private	April 21, 1777, Three Years	Third, Livermore	Dec 1777-June 1778 on furlough.
Henderson, Joseph Sergeant	Jan 1, 1777, Duration of War	First, Scott	Dec 1777 waggon master; Jan 1778 discharged.
Henderson/ Handerson, Zoath Private	Nov 15, 1776, Duration of War	First, Bell	Dec 1777-March 1778 on furlough; April-May 1778.
Herriman, Page Private	May 19, 1777, Three Years	First, Farwell	Dec 1777 sick in camp; Jan-April 1778; May 1778 sick in camp; June 1778 sick at Fish Kill.
Herrington/ Herinton, John Private	Jan 2, 1777, Duration of War	Third, Beal	Dec 1777-Jan 1778; Feb-March 1778 on command; April-June 1778.
Hewes, Samuel Corporal	April 18, 1777, Three Years	First, House	Dec 1777-Feb 1778; March 1778 on command; April-May 1778; June 1778 sick at Valley Forge.
Hewitt/Hewit, William Private	Feb 1, 1778, Three Years	First, Farwell	April 1778 in "M. Gard"; May 1778; June 1778 on General Lee's Guard.
Hicks, Benjamin Private		Second, Bell	Dec 1777 muster roll shows him as a prisoner on July 7, 1777, joined on September 20; Dec 1777-May 1778 on furlough.
Hill, David Private	Feb 2, 1778, Three Years	First, Emerson	June 1778 sick at Fish Kill.
Hill/Hills, Ebenezor, Private	April 21, 1777, Three Years	First, Scott	Dec 1777-March 1778 sick on furlough; April 1778; May 1778 on his march from New Hampshire; June 1778.

Name	Date	Company	Notes
Hill, Jonathan Private	Feb 14, 1777, Duration of War	Second, Robinson	Dec 1777 sick absent; Jan-June 1778.
Hill, Samuel Sergeant	April 10, 1777, Three Years	First, House	Dec 1777-June 1778 at Albany wounded.
Hillery, John Private	April 6, 1777, Three Years	Third, Livermore	Dec 1777; Jan-Feb 1778 on command; March 1778 on guard; April 1778; May 1778 sick in camp; June 1778 sick absent.
Hills, Joseph Private	April 21, 1777, Three Years	First, Scott	Taken prisoner June 30, 1777; Dec 1777-Jan 1778 at home returned from prison; Feb 1778 sick on furlough; March 1778 at home returned from prison; April 1778; May 1778 on his march from New Hampshire; June 1778 sick at Brookline.
Hilsgrove/ Hilgrove, John Corporal/Private	Jan 1, 1777, Duration of War	First, Scott	Dec 1777-Jan 1778 wounded and at Albany; Feb 1778 wounded on furlough; March 1778 on furlough; April 1778; May 1778 reduced to Private; May-June 1778.
Hilton, John Private	Jan 1, 1777, Duration of War	Second, Robinson	Dec 1777-May 1778 sick at Albany; June 1778 wounded at Albany.
Hilton/Hilten, Joseph/Josiah 2nd. Lt.	Nov 8, 1776	Third, McClary	Dec 1777 at Albany wounded; Jan-June 1778 on furlough.
Hilton, William Private	Jan 1, 1777, Duration of War	Second, Blodget	Dec 1777-June 1778.
Hoagg/Hogg, Huzza Private	Feb 26, 1777, Three Years	Third, Weare	Dec 1777; Jan 1778 on command; Feb-April 1778; May 1778 sick in camp; June-July 1778 sick at Valley Forge.
Hobart/Hubart, Joseph Private	March 10, 1777, Duration of War	Third, Stone	Dec 1777-June 1778.
Hodgden/Hogdon, Samuel Private	Jan 14, 1777, Duration of War	Third, Beal	Dec 1777 sick at Poughkeepsie; Jan-March 1778; April 1778 sick in camp; May 1778; June 1778 sick at Fishkill.
Hodgdon, Charles/Charls Private	April 20, 1777, Three Years	Third, Weare	Dec 1777; Jan 1778 after provisions; Feb-April 1778; May 1778 on guard; June-July 1778 sick at Valley Forge.
Hodgdon/ Hodgson, Phineas Private	Dec 1, 1776, Three Years	Second, Norris	Dec 1777-April 1778 on command artillery; May 1778; June 1778 sick at [Watsessen].

Name	Enlistment	Company	Remarks
Hodgers/Hoger, Robert Sergeant	March 24, 1777, Three Years	First, Frye	Dec 1777-Feb 1778; March 1778 on guard; April-June 1778.
Hodgskins/ Hodskins, William Private	April 6, 1777, Three Years	First, Hutchins	Dec 1777-June 1778.
Hogg, Abner Corporal	July 20, 1777, Three Years	Third, Livermore	Dec 1777-March 1778; April 1778 on guard; May-June 1778.
Hogg, William Private	Dec 1, 1776, Three Years	Second, Norris	Dec 1777-June 1778.
Hoit/Hoite, Benjamin Private	Jan 2, 1777, Three Years	Third, Beal	Dec 1777; Jan 1778 on command; Feb-March 1778; April 1778 on command at "Sweds Fort"; May 1778; June 1778 sick at Corryell's Ferry.
Hoit, Micah/Miah 2nd. Lt.	Nov 8, 1776	Second, Robinson	Dec 1777-Jan 1778 sick absent; Feb-June 1778 on furlough.
Hoit, Nathan Ensign	Nov 8, 1776	Third, Livermore	Dec 1777 on furlough; Jan 1778 sick absent; Feb-May 1778 on furlough; June 1778 sick absent.
Hoit/Hoite, Reuben, Private	April 13, 1777, Three Years	Third, Gray	Dec 1777; Jan 1778 sick in quarters; Feb-March 1778; April 1778 on a week's command for fatigue; May-June 1778.
Hoit/Hoyt, Thomas Private	May 10, 1777, Three Years	Third, Livermore	Dec 1777-Feb 1778 sick absent; March 1778 sick in hospital; April-May 1778 sick at Lancaster; June 1778 sick absent.
Hoite/Hoyte, Samuel Private	March 14, 1777, Three Years	First, Emerson	Dec 1777; Jan 1778 on duty; Feb-June 1778.
Holcomb/Holcom, Mathew Private	Nov 12, 1776, Duration of War	First, Morrill	Dec 1777 missing July 7, 1777 returned home lame Aug 1, 1777; Jan 1778 sick at Boscowin N. England; Feb-April 1778 sick at Boscowen; May 1778 deserted after being on furlough sick since July 9, 1777.
Holland, Nathaniel Private	April 13, 1777, Three Years	Third, Gray	Dec 1777; Jan 1778 on command; Feb 1778; March 1778 sick in General Hospital; April 28, 1778 died.
Holland, Robert Private	Feb 2, 1778, Three Years	First, Emerson	April 1778; May 1778 on Genl. Poor's Guard; June 1778 sick in Jerseys.
Holman, Jeremiah Sergeant	Nov 15, 1776, Three Years	First, Frye	Dec 1777 joined since last muster; Jan-May 1778; June 1778 sick at Valley Forge.

Name	Enlisted	Company	Service Record
Holmes/Holms, John, Private	March 10, 1777, Duration of War	Third, Stone	Dec 1777 on furlough sick; Jan-May 1778 on furlough; June 1, 1778 dead.
Holmes, Thomas, Private	Feb 17, 1777, Duration of War	Third, Livermore	Missing since Hubbardton Battle July 7, 1777; April 24, 1778 joined; April-May 1778; June 1778 sick absent.
Holt, Amos, Private	April 8, 1777, Three Years	Third, Frye	Dec 1777 sick absent; Jan-April 1778; May 1778 on command; June 1778 sick at Valley Forge.
Holt, Asa, Corporal/Sergeant	Feb 13, 1777, Three Years	First, Farwell	Dec 1777; Jan 1778 in the country by leave of ye Major; Feb 1778 sick in camp; March-April 1778; May 1, 1778 promoted to Sergeant; May-June 1778.
Holt, Nehemiah, Private	April 8, 1777, Three Years	Third, Frye	Dec 1777 sick absent; Jan 1778 on command; Feb-April 1778; May 1778 sick in camp; June 1778.
Honey, Peter, Private	Three Years	First, Emerson	Dec 1777; Jan-Feb 1778 on Genl Guard; March 1778 on command; April 1778 on command at Cross Road foraging; May 1778 on command for Tents; June 1778 on command driving waggon.
Honory/Honver, Jock/Jack, Private	April 1, 1778, Three Years	Third, McClary	May-June 1778 missing at Barren Hill.
Hopkinson, Jonathan, Private	Jan 1, 1777, Three Years	Second, Robinson	Nov 5, 1777 deserted; June 8, 1778 joined; June 1778.
Hosmore/Horsmore, Reuben, Private	April 23, 1777, Duration of War	Third, Frye	Dec 1777; Jan 1778 on command; Feb 1778 sick absent; March 1778 on command; April 1778; May 1778 on command; June 1778 sick at Valley Forge.
House, John, Captain	Jan 8, 1776	First, House	Dec 1777 on furlough; Jan 1778 on court martial; Feb 1778; March 4, 1778 resigned.
Hovey, Ivory, Surgeon	Nov 8, 1776	Third	Dec 1777 on furlough; Jan 1778 joined; Jan-March 1778; April 1, 1778 discharged.
How, Jonathan, Private	March 10, 1778, Two Years	Second, Clayes	June 1778 joined June 20, 1778, on guard.
How, Thomas, Private	May 1, 1777, Three Years	Second, Drew	Dec 1777-Jan 1778; Feb 1778 on command; March 1778 sick absent; April 1778 sick present; May 1778; June 1778 at Yellow Springs.

Name	Enlisted	Company	Service Record
Howard, Benjamin Private	April 13, 1777, Three Years	Third, Gray	Dec 1777 sick present; Jan-May 1778; June 1778 on command on General Lee's Guard.
Howard/Haward, Eleazor Private	Jan 22, 1778, Two Years	First, Wait	April 1778; May 1778 on guard; June 1778.
Howard, Rozel/Rozwell Private	April 18, 1777, Three Years	First, House	Dec 1777-Feb 1778; March 1778 on guard; April 1778; May 1778 sick in camp; June 12, 1778 dead.
Howe, Bezaleel/Bezeliel 2nd. Lt.	Nov 8, 1776	First, Morrill	Dec 1777 on duty; Jan-April 1778; May 1778 sick in camp; June 1778.
Howe/How, Richard Private	May 1, 1777, Three Years	Second, Robinson	Dec 1777; Jan 1778 on command; Feb-June 1778.
Hoyt/Hoit, Enoch/Enouch Private	July 3, 1777, Three Years	First, Hutchins	Dec 1777-April 1778 on furlough by General Gates; May 1778 on furlough New England; June 1778.
Hubart see Hobard			
Hubbard, Jonas Corporal	March 20, 1777, Three Years	First, House	Dec 1777 wounded on furlough by Genl. Gates; Jan-June 1778 on furlough wounded.
Hughes, Richard Sergeant	March 18, 1777, Three Years	Third, Frye	Dec 1777-Jan 1778; Feb 1778 on guard; March-April 1778; May 1778 on guard; June 1778.
Hull, Israel Private	April 25, 1777, Three Years	Second, Robinson	Dec 1777-May 1778; June 1778 sick at Valley Forge.
Hull, John Private	Feb 1, 1777, Three Years	Second, Bell	Dec 1777-Jan 1778 on command with the Commissary of Issues; Feb 1778 on command; March-April 1778 on command with Commissary; May 1778 on command January 10 with the Commissary.
Hull, Joseph Private	Feb 12, 1777, Three Years	Third, Beal	Dec 1777-Feb 1778; March 1778 on command; April 1778; May 1778 sick in camp; June-Oct 1778 sick at Valley Forge.
Hunking, Richard Private	May 1, 1777, Three Years	Second, Drew	Dec 1777-Jan 1778; Feb-March 1778 sick present; April 1778; May 1778 sick present; June 1778 sick at Princeton.
Hunt, Caleb/Caled Private	March 18, 1777, Three Years	Second, Blodget	Dec 1777-Jan 1778 wounded absent; Feb-June 1778 wounded at Albany.
Hunt, David, Private	Jan 1, 1778, Three Years	First, Emerson	June 1778.

Name	Enlisted	Company	Notes
Hunt, Enoch Private	March 11, 1777, Three Years	Third, Stone	Dec 1777-May 1778; June 1778 sick at General Hospital; July 1778 sick in Pennsylvania.
Hunt, Thomas Private	Feb 2, 1778, Two Years	First, Wait	April-May 1778; June 1778 sick at Kings Ferry.
Hunt, Willard Private	April 29, 1778	Second, Robinson	June 1778 sick at Valley Forge.
Hunt, Zachues Private	Feb 1, 1778, Three Years	First, Emerson	June 1778.
Huntoon, Joseph 1st. Lt.	Nov 8, 1776	Third, Gray	Dec 1777-June 1778 wounded on furlough.
Huntress, Jonathan Private	Nov 12, 1776, Duration of War	Second, Blodget	Dec 1777 muster roll shows him as missing on July 7, 1777, returned on October 19; Dec 1777-June 1778.
Huntriss, Christopher Private	May 1, 1777, Three Years	Second, Drew	Dec 1777-Jan 1778; Feb 1778 sick present; March-April 1778; May 1778 on guard; June 1778 sick Princeton.
Huntriss/Hunkers, Parson Private	May 10, 1777, Three Years	Second, Drew	Dec 1777 on command; Jan 1778; Feb-June 1778 on command.
Hurd, Zaduck Private	May 9, 1777, Eight Months	Third, Ellis	Dec 1777 sick at Albany.
Hutchins, James Private	April 1, 1777, Duration of War	First, Hutchins	Dec 1777-June 1778 lame at Ware.
Hutchins/ Hutchings, Moses Private	Nov 15, 1776, Three Years	First, Farwell	Dec 1777; Jan-Feb 1778 on present duty; March 1778 on command; April 1778 on command at ye lines; May 1778 sick in camp; June 1778 sick at Valley Forge.
Hutchins/Huchins, Nathaniel Captain	April 3, 1777	First, Hutchins	Dec 1777; Jan 1778 on command; Feb 1778 on furlough; March-May 1778; June 1778 on duty.
Hutchins/Hukhins, Simon/Simeon Private	April 2, 1777, Duration of War	First, Wait	Dec 1777 missing since July 7, 1777; Jan-June 1778.
Hutchins, William 2nd. Lt.	Nov 8, 1776	First, Hutchins	Dec 1777-June 1778.
Hutchinson, Elisha Private	April 20, 1778	First, Morrill	June 1778.
Hutchinson, James Private	March 25, 1777, Three Years	Third, Frye	Dec 1777 on duty; Jan 1778; Feb 1778 on guard; March 1778; April 1778 tending the sick. May 1778 muster roll shows he died on June 2, 1778.

Name	Enlisted	Company	Service Record
Hutchinson, John Private	Jan 26, 1777, Three Years	First, House	Dec 1777 on command with Captain; Jan-March 1778 sick in hospital; April-May 1778 sick in camp. June 1778 muster roll shows him sick at Downingtown. June 1778 payroll shows he died on June 22. June 1778.
Hutchinson, Levy Private	April 20, 1778	First, Morrill	
Hutchinson, Thomas Private	March 19, 1777, Three Years	Second, Blodget	Dec 1777 on command with the sick; Jan-March 1778 on command Albany; April-May 1778 on command Albany in hospital; June 1778.
Ingals, Israel Sergeant	Jan 27, 1777, Three Years	First, Emerson	Dec 1777-May 1778 sick at Albany; June 1778 sick in Jersey.
Inglish, William Private	May 1, 1778, Three Years	Third, Stone	June 1778.
Jackson, Clement Private	Jan 31, 1777, Three Years	Third, Beal	Dec 1777 sick at Albany; Jan 1778 dead.
Jackson, Daniel Private	Feb 1, 1777, Duration of War	Second, Drew	Dec 1777 wounded and in hospital; Jan 1778; Feb 1778 wounded Albany; March 1778 wounded at Albany; April-June 1778 wounded and at Albany.
Jamison, Hugh Private	April 19, 1778, One Year	First, Frye	June 1778.
Jamison/Jemeson, Thomas Private	Feb 2, 1778, Two Years	First, Hutchins	June 1778 joined since last muster; June 1778.
Jarvis/Jarves, Robert Private	May 30, 1777, Three Years	Third, Gray	Dec 1777 on duty; Jan-Feb 1778 on General Poor's Guard; March 1778 on command; April 1778 on guard; May 1778 sick present; June 1778 sick Valley Forge.
Jenkins/Jinkins, Peter Private	April 7, 1777, Three Years	First, Frye	Dec 1777; Jan 1778 on command thrashing; Feb 1778 on Potts Grove guard; March-May 1778; June 1778 sick at Downingtown.
Jennes, Jeb Private	Jan 28, 1777, Three Years	Third, Beal	Dec 1777 wounded at Albany; Jan 1778 dead.
Jennings, Ebenezer Corporal	March 10, 1778, Two Years	Second, Clayes	June 20, 1778 joined; June 1778.
Jenings/Jennings, Ephraim Private	May 12, 1777, Three Years	First, House	Dec 1777-June 1778 sick at Albany.

Name	Enlistment	Company	Service Record
Jenings/Jennings, Stephen Private/Corporal	May 12, 1777, Three Years	First, House	Dec 1777; Jan 1778 on command; Feb 1778 promoted to Corporal; March-May 1778 sick in camp; June 1778 sick at Downingtown.
Jewell, David, Private	Feb 7, 1777, Three Years	Third, Stone	June 1778 muster roll shows he was "Taken July 7th.1777 Joind"; June 1778.
Jewell, Enos Corporal	Jan 1, 1777, Three Years	Second, Robinson	Dec 1777-April 1778; May 1778 sick in camp; June 1778.
Jewell/Jewel, Joseph Corporal	Jan 17, 1777, Duration of War	Second, Bell	Dec 1777-May 1778.
Job/Gob, John Private	Nov 14, 1776, Three Years	Second, Carr	Dec 1777-April 1778; May 1778 sick in camp; June 1778 sick Valley Forge.
Johnson/Jonson, Asael/Asell Private	June 11, 1777, Three Years	Third, Ellis	Dec 1777 on furlough; Jan 1778 left sick at Albany Feb-April 1778 sick at Albany; May-June 1778 on furlough.
Johnson, David Private	Nov 14, 1776, Three Years	Second, Carr	Dec 1777-May 1778 sick absent; June 1778 sick on the road.
Johnson, Isaiah Private	May 7, 1777, Eight Months	Third, Stone	Dec 1777; Jan 10, 1778 discharged.
Johnson/Jonson, Philip Private	Jan 20, 1777, Three Years	Third, Weare	Dec 1777 on command with Commissary; Jan-Feb 1778 on command; March-May 1778 sick in camp; June 1778 sick General Hospital.
Johnson/Johnston, Samuel Private	Jan 30, 1777, Three Years	First, Farwell	Dec 1777-March 1778 sick at Albany N. City; March 20, 1778 discharged by ye Colonel.
Johnson/Jonston, Thomas Corporal	Dec 3, 1776, Three Years	First, Wait	Dec 1777-March 1778; April-May 1778 sick in camp; June 1778 sick at Corryell's Ferry.
Johnston/Jonston, David Private	Feb 16, 1777, Three Years	First, Wait	Dec 1777; Jan 1778 on command at the lines; Feb 1778; March 1778 on command at the lines; April-May 1778; June 1778 on guard.
Jones, Ephraim Private	April 16, 1777, Three Years	Second, Bell	Dec 1777-April 1778; May 1778 on guard.
Jones, John Quartermaster Sergeant	April 14, 1777, Three Years	Third, Beal	Dec 1777-April 1778; May 1778 sick in camp; June 1778.

Name	Enlistment	Company	Service Record
Jordan, John Corporal/Private/Sergeant	March 31, 1777, Three Years	First, Scott	Dec 1777; Dec 31, 1777 reduced to Private; Jan 1, 1778 promoted to Sergeant; Jan 1778 on command at the lines; Feb 1778 on duty; March 1778 sick present; April-June 1778.
Joyner/Joiner, Francis Private	Nov 13, 1776, Three Years	First, Wait	Dec 1777-Jan 1778; Feb 1778 on Commissary Generals guard; March-April 1778 on Commissary guard; May-June 1778.
Joyner, John Quartermaster Sergeant	Nov 19, 1776, Three Years	First	Dec 1777; Jan-May 1778 on furlough; June 1778.
Judkins, Ebenezer Private	Dec 27, 1777, Three Years	Second, Robinson	June 1778 on guard.
Judkins, Jonathan Private	April 10, 1777, Three Years	First, Hutchins	Dec 1777-June 1778.
Judkins/Judgkins, Jonathan Private	June 21, 1777, Three Years	First, Morrill	Dec 1777-April 1778 sick at Fish Kill; May 1778 muster roll shows he died March 4, 1778 at Fish Kill.
Judkins, Philip Corporal/Private	Aug 31, 1777, Three Years	First, Wait	Dec 1777; Jan 1778 on command; Feb-March 1778; April 1778 on command; May 1778 reduced to Private; May-June 1778.
Judkins/Judgkins, Samuel Drummer	April 17, 1777, Three Years	Third, Livermore	Dec 1777-April 1778; May 1778 sick in camp; June 1778.
Judkins/Jetkins, Samuel Private	Feb 25, 1777, Three Years	Third, McClary	Dec 1777-June 1778.
Karr, Benjamin Private	April 6, 1777, Three Years	Third, Livermore	Dec 1777 joined since Hubbarton Battle; Dec 1777; Jan-April 1778; May 1778 sick in camp; June 1778.
Kelley/Kelly, James Private	Nov 13, 1777, Three Years	Second, Blodget	Dec 1777 on command with the sick; Jan-June 1778.
Kelley, Jonathan Private	Nov 27, 1776, Three Years	First, Farwell	Dec 1777-May 1778; June 1778 on General Poor's guard.
Kelsey, Giles Private	April 18, 1777, Three Years	First, Farwell	Dec 1777 "on Presant Duty"; Jan 1778 on command; Feb 1778 on present duty; March-April 1778; May 1778 "in the Country for Necessarys for the Sick"; June 1778 sick at Cransburytown.

Name	Date, Term	Co., Capt.	Notes
Kelsey, Moses Sergeant/Private/Sergeant	Feb 6, 1777, Three Years	Third, McClary	Dec 1777; Dec 25, 1777 reduced to Private; Jan 10, 1778 promoted to Sergeant; Jan-March 1778; April 1778 on a weeks command at the Lines; May-June 1778.
Kelsey, Zach Private	May 1, 1777, Three Years	Second, Drew	Dec 1777 on guard; Jan-Feb 1778; March 1778 on guard; April-June 1778.
Kemp/Camp, Amos Private	April 14, 1777, Three Years	Second, Bell	Dec 1777-Jan 1778 wounded left at Albany; Feb-May 1778 on furlough.
Kenniston/Keniston, Samuel Private	Nov 15, 1776, Three Years	Second, Norris	Dec 1777 muster roll shows him as taken on July 7, 1777, joined October 15; Dec 1777-Jan 1778; Feb-March 1778 on guard; April-June 1778.
Kidder/Kider, Daniel Fifer	April 22, 1777, Duration of War	First, Morrill	Dec 1777-June 1778.
Kies, Stephen Private	March 20, 1778, Two Years	Third, Stone	May 1778 on guard; June 1778.
Kimball/Kimbell, John Private	Feb 17, 1778	Second, Robinson	April 25, 1778 joined; April-June 1778.
Kimbell/Kimball, Benjamin Paymaster	Nov 6, 1776	First	Jan-April 1778 on furlough; May-June 1778.
Kimble, Thomas Private	June 3, 1778, Three Years	First, Scott	June 1778.
Kindall/Kindal, Edward Sergeant	Feb 12, 1777, Duration of War	Third, Stone	Dec 1777; Jan 1778 on command; Feb-April 1778; May 1778 sick in camp; June 12, 1778 died.
Kingsberry, Elisha Private	May 12, 1777, Eight Months	Third, Livermore	Dec 1777 sick absent; Jan 10, 1778 discharged.
Kingsley/Kingsly, Alpheus Private	April 1, 1778, Two Years	First, Wait	June 1778 sick at Cakeatt.
Kinniston/Kennestone, Job/Joab Drummer	Jan 27, 1777, Three Years	Second, Bell	Dec 1777-May 1778.
Knap, Abial Private	May 9, 1777, Eight Months	Third, Ellis	Dec 1777 sick at Albany; Jan 10, 1778 discharged.
Knealy see Nealey			

Name	Enlisted	Company	Remarks
Knight/Night, Caleb Private	Feb 27, 1777, Three Years	Third, Stone	Missing since July 7, 1777; Dec 1777 joined; Jan 1778; Feb 1778 on command; March-May 1778; June 1778 sick at General Hospital.
Knott/Nott, Jessey/Jesse, Private	Nov 13, 1776, Three Years	First, Wait	Dec 1777-Feb 1778; on Generals guard; April 1778 in His Excellency's Guard.
Knowles/Knowls, Samuel Corporal	Jan 21, 1777, Three Years	Third, Beal	Dec 1777; Jan 1778 sick; Feb-May 1778; June 27, 1778 dead.
Knowles/Knowls, Simon Private	Nov 13, 1776, Duration of War	Third, Beal	Dec 1777-Jan 1778; Feb 1778 on command; March-June 1778.
Knowlton/Nolton, Asa Private	Nov 12, 1776, Duration of War	Second, Blodget	Dec 1777 muster roll shows he deserted on July 7, 1777, returned and pardoned; Jan-May 1778; June 1778 left sick at Valley Forge.
Knox, George Private	May 1, 1778, Three Years	First, House	June 1778.
Knox, Samuel Fifer	Feb 1, 1777, Three Years	First, Frye	Dec 1777 "Returned from Captivity Joyn'd Octor. 17th 1777"; Dec 1777-May 1778; June 1778 sick at Downingtown.
Lake, Jonathan Private	March 10, 1778, Two Years	Second, Clayes	June 20, 1778 joined; June 1778.
Lakin/Laking, William Private	April 1, 1777, Three Years	Second, Clayes	Dec 1777-Jan 1778 sick in hospital at Albany; Feb 1778 wounded in hospital Albany; March 1778 in hospital Albany; April-May 1778 wounded in hospital Albany; June 1778 sick at Albany.
Lamb, James Private	March 10, 1777, Three Years	First, Frye	Dec 1777 joined since last muster; Jan 1778 on picquet guard; Feb-June 1778.
Lambert, Paul Private	Jan 1, 1777, Three Years	Third, Beal	Dec 1777-Feb 1778; March 1778 sick in camp; April 1778; May 1778 on command paymasters servant; June 1778.
Lampory/ Lampree, Levi Private	Jan 20, 1777, Three Years	Third, Weare	Dec 1777-May 1778 on furlough; June 1778.
Lander, Johnathan/ Jonathan Private	Nov 15, 1776, Duration of War	Second, Drew	Dec 1777 guard; Jan-June 1778.
Lane, John Sergeant	March 18, 1777, Three Years	Second, Blodget	Dec 1777-April 1778; May 1778 sick in camp; June 1778.

Name	Enlistment	Company	Service Record
Lane, Samuel Private	May 9, 1777, Eight Months	Third, Ellis	Dec 1777; Jan 10, 1778 discharged.
Lang, William Corporal	Feb 18, 1777, Three Years	First, Hutchins	Dec 1777 sick at Reading; Jan 1778 absent with leave; Feb-March 1778 on command at Potts Grove; April-May 1778 sick at Potts Grove; June 1778.
Langmaid/ Langmad, Henry Private	Jan 25, 1777, Three Years	Third, Beal	Dec 1777-June 1778.
Lapish/Lapesh, John Private	Nov 17, 1776, Duration of War	First, Wait	Dec 1777 wounded October 7 and on furlough by General Gates; Jan 1778 wounded October 7 and on furlough; Feb 1778 wounded and on furlough; March 1778 on furlough; April 1778; May 1778 sick in camp; June 1778 sick at Downingtown.
Larrabee/Laraby, John Private	Nov 25, 1776, Three Years	First, Hutchins	Dec 1777 on duty; Jan 1778 on command; Feb-March 1778; April 1778 sick present; May 1778 sick at Yellow Springs; June 1778.
Larrabee/Larrabe, Samuel Private	Dec 26, 1776, Duration of War	First, Farwell	Dec 1777; Jan-Feb 1778 on present duty; March-May 1778; June 1778 sick at Valley Forge.
Larrance/ Lawrence, William Private	May 9, 1777, Eight Months	Third, Ellis	Dec 1777; Jan 10, 1778 discharged.
Lary/Leary, Stephen Private	Jan 30, 1777, Three Years	Third, Beal	Dec 1777; Jan 1778 on command; Feb-March 1778; April-May 1778 sick in camp; June 1778 sick at Valley Forge; August 1778 muster roll shows he died on June 22, 1778.
Laton/Laten, William Private	May 3, 1777, Duration of War	First, Farwell	Dec 1777-May 1778 sick at Albany; June 1778.
Lawrance/ Lawrence, Abraham Private	May 9, 1777, Three Years	Third, Ellis	Dec 1777; Jan 1778 on command; Feb-June 1778.
Lear, William Private	Jan 20, 1777, Three Years	Third, Beal	Dec 1777-April 1778; May 1778 on guard; June 1778 sick at Valley Forge; August 1778 muster roll shows he died on June 22, 1778.

Leary/Lary, John Corporal	Jan 4, 1777, Three Years	First, Morrill	Dec 1777-Jan 1778 on furlough by General Gates; Feb 1778 on furlough; March 1778 sick and on furlough; April 1778 sick at Lichfield; May 1778 deserted, went on furlough October 22, 1777.
Leather/Leathers, Edward Private	Feb 13, 1777, Three Years	Second, Drew	Dec 1777-March 1778; April 1778 sick present; May 24, 1778 dead.
Leathers, Jonathan Private/Corporal	Nov 15, 1776, Three Years	Second, Norris	Dec 1, 1777 promoted to Corporal; Dec 1777-June 1778.
Leavers/Leaver, William Private	Dec 1, 1776, Three Years	Second, Norris	Dec 1777-March 1778 sick at Albany; April-June 1778.
Leavitt/Levitt, Amos Private	May 13, 1777, Three Years	Second, Rowell	Dec 1777 on Genl. guard; Jan 1778 on duty; Feb-May 1778; June 25, 1778 missing.
Leavitt/Lavitt, Aratas/Aretus Private	April 23, 1777, One Year	Third, Weare	Dec 1777-Jan 1778; Feb 1778 sick absent; March 1778; April 26, 1778 discharged.
Leavitt, Edward Private	Nov 22, 1776, Duration of War	Second, Bell	Dec 1777-May 1778.
Leavitt, James Corporal	April 23, 1777, One Year	Third, Weare	Dec 1777; Jan 1778 sick in camp; Feb 1778; March 1778 on command; April 26, 1778 discharged.
Leavitt, Jonathan Private/Musician	Nov 15, 1776, Three Years	Second, Norris	Dec 1777-May 1778; June 4, 1778 promoted to Musician; June 1778.
Leavitt/Levett, Jonathan, Private	Jan 30, 1777, Three Years	Third, McClary	Dec 1777-March 1778 sick at Albany; April 1778 sick at Fishkill; May-June 1778 on command at Portsmouth
Leavitt, Nathaniel Ensign	Nov 8, 1776	Third, Weare	Dec 1777-June 1778.
Leavitt, Nehemiah Private	Feb 5, 1778, Three Years	Second, Rowell	April 24, 1778 joined; April 1778; May 1778 sick in camp; June 1778 sick at Yellow Springs.
Leavitt/Levett, Nehemiah Corporal	Feb 6, 1777, Three Years	Third, McClary	Dec 1777; Jan 1778 sick in camp; Feb-March 1778 sick in General Hospital; April 1778 sick in Red Lion Hospital; May-June 1778.
Leavitt, William Private	Jan 1, 1777, Duration of War	Second, Robinson	Nov 7, 1777 deserted; June 8, 1778 joined; June 1778.
Lee, Samuel Private	Jan 1, 1777, Duration of War	First, Scott	Dec 1777-Feb 1778; March 24, 1778 died.
Lee, William 2nd. Lt.	Nov 8, 1776	First, Emerson	Dec 1777; Jan 9, 1778 resigned.

Name	Enlistment	Company	Service Record
Leech, Benjamin Private	Feb 7, 1778, Duration of War	Second, Robinson	June 1778 sick Brunswick.
Lewis, Joseph Private	March 17, 1777, Three Years	Third, Frye	Dec 1777; Jan 1778 on command; Feb-April 1778; May 1778 on command; June 1778 sick in General Hospital; July 1778 sick at Hospital Pennsylvania.
Libby/Libbe, Luke Private	April 1, 1777, Three Years	Third, McClary	Dec 1777 on command; Jan-April 1778; May 1778 sick in camp; June 1778.
Light, Ebenezer 2nd. Lt.	Nov 8, 1776	Second, Bell	Dec 1777-Jan 1778; Feb 1778 sick with the smallpox out of camp; March-April 1778; May 1778 on guard.
Lines/Lynes, Charles Private	Jan 14, 1777, Three Years	First, Farwell	Dec 1777 wounded and at Albany; Jan-March 1778 wounded at Albany; April 1, 1778 died.
Liscomb, Samuel Private	May 8. 1777, Duration of War	First, Farwell	Dec 1777-March 1778 on command in Armory, Albany; May-June 1778.
Livermore, Daniel Captain	Nov 8, 1776	Third, Livermore	Dec 1777-Feb 1778; March 1778 on command; April-June 1778.
Livingstone/ Livingston, Robert Sergeant	March 31, 1777, Three Years	Third, Livermore	Dec 1777-April 1778; May 1778 sick in camp; June 1778.
Lock, Joshua Private	Jan 27, 1777	Second, Bell	May 1778 sick in hospital.
Lock, Moses Private	Jan 1, 1777, Duration of War	First, Morrill	Dec 1777; Jan 1778 on command; Feb-June 1778.
Lock, Richard Private	Jan 27, 1777, Three Years	Third, Beal	Dec 1777-Feb 1778 on command; March 1778; April 1778 sick in camp; May-June 1778.
Lock, Samuel Private	Feb 1, 1777, Duration of War	First, Morrill	Dec 1777; Jan 1778 sick present; Feb 1778 sick in camp; March-June 1778.
Long, Paul Private	April 23, 1777, Eight Months	Third, Weare	Dec 1777; Jan 10, 1778 discharged.
Lord, Stephen/Sephen Private	Feb 1, 1777, Three Years	First, Hutchins	Dec 1777 tending the sick; Jan 1778 sick present; Feb-May 1778; June 1778 sick Valley Forge.
Lougee/Louge, Moses Fifer	Jan 1, 1777, Duration of War	Second, Robinson	Dec 1777-June 1778.
Lovejoy, Abel Private	Feb 1, 1777, Three Years	First, House	Dec 1777; Jan 1778 on duty; Feb-June 1778.

Name	Enlistment	Company	Service Record
Lovejoy, Asa Drummer	July 1, 1777, Three Years	First, House	Dec 1777-Feb 1778; March-April 1778 sick in camp; May 1778; June 1778 sick at Fish Kill.
Loverin/Lovering, Simon D. Corporal/Private	Jan 23, 1777, Three Years	Third, Weare	Dec 1777-March 1778; April 1778 sick in camp; April 28, 1778 reduced to Private; May 1778; June 1778 General Hospital.
Lovering/ Loverign, Benjamin Private	Aug 27, 1777, Eight Months	Second, Blodget	Dec 12, 1777 deserted.
Lovering, Theophilus Private	May 13, 1777 or Oct 23, 1777, Three Years	Second, Rowell	Sept 1777 muster roll shows he enlisted on May 13, 1777 and was missing on July 7, 1777. June 1778 muster roll shows he enlisted on Oct 23, 1777 and joined on July 20, 1778. Possibly two different individuals.
Lucy, William Corporal	April 1, 1777, Three Years	First, Frye	Dec 1777 sick absent; Jan-April 1778 sick at Albany; May 1778 [att] N. England; June 1778 sick at Albany.
Lufkin, Philip Private	April 13, 1777, Three Years	Third, Gray	Dec 1777 sick absent; Jan 1778 sick in camp; Feb 1778 sick absent; March 20, 1778 died.
McAllester/ M'allester, Benjamin Sergeant	Nov 13, 1776, Duration of War	First, Morrill	Dec 1777-Feb 1778; March 7, 1778 died.
McAllester/ McAlester, Reuben Private		Second, Clayes	Dec 1777-Feb 1778; March 1778 on guard; April-June 1778.
McBride/Bride, Jabez Private	Nov 14, 1776, Three Years	Second, Clayes	Dec 1777-Jan 1778; Feb 1778 on duty; March-May 1778; June 1778 sick Valley Forge.
McCalley/ M'Cauley, Florance Private	Nov 12, 1776, Duration of War	First, Morrill	Dec 1777; Jan-Feb 1778 wounded and at Albany; March 1778 wounded and on furlough; April 1778 on command at the lines; May 1778; June 1778 on guard.
McCalley/ McColley, Nathaniel 1st. Lt.	Nov 8, 1776	First, Morrill	Dec 1777; Jan-May 1778; June 1778 on command at Valley Forge.
McClary, Michael Captain	Nov 6, 1776	Third, McClary	Dec 1777-June 1778.

Name	Enlisted	Company	Notes
McClellen, John Private	April 1, 1777, Three Years	First, Emerson	Dec 1777; Jan 1778 on duty; Feb-March 1778; April 1778 on the main guard; May 1778; June 1778 sick in Pennsylvania.
McClintick, John Private	April 14, 1777, Three Years	First, Wait	June 1778 payroll shows he joined on April 1, 1778. The June 1778 muster roll shows him as "formerly deserted but since joined."
McClure/McCluer, Benjamin Corporal	March 13, 1778	Third, Weare	May 16, 1778 joined; May 1778; June 1778 sick at New Brunswick.
McClurge, Robert Private	Jan 1, 1777, Three Years	Second, Clayes	June 1778 payroll shows he was "taken pisoner July 7 1777 Joyned June 1778"; June 1778.
McCoye, Daniel Private	March 12, 1778, Three Years	First, Frye	June 1778 on guard.
McCoye, Jonathan Private	March 11, 1778, Three Years	First, Frye	June 1778 joined since last muster; June 1778.
McDanniel/McDaniels, James Private	April 10, 1777, Three Years	Second, Bell	Dec 1777-May 1778.
McDorman, John Private	Three Years	Third, Stone	June 1778.
McEllery/McElery, James Private	Eight Months	Third, Livermore	Dec 1777; Jan 10, 1778 discharged.
McElvin/McElvan, Ebenezer Private	Jan 1, 1777, Three Years	Second, Carr	Dec 1777-May 1778 sick absent; June 1778.
McFarland/McFarlin, Joseph Private	April 28, 1777, Three Years	First, Frye	Dec 1777 on command with Lieutenant How; Jan 1778; Feb 1778 sick in camp; March-April 1778; May 1778 sick present; June 1778 sick at Downingtown.
McGaffey/McGaffe, Andrew 1st. Lt.	Nov 8, 1776	Third, McClary	Dec 1777; Jan 1778 on guard; Feb 1778 sick with the smallpox; Feb-June 1778.
McGaffey/McGaffe, Neal Sergeant	Jan 25, 1777, Three Years	Third, McClary	Dec 1777-May 1778 on furlough; June 1778.
McGee/McGie, John Private	Dec 10, 1776, Duration of War	First, Wait	Dec 1777; Jan 1778 sick in camp; Feb-March 1778 on guard; April 1778 on command; May 1778 sick in camp; June 1778 sick at Valley Forge.
McGee/McGie, William Private	Dec 10, 1776, Duration of War	First, Wait	Dec 1777-March 1778; April 1778 sick in camp; May 1778; June 1778 sick at Valley Forge.

Name	Enlistment	Company	Service Record
McGinness/ McGinniss, John Private	Nov 10, 1776, Duration of War	First, Wait	Dec 1777-April 1778; May 1778 sick in camp; June 17, 1778 died.
McGlaughlin, Thomas Private	March 12, 1778, Three Years	First, Frye	June 1778 joined since last muster, sick at Valley Forge; June 1778.
McGregore/ MacGregore, David 1st. Lt.	Nov 8, 1776	Third, Livermore	Dec 1777-Feb 1778 on command; March 1778 sick in camp; April 1778 sick present; May 1778 sick in camp; June 1778.
McIntire/M'intire, Andrew Private	Feb 1, 1777, Duration of War	First, Morrill	Dec 1777-Feb 1778; March-April 1778 sick in camp; May 1778; June 1778 sick at Valley Forge.
McIntire/M'intier, John Private	March 28, 1777, Three Years	First, Morrill	Dec 1777-Feb 1778; March 1778 on guard; April-May 1778; June 1778 sick at Valley Forge.
McLane/McClain, Obed Private	Nov 12, 1777, Three Years	First, Frye	Dec 1777; Jan 1778 on command; Feb-May 1778; June 1778 sick at Valley Forge.
McMaster, Alexander, Private	Nov 13, 1776, Three Years	First, Frye	Dec 1777 on command after leather; Jan 1778 on command in the country; Feb-March 1778; April 1778 sick present; May-June 1778.
McMehorn, John Private	Nov 14, 1776, Three Years	Second, Carr	Dec 1777 sick in camp; Jan-June 1778.
McMurphy, George Private	Three Years	First, Frye	Dec 1777 on command with Lieutenant [Howe]; Jan-May 1778; June 1778 sick at Downingtown.
McMurphy, John Private	April 28, 1777, Three Years	First, Frye	Dec 1777 returned from captivity joined since last muster; Jan-June 1778.
McNeal, Thomas Privatep	April 5, 1777, Duration of War	First, Scott	Dec 1777 sick at Fish Kill; Jan-Feb 1778; March 1778 sick present; April-June 1778.
Mach, John Private	May 2, 1777, Three Years	First, Frye	Dec 1777 wounded absent; Jan-May 1778 wounded and on furlough; June 1778.
Mack, Joseph Private	April 2, 1777, Three Years	First, Frye	Dec 1777 wounded absent; Jan-May 1778 wounded and on furlough; June 1778 sick at Albany.
Magoon, Alexander Private	May 15, 1777, Three Years	Second, Robinson	Dec 1777; Jan 1778 on command at Bridge; Feb 1778 sick absent; March 1778 on command; April 1778; May 1778 on command at hospital; June 1778 sick Valley Forge.

Name	Date	Company	Notes
Mahane, Philip, Private	Dec 1, 1776, Duration of War	First, Scott	March 1, 1777 deserted; May 1778 "Joined May 1 who had been returned Deserted"; May 1778; June 1778 muster roll shows he died on July 1, 1778.
Mallen, William Private	April 7, 1777, Three Years	Third, Gray	Dec 1777 on duty; Jan-March 1778; April 1778 sick in camp; May-June 1778.
Man, Nathan Private	April 1, 1777, Three Years	First, Scott	Dec 1777-May 1778; June 1778 sick at Valley Forge.
Man, William Private	April 1, 1777, Three Years	First, Scott	Dec 1777 on duty; Jan-April 1778; May 1778 sick in camp; June 1778.
Manning, Eliphalit/Eliphalet Private	April 14, 1777, Three Years	First, Emerson	Dec 1777-March 1778; April 1778 on command at Rednigh; May 1778 sick in camp; June 1778.
Manning, John Corporal	April 17, 1777, Three Years	First, Emerson	Dec 1777-April 1778 "Retaken at Ticonderoga and gone to New England with Prisoners"; May 1, 1778 joined; May-June 1778.
Mansfield, Elijah Private	March 18, 1777, Three Years	Third, Frye	Dec 1777-March 1778 on furlough; April 1778 sick in camp; May 14, 1778 died.
March/Marsh, Stephen Private	May 1, 1777, Eight Months	Third, Stone	Dec 1777; Jan 10, 1778 discharged.
Marden, James Private	March 8, 1777, Three Years	Second, Carr	Dec 1777 guard; Jan-March 1778; April-May 1778 on guard; June 1778.
Mardin/Marden, John Private	Jan 25, 1777, Three Years	Third, Beal	Dec 1777-March 1778; April-June 1778 sick in camp.
Margery/Mergery, Jonathan Private	Jan 10, 1777, Three Years	Second, Clayes	Dec 1777 sick in hospital at Albany; Jan-April 1778 wounded in hospital Albany; May 1778 wounded at Albany; June 1778.
Marsdon/Marsden, Nathaniel Private	Jan 1, 1777, Three Years	Second, Blodget	Dec 1777-April 1778; May 1778 sick in camp; June 1778 left sick at Valley Forge.
Marsh/Mash, John Private	April 14, 1777, Three Years	Second, Bell	Dec 1777-May 1778.
Marsh/Mash, Joseph Private/Corporal	April 2, 1777, Three Years	First, Frye	Dec 1777 on command General's guard; Jan 1778 on command with General Poor; Feb 1778 on ye [ ] guard; March 1778; April 1778 on command at the lines; May 1778; June 8, 1778 promoted to Corporal; June 1778.

Name	Enlisted	Company	Notes
Marsh/Mash, Noah, Private	March 1, 1777, Three Years	Second, Robinson	Dec 1777-June 1778 sick at Albany.
Marston, James, Private	April 16, 1777, Three Years	Third, Gray	Dec 1777 on duty; Jan-April 1778; May 1778 sick present; June 1778 sick at Valley Forge.
Marston, Matthias, Private	May 7, 1777, Eight Months	Third, Weare	Dec 1777 sick hospital; Jan 10, 1778 discharged.
Marston, Nathaniel, Private	May 7, 1777, Eight Months	Third, Weare	Dec 1777 left sick at Bennington; Jan 10, 1778 discharged.
Marston, Samuel, Private	June 4, 1778, Three Years	Third, Weare	First appears on the July 1778 muster roll.
Martin/Marten, Christopher, Corporal	April 8, 1777, Three Years	Third, Frye	Dec 1777-Jan 1778; Feb 1778 on guard; March-May 1778 sick in camp; June 1778.
Martin, Ealepser/Eleazer, Corporal	May 9, 1777, Eight Months	Third, Ellis	Dec 1777 on furlough; Jan 10, 1778 discharged.
Martin, Edward, Private	Nov 15, 1776, Duration of War	Second, Rowell	April 1778 muster roll shows him as missing July 7, 1777, joined April 30, 1778; April-June 1778.
Martin/Marten, Ichabod, Private	Nov 13, 1776, Three Years	First, Frye	Dec 1777-Feb 1778; March 1778 on command; April-June 1778.
Martin, John, Private	April 20, 1777, Three Years	Third, Livermore	Dec 1777-May 1778; June 1778 on command with the sick.
Martin/Marten, Timothy, Private	March 8, 1777, Three Years	First, Morrill	Dec 1777-June 1778.
Mason, Benjamin, Private	Jan 22, 1777, Duration of War	Third, Weare	Dec 1777; Jan-Feb 1778 after provisions; May 1778 on guard; June 30, 1778 died.
Mason, Edward, Sergeant/Private/Sergeant/Private/Sergeant	Jan 30, 1777, Three Years	Third, McClary	Dec 1777; Dec 25, 1777 reduced to Private; Jan 10, 1778 promoted to Sergeant; Jan-March 1778; March 6, 1778 reduced to Private; March-April 1778; April 13, 1778 "Restor'd to a Serjt.;" May 1778 sick in camp; June 1778.
Mason, James, Private	March 27, 1777, Duration of War	Third, Gray	Dec 1777-Feb 1778 sick at Albany; March-June 1778 on furlough.
Mason, Jeremiah, Private	Nov 15, 1776, Duration of War	Second, Blodget	Dec 1777; Jan-March 1778 on command at Albany.
Mason, Lemuel/Elimuel, Private	Nov 15, 1776, Duration of War	Second, Rowell	Dec 1777-March 1778 on furlough; April-June 1778.

Name	Enlistment	Company	Service Record
Mason, Robert Private	March 17, 1778, Three Years	First, House	June 1778.
Mason, Simon/Simeon Private	April 1, 1777, Three Years	Second, Norris	Dec 1777 on command Albany; Jan-March 1778 on command hospital; April 1778 on command hospital Albany; May 1778 on command hospital; June 1778 on guard.
Mathes/Mathace, Thomas Private	April 25, 1777, Three Years	First, Frye	Dec 1777 wounded absent; Jan-March 1778 wounded and on furlough; April-June 1778.
Mathews, Ebenezer Private	March 12, 1778, Three Years	First, Farwell	May 1778; June 1778 on General Poor's guard.
Mathies/Mathes, John Private	Dec 1, 1776, Duration of War	First, Scott	March 1, 1777 deserted; May 1778 "Joined May 1 who had been returned deserted"; May-June 1778.
Matthews, Thomas Private	March 19, 1778, Three Years	Second, Robinson	June 1778.
Meader, Stephen Private	May 1, 1777, Three Years	Second, Drew	Dec 1777 muster roll shows him as missing on July 7, 1777, and returned on Sept 20; Dec 1777-March 1778 on furlough; April 1778; May 1778 on guard; June 1778 sick at Valley Forge.
Melcher, Ward Private		Third, Robinson	June 8, 1778 joined; June 1778.
Meloon/Meloone, Josiah Ensign	Nov 8, 1776	Second, Norris	Dec 1777; Jan 1778 on command; Feb-May 1778 on furlough; June 1778.
Mercy/Mercey, Cato Private	Jan 26, 1777, Three Years	First, Wait	Dec 1777-April 1778; May 27, 1778 died.
Merrill/Merril, Abel Private	April 1, 1777, Three Years	First, Scott	Dec 1777 on command at the lines; Jan-April 1778; May 1778 on guard; June 1778 sick at Princeton.
Merrill/Merill, Barnard Private	April 4, 1777, Three Years	First, Emerson	Dec 1777-May 1778 sick at Albany; June 1778.
Merrill, David Private	March 1, 1777, Three Years	First, Morrill	Dec 1777; Jan-March 1778 sick at Albany; April 1778 sick at Derefield; May 1778 sick and on furlough; June 1778.

Name	Enlisted	Company	Notes
Merrill/Merriel, James Private	Three Years	First, Wait	April 1778 muster roll shows he joined on April 22, 1778. May 1778 muster roll shows he deserted Nov 17, 1776 and joined Jan 24, 1778. April-June 1778.
Merrill/Merill, John Private	Nov 12, 1776, Duration of War	First, Morrill	Dec 1777-May 1778; June 1778.
Merrill/Merril, Nathaniel/ Nethaniel Private	May 12, 1777, Eight Months, Oct 12, 1777, Three Years	Third, Livermore/ Ellis	Dec 1777 enlisted into Capt. Ellis's Co.; Jan 10, 1778 discharged. Apparently re-enlisted and transferred to Ellis' Company. Dec 1777-March 1778 on furlough; May-June 1778.
Merrill, Simon Ensign	Nov 8, 1776	First, Emerson	Dec 1777; Jan-May 1778 on furlough; June 1778.
Merrow, Joshua Ensign	April 2, 1777	Second, Rowell	May 1778 muster roll shows him as a prisoner on July 7, 1777; May 16, 1778 joined; May-June 1778.
Miles/Miales, Moses Private	April 2, 1777, Three Years	Second, Bell	Dec 1777-May 1778.
Miller, Farrer/Farren Private	Nov 28, 1776, Three Years	Second, Carr	Dec 1777 waiter Genl.; Jan-March 1778 Genl. waiter; April-June 1778.
Miller/Millar, John Private	Jan 21, 1777, Three Years	Third, Beal	Dec 1777-Feb 1778; March 1778 on command; April-June 1778.
Miller, Jonathan Private	Jan 24, 1777, Three Years	Third, Weare	Dec 1777; Jan 1778 after provisions; Feb-April 1778; May 1778 sick in camp; June-1778 sick General Hospital.
Miller, Matthew Private	Feb 17, 1777, Three Years	First, House	Dec 1777-April 1778; May 1778 sick in camp; June 1778 on duty.
Miller, Robert Private/Corporal/ Sergeant	Feb 23, 1777, Three Years	First, House	Dec 1777-Jan 1778; Jan 4, 1778 promoted to Corporal; Feb 24, 1778 promoted to Sergeant; Feb-March 1778 sick in hospital; April 1778 sick in camp; May-June 1778.
Millet, John Private	Feb 15, 1777, Duration of War	First, Scott	Dec 1777; Jan 1778 on command; Feb-June 1778.
Millitt/Millett, Morris Sergeant	Jan 1, 1777, Duration of War	First, Scott	Dec 1777; Jan 1778 absent with leave; Feb-May 1778; June 1778 sick at Fish Kill.
Mills, Johnathan/ Jonathan Private/Corporal	Feb 27, 1777, Three Years	Second, Drew	Dec 1777-Feb 1778; Feb 28, 1778 promoted to Corporal; March 1778; April-May 1778 on guard; June 1778.

Name	Enlisted	Company	Service Record
Mitchel, Francis Private	April [15], 1778, Three Years	First, Frye	June 1778.
Mitchell/Mitchel, Isaac Private	Nov 15, 1776, Duration of War	First, Farwell	Dec 1777; Jan 1778 on command with General Greene; Feb 1778 on present duty; March 1778 on command; April 1778 sick present; May-June 1778.
Mitchell, Isaac Private	March 3, 1778, Two Years	Second, Robinson	June 1778.
Mitchell, Joshua Private	Jan 1, 1777, Duration of War	Second, Robinson	Dec 1777-March 1778; April 1778 sick in camp; May-June 1778.
Montgomery/ Mountgomery, Martin Corporal	Nov 28, 1776, Three Years	Second, Carr	Dec 1777-April 1778; May 1778 sick in camp; June 1778 sick Valley Forge.
Moor/Moore, Isaac Drummer	Feb 6, 1777, Three Years	Third, McClary	Dec 1777-Jan 1778; Feb 1778 sick in camp; March 1778 sick in the General Hospital; April-June 1778.
Moore/Moor, James Private	Feb 15, 1777, Duration of War	First, Scott	Dec 1777-April 1778; May 1778 sick in camp; June 1778 sick at Princeton.
Moore/Moor, John Lt.	Nov 8, 1776	First, Frye	Dec 1777; Jan-June 1778 on furlough.
Moore, William Sergeant	April 1, 1777, Three Years	Second, Robinson	June 8, 1778 joined; June 1778.
Moores, Elkins/ Elkinese Private		Second, Robinson	Dec 1777; Jan 1778 lame in camp; Feb-June 1778.
Morgan/Morgon, David Sergeant	Nov 10, 1776, Duration of War	Second, Carr	Dec 1777-March 1778 on furlough; April 24, 1778 joined; April 1778; March 1778 on guard; June 1778.
Morgan/Morgon, John Corporal/Private	April 7, 1777, Three Years	Second, Carr	Dec 1777; Jan 1, 1778 reduced to Private; Jan-Feb 1778; March 1778 on command; April 1778 on command waggoner; May 1778 on command; June 1778.
Morrell/Morrill, Abel Private	Nov 14, 1776, Duration of War	Second, Drew	Dec 1777-Jan 1778; Feb 1778 sick present; March-April 1778; May 1778 on guard; June 1778 on command with armourer.
Morrell/Morrill, Jacob Private	March 15, 1778, Duration of War	Second, Robinson	Dec 1777 on command; Jan 1778; Feb 1778 sick in camp; March-April 1778; May 1778 sick in camp; June 2, 1778 died.

Name	Date	Company	Notes
Morrill/Morril, Amos Captain	Nov 8, 1776	First, Morrill	Dec 1777; Jan-April 1778 on furlough; May 1778 on court martial; June 1778.
Morrill, Robert Private	April 1, 1777, Three Years	Third, Livermore	Dec 1777-June 1778 on furlough.
Morrison, John Private	April 20, 1777, Three Years	Third, Gray	Dec 1777; Jan 1778 on command; Feb-March 1778; April 1778 sick in camp; May 1778; June 1778 on command at Valley Forge.
Morrison, Samuel Private	Jan 1, 1777, Duration of War	First, Scott	Dec 1777-June 1778.
Morse/Moss, Enoch Fifer	Feb 2, 1777, Three Years	First, Wait	Dec 1777-May 1778 sick at Fish Kill; June 1778.
Morse/Mors, Isaac Private	April 25, 1777, Three Years	Second, Robinson	Dec 1777-Feb 1778; March 1778 on guard; April 1778; May 1778 sick in camp; June 1778.
Moss, Daniel Fifer	March 5, 1777, Duration of War	Third, Stone	Dec 1777 missing since July 7, 1777; May-June 1778.
Moss, Jonathan Private	April 2, 1778, One Year	First, House	June 1778.
Moulton, James Private	Feb 16, 1777, Three Years	Third, Weare	Dec 1777-June 1778.
Moulton, Josiah Fifer	April 23, 1777, Three Years	Third, Weare	Dec 1777-May 1778; June 1778 sick at Amwell.
Moulton, Nathaniel Private	Nov 11, 1776, Duration of War	First, Morrill	Dec 1777; Jan 1778 sick present; Feb 1778; March 1778 on command at the lines; April 1778 on guard; May-June 1778.
Moulton/Molton, Nathaniel Private	April 28, 1777, Three Years	First, Wait	Dec 1777 on furlough by General Gates wounded October 7; Jan-Feb 1778 wounded on furlough; March 1778 on furlough; April-May 1778 sick in camp; June 2, 1778 died.
Moulton, Simeon Private	March 22, 1778, Three Years	Second, Carr	June 1778.
Muchemore/ Mutchemore, James Private	Jan 23, 1777, Three Years	First, Frye	Dec 1777; Jan 1778 on command a baker; Feb 1778 sick in camp; March 1778 on command; April 1778; May 1778 on command a baker; June 1778.
Mudget/Muget, John Private/Corporal	April 23, 1777, Three Years	Third, Gray	Dec 1777; Jan 1778 on guard; Feb-March 1778 on command; April 1778; May 1, 1778 promoted to Corporal; May 1778; June 1778 sick at Yellow Springs.

Munro, Josiah 2nd. Lt.	Nov 8, 1776	First, Scott	Dec 1777; Jan-March 1778 on furlough; April 1778; May 1778 on furlough; June 1778.
Murdough/ Mourdough, Thomas Private	Feb 1, 1777, Three Years	Second, Clayes	Dec 1777-Jan 1778 on furlough by Genl. Poor; Feb-May 1778 on furlough; June 1778 sick at Valley Forge.
Murphy/Murfey, Patrick Private		Second, Carr	April 1778 muster roll shows him missing on July 7, 1777, April 30, 1778 joined; April 1778; May 1778 on guard; June 1778.
Neal, Johnathan/ Jonathan Sergeant	Jan 27, 1777, Three Years	Second, Drew	Dec 1777-June 1778 on furlough.
Nealey/Neele, William Private	Nov 12, 1776, Duration of War	First, Morrill	Dec 1777 at Albany wounded; Jan-March 1778 wounded and at Albany; April 1778 on furlough wounded; May-June 1778 wounded and on furlough.
Nealy, Joseph Private	March 17, 1777, Duration of War	Third, Weare	Dec 1777-Feb 1778; March 1778 on command; April-May 1778; June 1778 sick at Valley Forge.
Neas, Elisha Sergeant	April 1, 1778, Three Years	Third, McClary	June 1778.
Needham/ Nedham, Nathaniel Private	March 1, 1777, Three Years	First, Wait	Dec 1777; Jan 1778 on command; Feb-April 1778; May 1778 on quarter guard; June 1778 sick at Cakoatt.
Neils/Niels, Gais Private	Nov 16, 1776, Duration of War	First, Wait	Dec 1777-May 1778; June 1778 on guard.
Nesmith, James Private	April 5, 1777, Three Years	Third, Livermore	Dec 1777 joined since Hubbardton Battle; Dec 1777-June 1778 on furlough.
Newman, Thomas Private	March 1, 1777, Three Years	First, House	Dec 1777 missing on scout Aug 19, 1777; Jan 23, 1778 joined; Jan 1778; Feb 1778 on command; March 1778 sick in hospital; April 1778 sick at Yellow Springs; May-June 1778.
Newton, Timothy Private	Nov 16, 1776, Duration of War	First, Farwell	Dec 1777-April 1778; May 1778 on guard; June 1778 at Valley Forge nursing sick.
Nicholls/Nichols, John Private	Jan 1, 1777, Duration of War	Second, Robinson	April 1778 muster roll shows him as a prisoner on July 7, 1777, joined April 25, 1778; April 1778 on guard; May-June 1778.
Nichols, James 2nd. Lt.	April 2, 1777	Second, Norris	Dec 1777-June 1778.
Night see Knight			

Name	Enlistment	Company	Service
Noble, Stephen Sergeant	Feb 1, 1777, Duration of War	Second, Bell	Dec 1777; Jan 1778 on command; Feb-May 1778 on furlough.
Nock, Jonathan Private	Three Years	First, Emerson	Dec 1777-March 1778 sick at Albany; April-June 1778.
Nolton see Knowlton			
Norris, Eliphalet Sergeant	Jan 27, 1777, Three Years	Second, Norris	Dec 1777-June 1778.
Norris, James Fifer/Private	Nov 15, 1776, Three Years	Second, Norris	Feb 1778 muster roll shows he was taken July 7, 1777, joined Feb 28, 1778; Feb-March 1778; March 10, 1778 reduced to Private; April-June 1778.
Norris, James Private	Jan 1, 1777, Duration of War	Second, Robinson	Dec 1777-April 1778; May-June 1778 on command Adjutant General.
Norris, Samuel Private	Jan 1, 1777, Duration of War	Second, Robinson	Dec 1777; Jan 1778 on guard; Feb-June 1778.
Norton, John Private	Jan 18, 1777, Duration of War	Second, Bell	Dec 1777-March 1778; April 1778 on guard; May 1778 prisoner in camp.
Norwood, Francis Private	May 9, 1777, Eight Months	Third, Ellis	Dec 1777 missing; Jan 10, 1778 discharged.
Nott see Knott			
Nowls/Noles, Simon Private	March 12, 1777, Duration of War	First, Morrill	Dec 1777-Jan 1778; Feb 1778 sick in hospital; March-June 1778.
Nute, Jotham Private	Feb 1, 1777, Duration of War	Second, Rowell	June 1778 muster roll shows him as missing on July 7, 1777; June 1778.
OBriant, Joseph Private	April 12, 1778, Two Years	Third, Livermore	June 1778.
Obrion/Obriant, John Private	April 9, 1777, Three Years	First, Frye	Dec 1777; Jan 1778 on command to Lancaster; Feb 1778; March 1778 sick in hospital; April 1778 sick at the French Creek Hospital; May 1778 sick in hospital at French Creek; June 1778.
Odiorne/Odiorn, John Fifer	April 11, 1777, Three Years	Third, Beal	Dec 1777-March 1778; April 1778 sick in camp; May 1778 on guard; June 1778.
Odiorne/Odiorn, Samuel Fifer	Jan 10, 1777, Duration of War	Third, Beal	Dec 1777-June 1778.
Onastose/ Onasteas, Vinsent/Vencient Private	April 1, 1778, Three Years	Third, McClary	May 1778; June 1778 sick at Englishtown.

Name	Enlistment	Company	Service Record
Orr, James Private	March 8, 1777, Three Years	First, Morrill	Dec 1777-April 1778; May 1778 sick in camp; June 1778 sick at Valley Forge.
Osgood, Thomas Private	March 12, 1778	First, Farwell	June 1778 on waggon guard.
Otis, John/ Jonathan Private	May 1, 1777, Three Years	Second, Drew	Dec 1777-June 1778.
Otis, Paul Corporal	May 1, 1777, Three Years	Second, Drew	Dec 1777-Jan 1778; Feb 1778 sick present; March 1778 on guard; April-June 1778.
Oxford, Derick/Derrick Private	May 3, 1777, Three Years	First, House	Dec 1777 sick at Albany; Jan-Feb 1778 on furlough; March 1778 sick at Albany; April-May 1778 sick at Lebanon; June 1778 sick at New Hampshire.
Pace, Thomas Private	Nov 15, 1776, Three Years	Second, Norris	Dec 1777-May 1778; June 1778 sick at [Watsessen].
Page, Abraham Private	Feb 10, 1777, Three Years	Third, McClary	Dec 1777; Jan 1778 on command; Feb-April 1778; May 1778 on command; June 1778.
Page, Benjamin Private	Jan 20, 1777, Three Years	Third, Weare	Dec 1777-May 1778; June 1778 on command on Commissary's Guard.
Page, Chase Private	Feb 22, 1777, Three Years	Third, McClary	Dec 1777 nursing in hospital; Jan-May 1778 on furlough; June 1778.
Page, David Private	April 4, 1777, Duration of War	Second, Drew	Dec 1777 muster roll shows he deserted on July 15, 1777, joined October 5; Dec 1777-Jan 1778; Feb 1778 sick present; March 1778 sick absent; April 1778; May 1778 on command; June 1778 sick at [ ].
Page, Moses Sergeant	March 28, 1777, Three Years	Third, Livermore	Dec 1777-May 1778; June 1778 sick absent.
Page, William Private	March [1], 1778, Duration of War	First, Farwell	June 1778 sick at Watt [ ].
Palmer, Ebenezer Private	April 14, 1777, Three Years	Second, Bell	Dec 1777-April 1778; May 1778 sick in camp.
Palmer/Palmar, William Private	Three Years	Second, Carr	Dec 1777 guard; Jan-March 1778 sick in camp; April-May 1778; June 1778 on General's guard.
Parker, Amasa Sergeant	Feb 28, 1778	Third, Ellis	June 1778.
Parker, James Private	Jan 21, 1777, Three Years	Third, Beal	Dec 1777-Feb 1778; March 1778 under guard; April 1778 sick in camp; May 7, 1778 died.

Name	Enlisted	Co./Capt.	Service Record
Parker, Robert Corporal	Aug 31, 1777, Three Years	First, Wait	Dec 1777-March 1778; April-May 1778 sick in camp; June 1778 sick at Valley Forge.
Parker, William Surgeon	Nov 8, 1776	Second	Dec 1777-June 1778.
Parks, Michael Sergeant	April 16, 1777, Three Years	Third, Gray	Dec 1777-June 1778.
Parsley, George Private	May 1, 1777, Three Years	Second, Drew	Dec 1777-May 1778 on command with Captain Drew; June 1778 sick at Valley Forge.
Parsley, Thomas Private/Fifer	May 1, 1777, Three Years	Second, Drew	Dec 1777-March 1778; April 1778 promoted to Fifer; April-June 1778.
Paton/Pattan, Nathaniel Private	Jan 1, 1778, Two Years	First, Frye	May 1778 joined; May-June 1778.
Patten/Pattin, James Private	Nov 13, 1776, Duration of War	Second, Blodget	Dec 1777 muster roll shows him as missing on July 7, 1777, returned on October 19; Dec 1777-Feb 1778; March 1778 on command; April-June 1778.
Pattin, Nathaniel Private	Feb 1, 1777, Three Years	First, House	Dec 1777-April 1778; May 1778 on command; June 1778 sick in camp.
Pattingill, Jethro Private	March 1, 1778, Three Years	First, Frye	June 1778 joined since last muster; June 1778.
Pearce/Peirce, Asa Private	March 21, 1778, Three Years	Third, Frye	June-July 1778 sick at Valley Forge.
Pearl, Joseph Private	May 1, 1777, Three Years	Second, Rowell	June 1778 muster roll shows him as missing on July 7, 1777, joined on June 7, 1778; June 1778 sick at Valley Forge.
Pearl, Simeon Private	April 20, 1777, Three Years	Second, Rowell	Dec 1777-Feb 1778 sick at Fish Kill; March 1778 muster roll shows he died on Feb 8, 1778.
Pendal, John Private		Second, Blodget	June [24], 1778, joined; June 1778.
Penniman, Adna 2nd. Lt.	Nov 8, 1776	Third, Gray	Dec 1777-Jan 1778; Feb 1778 sick with the smallpox; March 1778 on command; April-June 1778.
Perkins/Parkins, Adam Private	Jan 27, 1777, Duration of War	Second, Rowell	Dec 1777; Jan 1778 on duty; Feb 1778 on command; March-June 1778.
Perkins, Benjamin Private	Feb 2, 1777, Three Years	First, Wait	Dec 1777-March 1778; April 1778 sick in camp; May-June 1778.

Perkins, Jonathan Ensign	July 29, 1777	First, Wait	Dec 1777 on furlough by General Gates; Jan-March 1778 wounded and on furlough; April-June 1778.
Perkins, Jonathan Private	April 11, 1777, Three Years	Second, Robinson	Dec 1777-Feb 1778; March 1778 sick in camp; April 9, 1778 dead.
Perrey, John Private	Feb 19, 1777, Three Years	First, Emerson	Dec 1777-April 1778; May 1778 sick in camp; June 1778.
Perry, Abraham Private	Jan 1, 1777, Duration of War	Second, Robinson	Dec 1777-Jan 1778 a butcher; Feb-March 1778; April 1778 a butcher; May 1778 sick in camp; June 1778 on command commissary.
Perry/Perrey, Ichabod Private	May 3, 1777, Three Years	Third, Frye	Dec 1777-Feb 1778; March 1778 on guard; April-May 1778; June-Aug 1778 sick at Valley Forge.
Perry, Jonas Private	March 25, 1778	Third, Frye	June-August 1778 sick at Valley Forge; Sept 1778 died.
Perry/Perrey, Samuel Private	Jan 4, 1777, Duration of War	Third, Beal	Dec 1777 sick at "Poukepsie"; Jan 1778 sick at Albany; Feb-May 1778 sick at Fishkill; June 1778 dead.
Peters, Philip Private	May 1, 1778, Three Years	First, Farwell	June 1778.
Petiss, John Private	Three Years	Third, Stone	June 1778.
Pettingill/Petingill, Benjamin Private	Nov 10, 1776, Duration of War	First, Morrill	Dec 1777; Jan 1778 on command; Feb 1778; March 1778 on command at the lines; April-June 1778.
Pettingill/ Patinggill, Jonathan Private	April 19, 1777, Three Years	First, Farwell	Dec 1777-June 1778.
Pettengill, William Private	April 8, 1777, Three Years	Third, Frye	Dec 1777; Jan 1778 on command; Feb-May 1778; June-July 1778 sick at Valley Forge.
Pettigrew, William Private	March 16, 1778, Three Years	First, Scott	May 1778 on guard, enlisted March 16, 1778 "to Complete the Terim of 3 Years from ye 1st. of Jany. 1777"; June 1778.
Peverly/Pevely, John Corporal	Feb 13, 1777, Three Years	Third, Beal	Dec 1777-Feb 1778; March 1778 on command; April-May 1778; June-July 1778 sick Valley Forge.

Name	Enlistment	Regiment	Service
Phelps/Phalps, Samuel, Private	Nov 15, 1776, Three Years	First, Farwell	Dec 1777 wounded at Sanakady; Jan-March 1778 wounded at Sanahady; April 1778 on main guard; May 1778; June 1778 on Cloathier General guard.
Philbrick, Daniel, Private	May 16, 1777, Three Years	Third, Gray	Dec 1777; Jan 1778 on command; Feb-March 1778; April 1778 sick in camp; May-June 1778.
Phillips/Philips, John, Private	March 27, 1777, Duration of War	Third, Stone	Dec 1777-May 1778; June 1778 sick at General Hospital.
Pierce, Nehemiah, Private	April 10, 1777, Eight Months	First, House	Dec 1777 on furlough by General Gates; Jan 6, 1778 discharged.
Pike, John, Private	Dec 5, 1776, Duration of War	First, Farwell	Dec 1777 sick at Albany New City; Jan-April 1778 sick Albany N. City; May-June 1778 sick at Albany.
Pinkham, Isaac, Drummer	Feb 13, 1777, Three Years	Second, Drew	Dec 1777-May 1778; June 1778 sick absent Princeton.
Pinkham, Paul, Private	Dec 15, 1776, Three Years	Second, Drew	Dec 1777-May 1778; June 1778 sick Princeton.
Pinner, Benjamin, Private	Jan 19, 1777, Duration of War	Second, Rowell	Dec 1777-May 1778 wounded at Albany; June 1778 sick at Albany.
Piper, David, Private	May 30, 1777, Three Years	Third, Gray	Dec 1777-Jan 1778; Feb 1778 on guard; March-May 1778; June 1778 sick at Princeton.
Piper, John, Private	May 23, 1777, Three Years	Third, Gray	Dec 1777 sick present; Jan-April 1778; May 1778 sick present; June 1778.
Piper, Thomas, Private	May 24, 1777, Three Years	Third, Gray	Dec 1777-Feb 1778; March 1778 on his Excellency's Guard; March 19, 1778 transferred to the Commander-in-Chief's Guard.
Pitman, Joseph, Private	Nov 15, 1776, Duration of War	Second, Drew	Dec 1777 not fit for duty; Jan-April 1778; May 1778 sick present; June 1778 at Valley Forge sick.
Pitts/Pitt, Thomas, Private	April 21, 1777, Three Years	Third, Livermore	Dec 1777; Jan 1778 sick in camp; Feb 1778; March 1778 on command; April 1778 on command at the Lines; May 1778 sick in camp; June 1778 sick absent; July 1778 sick at Valley Forge.
Plummer/Plumer, Davise, Private	April 7, 1777, Three Years	First, Frye	Dec 1777-May 1778; June 1778 sick present.

Plummer/Plumer, Nathan Private	April 7, 1777, Three Years	First, Frye	Dec 1777; Jan 1778 on piquet guard; Feb-June 1778.
Pollard, Elijah Private	May 19, 1778, Three Years	Second, Robinson	June 1778.
Pollard, Ezekiel Private	Feb 15, 1778, Three Years	Second, Robinson	June 1778.
Polley, Joseph Fifer	April 11, 1777, Three Years	First, Frye	Dec 1777-June 1778.
Pomp, Peter Private	Jan 24, 1777, Duration of War	Third, McClary	Dec 1777; Jan-Feb 1778 sick in camp; March 15, 1778 died.
Pool/Poole, Jonathan Surgeons Mate	April 2, 1777	First	Jan-May 1778; June 1778 on command at Corryell's Ferry.
Poor, Enoch Brigadier General	Feb 21, 1777		Poor commanded a brigade comprised of the three New Hampshire Regiments and the Second and Fourth New York Regiments. He was present during the entire Encampment and took the Oath of Allegiance at Valley Forge on May 12, 1778
Porter, Joseph Private	April 1, 1777, Three Years	Third, Livermore	Dec 1777; Jan 1778 on command; Feb-March 1778; April 27, 1778.
Porter, Noah Private	Jan 1, 1778, Three Years	First, Farwell	April 1778; May 1778 on command with waggons; June 1778.
Potter, Joseph 2nd. Lt.	Nov 8, 1776	Second, Clayes	Dec 1777-June 1778.
Potter, Samuel Corporal	Nov 15, 1776, Duration of War	First, Farwell	Dec 1777 wounded absent; Jan-March 1778 wounded at Sanahedy; April-May 1778; June 1778 sick at Valley Forge.
Powel, Samuel Private	May 8, 1778, One Year	First, Hutchins	June 1778 joined since last muster.
Powel, William Private	May 8, 1778, One Year	First, Hutchins	June 1778 joined since last muster.
Powell, Thomas Drum Major	March 1, 1777	Third	Dec 1777-June 1778.
Powell, William Private	June 15, 1777, Three Years	First, Emerson	Dec 1777; Jan 1778 on duty; Feb-March 1778; April 1778 on command Rednigh; May 1778; June 1778 on guard.
Powers, Abner, Private	Feb 13, 1778, Three Years	First, Farwell	June 1778.
Powers, Jonathan Private	Jan 1, 1777, Three Years	First, Emerson	Dec 1777; Jan-Feb 1778 sick present; March-June 1778.

Name	Enlisted	Company	Service
Powers, Joseph Private	Jan 1, 1778, Three Years	First, Farwell	April 1778; May 1778 on guard; June 1778.
Powers, Josiah Private	April 25, 1777, Three Years	Third, Ellis	Jan 1778 sick at Albany; Feb-June 1778 on furlough.
Powers, Nathaniel Private	Feb 13, 1778, Three Years	First, Farwell	June 1778.
Powers, Simeon Private	May 5, 1777, Duration of War	First, Farwell	Dec 1777 wounded absent; Jan-May 1778 wounded and on furlough; June 1778.
Powers, Stephen Private	May 6, 1777, Eight Months	Third, Frye	Dec 1777; Jan 10, 1778 discharged.
Pratt, Thomas Private	Feb 1, 1777, Three Years	First, House	Dec 1777 on furlough by General Gates; Jan-June 1778 on furlough.
Pratt, William Private	April 18, 1777, Three Years	First, House	Dec 1777-Jan 1778 sick at Reding; Feb-March 1778 sick in hospital; April 1778 muster roll shows he died on Dec 20, 1777.
Presby/Presbee, Richard Private	Nov 22, 1776, Duration of War	Second, Bell	Dec 1777-Jan 1778; Feb 1778 on command; March-May 1778.
Prescutt/Prescott, Jonathan Private	Feb 7, 1777, Three Years	Third, McClary	Dec 1777; Jan 1778 sick in camp; Feb 1778 sick in the country; March 1778 sick in camp; April-June 1778.
Presson, Benjamin Private	March 10, 1777, Three Years	Third, Stone	Dec 1777-Feb 1778; March 1778 sick in camp; April 1778 on guard; May 1778 on command; June 1778.
Presson/Preston, William Corporal/ Sergeant	Feb 10, 1777, Three Years	Third, Stone	Dec 1777; Jan 1778 on command; Feb-June 1778; June 12, 1778 promoted to Sergeant.
Preston, Abner Drummer	Feb 1, 1777, Three Years	First, Farwell	Dec 1777-June 1778.
Prichard, Jeremy/Jeremiah 2nd. Lt.	Nov 8, 1776	First, Farwell	Dec 1777-June 1778.
Prichard, William Private	Nov 16, 1776, Three Years	First, Farwell	Dec 1777; Jan 1778 sick present; Feb-June 1778.
Proctor, Joel Private		First, House	June 1778.
Prowse/Prows, Thomas Private	March 8, 1777, Three Years	Third, Beal	Dec 1777-May 1778 sick at Albany; June 1778 sick at Corryell's Ferry.
Putnam, Daniel Private	Feb 13, 1777, Three Years	First, House	Dec 1777 on command in the armory at Albany; Jan-March 1778 on command with the armorers at Albany.

Name	Enlisted	Company	Notes
Quimbey/Quinby, Eliphelate/ Eliphalet, Sergeant	April 1, 1777, Three Years	First, Hutchins	Dec 1777; Jan 1778 absent with leave; Feb-May 1778; June 1778 sick Yellow Springs.
Quimby, Eleazer Private	April 25, 1777, Three Years	Second, Robinson	June 1778 muster roll shows him as taken on July 7, 1777, joined June 8, 1778; June 1778.
Quimby, James Private	April 20, 1777, Three Years	Second, Rowell	April 1778 muster roll shows he was taken prisoner on July 7, 1777, joined on April 24, 1778; April-May 1778.
Quimby, Johnathan/ Jonathan Private	March 11, 1777, Three Years	Second, Carr	Dec 1777 sick in camp; Jan-May 1778; June 1778 sick Valley Forge.
Quinby/Quimby, Benjamin, Private	May 23, 1777, Three Years	Third, Gray	Dec 1777-May 1778; June 1778 sick at Corryell's Ferry.
Quinby/Quimby, Zachariah Private	April 16, 1777, Three Years	Third, Gray	Dec 1777; Jan-Feb 1778 sick present; March 1778; April 1778 sick in camp; May-June 1778.
Quint, Thomas Private	Jan 28, 1777, Three Years	Second, Carr	Dec 1777 guard; Jan 1778 on command; Feb-May 1778; June 1778 on command Valley Forge.
Raine/Rane, John Corporal	April 26, 1777, Duration of War	First, Scott	Dec 1777; Jan 1778 absent with leave; Feb-April 1778; May 1778 sick in camp; June 1778 sick at Valley Forge.
Rand, John Private	Feb 6, 1777, Three Years	Third, Beal	Dec 1777 sick at N. City; Jan-June 1778 sick at Albany.
Randall/Randell, James Private	March 12, 1777, Duration of War	First, Morrill	Dec 1777; Jan-April 1778 sick at Manchester; May 1778 muster roll shows he deserted after being on furlough since July 9, 1777.
Randel, William Private	March 10, 1778, Two Years	Second, Clayes	June 20, 1778 joined; June 1778.
Rankin, Jonathan Private	April 4, 1777, Three Years	First, Emerson	Dec 1777-April 1778 sick at Albany; June 1778 muster roll shows he died on March 28, 1778.
Rawlins/Rollins, Daniel Private	Jan 20, 1777, Three Years	Third, Beal	Dec 1777 sick in camp; Jan 1778 on command; Feb-March 1778; April 1778 on guard; May 1778 sick in camp; June-Aug 1778 sick Valley Forge.
Rawlins/Rawlings, Eliphalet/Eliphlet Private	Jan 24, 1777, Three Years	Third, Weare	Dec 1777 on command; Jan 1778 after provisions; Feb-May 1778; June 1778 sick General Hospital.

Name	Enlistment	Regiment, Company	Service Record
Rawlins/Rawlings, John, Private	Feb 3, 1777, Three Years	Third, Weare	Dec 1777; Jan 1778 sick in camp; Feb-May 1778; June 1778 tending on sick at Valley Forge.
Rawlings/Rawlings, Joseph, Private	April 3, 1777, Three Years	Third, Weare	Dec 1777-June 1778 left wounded at Albany.
Rawlings/Rawlins, Aaron, Private	Nov 13, 1776, Duration of War	Second, Blodget	Dec 1777 muster roll shows him as missing on July 7, 1777, and returned on October 19; Dec 1777-April 1778; May 1778 on guard; June 1778 left sick at Valley Forge.
Rawlings, Aaron, Private		Second, Clayes	June 20, 1778 joined; June 1778. In July 1778 he appears on the rolls of Drew's Company.
Rawlings, Robert, Private		Second, Clayes	June 20, 1778 joined; June 1778. In July 1778 he appears on the rolls of Drew's Company.
Ray, Silas/Silus, Private	May 10, 1777, Eight Months/ Three Years	Third, Livermore/ Ellis	Dec 1777; Jan 10, 1778 discharged; Jan 1778 enlisted into Captain Ellis's Company; Jan-June 1778 on furlough.
Razey, Peltiah, Private	Feb 28, 1778, Three Years	Third, Ellis	June 1778.
Read/Reed, Alpheus/Elphus, Corporal	Jan 17, 1777, Three Years	Third, Beal	Dec 1777 wounded and on furlough; Jan-April 1778 wounded. May 1778 muster roll shows he deserted on Jan 10, 1778.
Redfield, William, Sergeant	Jan 1, 1777, Duration of War	First, Scott	Dec 1777-Jan 1778; Feb 1778 sick in camp; March-June 1778.
Reed, James, Sergeant	Jan 1, 1777, Three Years	Second, Clayes	Dec 1777 shows he deserted on July 27, 1777, and rejoined on Sept 1; Dec 1777-May 1778; June 1778 sick Valley Forge.
Reed/Reid, John, Private	May 18, 1777, Three Years	First, Frye	Dec 1777 sick at Fish Kill; Jan-June 1778.
Reed, John, Private	Three Years	Third, Weare	Dec 1777 left wounded at [ ].
Reed/Read, Zadock, Private	Nov 12, 1776, Duration of War	First, Morrill	Dec 1777; Jan-April 1778 sick at Albany; June 1778.
Reid, George, Lt. Col.	April 2, 1777	First	Dec 1777; Jan-March 1778 on furlough; April-June 1778.
Rendall/Rendal, James, Private	Feb 6, 1777, Three Years	Third, Beal	Dec 1777-June 1778 on furlough.

Name	Enlisted	Company	Service Record
Rendall/Rendal, James, Jr. Private	Feb 6, 1777, Three Years	Third, Beal	Dec 1777-Feb 1778; March 1778 on guard; April 1778; May 1778 sick in camp; June-Aug 1778 sick at Valley Forge; August 31, 1778 died.
Rendell/Randell, Edward Private	Jan 24, 1777, Duration of War	Second, Bell	Dec 1777-May 1778 on furlough.
Riant, John Private	Feb 12, 1777, Duration of War	Third, Stone	Dec 1777; Jan 1778 on command; March-June 1778 on command.
Riant, Joseph Private	April 12, 1778, Two Years	Third, Livermore	Does not appear on a muster roll until Oct 1779.
Rice/Royce, Amos Private	May 1, 1777, Three Years	First, Scott	Dec 1777 on duty; Jan-Feb 1778; March 1778 sick in camp; April 1778; May 5, 1778 dead.
Rice/Royce, Joel Private	May 1, 1777, Three Years	First, Scott	Dec 1777 on duty; Jan-Feb 1778; March 1778 absent; April-June 1778.
Rice, Jedediah/Juddiah Private	Jan 22, 1778, Two Years	First, Wait	April-June 1778.
Rice, Lemuel Private	Feb 4, 1778, Three Years	First, Farwell	June 1778.
Richards, Bradley/Bradlee Sergeant	Jan 27, 1777, Three Years	Third, Stone	Dec 1777-June 1778.
Richardson, Daniel Private	April 14, 1777, Three Years	Second, Bell	Dec 1777-May 1778.
Richardson, Joseph Sergeant	Feb 28, 1777, Three Years	Second, Bell	Dec 1777-May 1778.
Richardson, Nathaniel Private	Jan 1, 1777, Duration of War	Second, Robinson	Dec 1777-Jan 1778; Feb 1778 sick in camp; March-April 1778; May 1778 sick in camp; June 1778 sick Valley Forge.
Richardson, Paris Private	Feb 13, 1778, Three Years	First, Farwell	June 1778.
Richardson, Richard Private	April 3, 1777, Three Years	First, Wait	Dec 1777-Feb 1778; March-April 1778 sick in camp; May 1778; June 1778 sick at Corryell's Ferry.
Richardson, Stephen Private	April 1, 1777, Three Years	Third, Frye	Dec 1777-Jan 1778; Feb 1778 on command; March 1778 sick in camp; April 1778; May 1778 sick in camp; June 1778 sick in General Hospital.

Name	Enlisted	Company	Service Record
Richardson, William, Private	Jan 1, 1777, Three Years	First, Emerson	Dec 1777; Jan 1778 on duty; Feb-April 1778; April 1, 1778 promoted to Sergeant; May 1778 on command with Captain McLane; June 1778 sick in Pennsylvania.
Ricker, Timmey/ Timothy, Private	May 22, 1777, Three Years	Second, Carr	Dec 1777-Feb 1778; March 1778 General's Life Guard; March 19, 1778 transferred to the Commander-in-Chief's Guard.
Riddel, John, Private	March 7, 1778, Three Years	First, Frye	June 1778 joined since last muster, sick Valley Forge.
Riddle/Riddel, James, Private	March 23, 1777, Three Years	First, Frye	Dec 1777 wounded absent; Jan-May 1778 wounded and on furlough; June 1778 sick at Valley Forge.
Rider, James, Private	Nov 17, 1776, Duration of War	First, Wait	Dec 1777-June 1778.
Right see Wright			
Robarts/Robards, Moses, Private	Nov 15, 1776, Three Years	Second, Norris	Dec 1777 muster roll shows he was taken prisoner on July 7, 1777; joined October 3, deserted on Nov 1; April 1778 muster roll shows he joined on April 23, 1778; April 1778; May 1778 on guard; June 1778.
Roberts, Cornelius, Private	May 13, 1777, Eight Months	Third, Livermore	Dec 1777; Jan 10, 1778 discharged.
Roberts/Robards, Reubin/Ruben, Private	Nov 24, 1776, Three Years	First, Hutchins	Dec 1777; Jan 1778 on command with General Greene; Feb 1778 sick in camp; March-April 1778 sick present; May 1778; June 1778 sick Yellow Springs.
Robertson/ Robartson, Richard, Corporal/ Sergeant	Aug 9, 1777, Three Years	First, Wait	Dec 1777-Feb 1778; March 1778 sick in camp; April 1778; May 1, 1778 promoted to Sergeant; May-June 1778.
Robinson, Caleb, Captain		Second, Robinson	July 7, 1777 taken prisoner at Hubbardton.
Robinson/Robison, James, Private	Nov 28, 1776, Three Years	Second, Carr	Dec 1777; Jan 1778 on command Albany; Feb-March 1778 on command; April 1778; May 1778 sick absent; June 1778 sick on the road.

Name	Enlisted	Company	Notes
Robinson, John Private	Jan 1, 1777, Duration of War	Second, Blodget	Dec 1777 muster roll shows him as missing on July 7, 1777, and returned on October 19; Dec 1777-March 1778; April 1778 on guard; May-June 1778.
Robinson, Noah 2nd. Lt.	Nov 8, 1776	Second, Blodget	Dec 1777 wounded near camp; Jan-May 1778; June 1778 "Taken for the [ ] of June 1778"; July 1778 on detachment.
Rollings, Jeremiah Private	Three Years, April 25, 1777	Third, McClary	June 8, 1778 joined; June 1778 sick at Rocky Hill.
Rollings/Rolings, Thomas Private	Jan 1, 1777, Duration of War	Second, Robinson	Dec 1777-Jan 1778; Feb 1778 sick in camp; March-June 1778.
Roose, James Private	Feb 1, 1777, Three Years	First, House	Dec 1777 wounded on furlough by General Gates; Jan-March 1778 on furlough wounded; April-May 1778 sick in camp; June 1778.
Roundy, Asel Private	May 1, 1777, Three Years	First, Hutchins	Dec 1777; Jan 25, 1778 dead.
Rowe/Row, John Private	April 15, 1777, Three Years	First, Emerson	Dec 1777; Jan 1778 on command for provisions; Feb-May 1778; June 1778 on Commissary guard.
Reave, John Private	April 1, 1778, Three Years	Third, McClary	June 1778.
Rowe/Row, William Private	April 12, 1777, Three Years	Third, Livermore	Dec 1777-June 1778 on furlough.
Rowel, Phillip, Private	May 10, 1777, Three Years	Third, Livermore	Dec 1777-June 1778 on furlough.
Rowell, Lemuel/Lamuel Private	May 30, 1777, Three Years	Third, Gray	Dec 1777; Jan 1778 sick in camp; Feb-March 1778 on command; April 1778 sick present; May 1778; June 1778 sick Valley Forge; July 1778 sick Yellow Springs.
Rowell, William Captain	April 2, 1777	Second, Rowell	Dec 1777; Jan-March 1778 on furlough; April-May 1778 on furlough to New Hampshire; June 1778.
Rowen, Andrew Private	April 21, 1777, Three Years	Third, Gray	Dec 1777 sick absent; Jan-Feb 1778 sick at Albany; March 20, 1778 died.
Rowen, John Private	April 30, 1777, Three Years	Third, Gray	Dec 1777; Jan 1778 on command; Feb-April 1778; May 1778 sick present; June 1778 sick at Valley Forge.

Name	Enlistment	Company	Notes
Rowley, Joseph Corporal	April 21, 1777, Three Years	Second, Bell	Dec 1777-Jan 1778 on furlough; Feb 1778 muster roll shows he died on November 16, 1777.
Royce, Jacob Private	Jan 1, 1778, Two Years	First, Scott	June 1778.
Rundlett/Runlett, William Corporal	Jan 30, 1777, Three Years	Third, McClary	Dec 1777-June 1778.
Runlett, James Sergeant	Feb 14, 1777, Three Years	Second, Norris	June 1778 muster roll shows he was taken on July 7, 1777, joined June 8, 1778; June 1778.
Runnels/Runnells, Isreal/Israel Private	April 14, 1777, Duration of War	Second, Bell	Dec 1777; Jan 1778 on command; Feb-March 1778; April 1778 on command; May 1778.
Runnels/Runnells, Moses Private	April 10, 1777, Duration of War	Second, Bell	Dec 1777; Jan-March 1778 on command; April 1778 on command at the Bridge; May 1778.
Runnels/Runels, Samuel Private	May 1, 1777, Three Years	Third, McClary	May-June 1778 on command with General Sullivan.
Runnels/Runnells, Stephen Private	Jan 24, 1777, Duration of War	Second, Bell	Dec 1777-Jan 1778; Feb 1778 on command; March-April 1778; May 1778 sick in camp.
Russell, Daniel/David Private	March 20, 1777, Three Years	Second, Blodget	Dec 1777 wounded absent; Jan-March 1778 on furlough; April-June 1778 on furlough to New Hampshire.
Russell, Jacob Private	Nov 15, 1776, Three Years	Second, Carr	Dec 1777-May 1778; June 1778 sick Brunswick.
Russell, John Private	Feb 3, 1777, Three Years	First, Frye	Dec 1777 sick at White Marsh; Jan-Feb 1778 sick at Reading; March 29, 1778 dead.
Russell, William Private	March 24, 1777, Three Years	Third, Beal	Dec 1777-Jan 1778; Feb-March 1778 on command; April-May 1778; June 1778 sick at Corryell's Ferry.
Sampson/Samson, John Private	Nov 15, 1776, Three Years	First, Frye	Dec 1777-March 1778; April 1778 on command in country; May 1778; June 1778 on guard.
Sanborn/Samborn, John Private	April 1, 1777, Three Years	First, Morrill	Dec 1777-Feb 1778; March 1778 sick in camp; April-May 1778; June 1778 sick at Ward [Sesion].
Sanborn/Sandborn, John Sergeant	March 15, 1777, Three Years	Second, Norris	Dec 1777 muster roll shows he deserted on October 3, 1777; April 30, 1778 joined; April-June 1778.

Name	Date/Term	Regt/Co	Notes
Sanborn/Sanburn, Joseph Private	Nov 24, 1776, Three Years	First, Hutchins	Dec 1777-April 1778 on furlough by General Gates; May 1778 on furlough New England; June 1778 tending sick Valley Forge.
Sanborn/Sanbins, Joseph Private	April 16, 1778, Three Years	Third, Gray	Dec 1777; Jan 1778 on command; Feb-March 1778; April 1778 sick in camp; May-June 1778.
Sanborn, Matthew N. Private	Jan 22, 1777, Duration of War	Third, Weare	Dec 1777-June 1778.
Sanborn/Sandbourn, Paul/Pall Private	March 11, 1777, Three Years	Second, Carr	Dec 1777-March 1778; April 1778 on command; May-June 1778.
Sanburn, Moses Private	May 8, 1778, One Year	First, Hutchins	June 1778 joined since last muster, on guard.
Sanderson, David Private	Feb 1, 1777, Three Years	First, House	Dec 1777-May 1778; June 1778 on duty.
Sanderson/Saunderson, Thomas Private	April 1, 1777, Duration of War	First, Scott	Dec 1777-Feb 1778; March 1778 on duty; April-May 1778; June 1778 on picket guard.
Sarjant/Sargent, Valintine/Valtine Private	Dec 1, 1776, Three Years	Second, Carr	Dec 1777 with Artillery; Jan 1778 in the Train; Feb 1778 in the Artillery; March 1778 with Artillery.
Sarjent/Sarjeant, John Private	Jan 10, 1777, Duration of War	Second, Bell	Dec 1777-May 1778.
Sartwell, Simon 1st. Lt.	Nov 8, 1776	First, Hutchins	Dec 1777-Jan 1778; Feb 1778 sick absent; March-April 1778; May 1778 sick present; June 1778.
Sawyer/Sawer, Jonathan Private	April 4, 1777, Three Years	First, Hutchins	Dec 1777; Jan 1778 on command at Lancaster; Feb-June 1778.
Scales, Matthew Private	April 18, 1777, Three Years	Third, Gray	Dec 1777; Jan-March 1778 sick absent; April-June 1778 sick at Yellow Springs.
Scammell, Alexander Colonel/Adjutant General	Nov 8, 1776	Third	Dec 1777; Jan 15, 1778 appointed Adjutant General and was at Valley Forge throughout the Encampment period.
Scott, Thomas Corporal	Nov 10, 1776, Duration of War	First, Morrill	Dec 1777 assistant to the Waggon Master; Jan 1778 on duty; Feb-June 1778.
Scott, William Captain	Nov 8, 1776	First, Scott	Dec 1777-March 1778; April-June 1778.

Name	Enlistment	Company	Service Record
Scott/Stoct, William Private	March 1, 1777, Three Years	Second, Carr	Dec 1777 guard; Jan-March 1778; April 1778 on command; May-June 1778.
Seavy, Jonathan Private	May 7, 1777, Eight Months	Third, Weare	Dec 1777; Jan 10, 1778 discharged.
Seavy, Levi Private	May 7, 1777, Eight Months	Third, Weare	Dec 1777; Jan 10, 1778 discharged.
Seeley see Cilley			
Senter, Abraham Private	Nov 14, 1776, Three Years	Second, Carr	Dec 1777 on command with General Surgeon; Jan-Feb 1778 on command Albany; March-April 1778 on command; May-June 1778 on command Albany.
Senter, Asa 2nd. Lt.	Nov 8, 1776	First, Frye	Dec 1777 now returning from captivity; Jan 1778 exchanged from being a prisoner; Feb 1778 exchanged from captivity; March 1778 at New England.
Sergent/Serjeant, Benjamin Private	March 31, 1777, Three Years	Third, Livermore	Dec 1777-May 1778 on furlough; June 1778 sick absent.
Sergent/Sargent, Samuel Corporal	May 8, 1777, Three Years	Third, Stone	Dec 1777; Jan-May 1778 on furlough; June 1778.
Serjent, Ephriem Private	May 8, 1778, One Year	First, Hutchins	June 1778 joined since last muster, sick Princeton.
Serjents/Sergents. Ebenezer Private	April 7, 1777, Three Years	Second, Clayes	Dec 1777-May 1778; June 1778 sick Valley Forge.
Seshings/Shesings, John Private	Feb 21, 1777, Three Years	Third, Stone	Dec 1777-June 1778.
Severance, Thomas Private	March 21, 1777, Three Years	First, Hutchins	Dec 1777 sick present; Jan 1778; Feb 1778 sick in camp; March-June 1778.
Shadock see Chadwick			
Shail, James Private	April 18, 1777, Three Years	First, Scott	June 1778.
Sharp, Jonathan Private	Jan 31, 1777, Duration of War	Second, Rowell	Dec 1777-Feb 1778; March-May 1778 sick in camp; June 1778 sick at Yellow Springs.
Shaw, Thomas Sergeant	Jan 3, 1777, Duration of War	Third, Beal	Dec 1777-Jan 1778; Feb 1778 on guard; March-May 1778; June 1778 sick at Slaughter[sdam].
Shaw, William Private	July 15, 1777, Duration of War	First, Scott	Dec 1777; Jan 1778 sick absent; Feb 1, 1778 deserted.

Name	Enlisted	Company	Service Record
Shepard/Shepherd, George/Georg Corporal	Feb 10, 1777, Duration of War	Third, Stone	Dec 1777-Feb 1778; March 1778 on command; April 1778 sick in camp; May 1778; June 1778 General Hospital.
Shepperd, Jonathan/Johnathan Corporal	Nov 15, 1776, Duration of War	Second, Drew	Dec 1777-Jan 1778; February 28, 1778 deserted.
Sherer/Sheror, David Private	April 5, 1777, Three Years	First, Hutchins	Dec 1777-Jan 1778; Feb 1778 on command; March-May 1778; June 1778 on guard.
Sherman/Sharman, Richard Private	Jan 3, 1777, Duration of War	Third, Beal	Dec 1777-March 1778 wounded at Albany; April-June 1778.
Shipman, Eliphas Private	Feb 20, 1777, Three Years	Third, Ellis	Dec 1777-April 1778 sick at Albany; May-June 1778 sick at Westminster.
Shirley, Daniel Private	April 3, 1777, Three Years	First, Emerson	Dec 1777 on duty; Jan-March 1778; April 1778 on a fortnight command; May 1778 sick at Killen Mill; June 1778.
Shrowder/Schrowder, Thomas Private	Nov 19, 1776, Three Years	First, Frye	Dec 1777-Jan 1778; Feb-March 1778 lame in hospital; April 15, 1776 died.
Shute, Jonathan Private	March 29, 1777, Three Years	Third, Beal	Dec 1777-June 1778.
Silk, Michael Private	July 23, 1777, Duration of War	First, Scott	Dec 1777 sick in camp; Jan 1778 on guard; Feb 1778; March 1778 on command; April 1778; May-June 1778 on command to the Adjutant General.
Sillingham/Sellingham, Henry Private	April 12, 1778, Two Years	Third, Livermore	June 1778.
Sillingham/Sellingham, Jacob Private	April 12, 1778, Two Years	Third, Livermore	June 1778.
Silver, Samuel Private	May 30, 1777, Three Years	Third, Gray	Dec 1777-Jan 1778; Feb 1778 on command; March 1778 sick in camp; April 1778; May 1778 on guard; June 1778 sick at Valley Forge.
Simonds, Levi Private	Feb 3, 1778, Three Years	First, Farwell	June 1778.
Simons/Simonds, James Private	Duration of War	First, Farwell	April 1778 taken prisoner July 7, 1777, rejoined April 30, 1778; May-June 1778 on guard.

Name	Enlisted	Company	Notes
Simons/Simonds, John Private	Jan 1, 1778, Three Years	First, Farwell	April-June 1778.
Simons/Simonds, Silas Private	Jan 1, 1778, Three Years	First, Farwell	April 1778; May-June 1778 on guard.
Simpson, Robert/Robard Private	Feb 10, 1777, Three Years	Third, Weare	Dec 1777-May 1778 on furlough; June 1778.
Simpson, Thomas 2nd. Lt.	Nov 6, 1776	Third, Weare	Dec 1777-March 1778 on furlough; April-June 1778.
Simson/Simpson, William Private	Jan 1, 1777, Three Years	First, Frye	Dec 1777; Jan 1778 on command; Feb-April 1778; May 1778 "as Qr Mastr. Sergt."; June 1778 assistant to the Forage Master.
Sincler/Sinckler, Noah Private	Feb 10, 1777, Three Years	Third, McClary	Dec 1777 nursing in hospital; Jan-March 1778 on furlough.
Sinkler, Bradbury Private	June 21, 1777, Three Years	First, Morrill	Dec 1777; Jan 1778 sick in hospital; Feb 1778 muster roll shows he died on March 5, 1778.
Sinkler/Sinclair, Joshua Private	June 21, 1777, Three Years	First, Morrill	Dec 1777; Jan 1778 on command; Feb 1778 sick in camp; March-June 1778.
Sinkler/Sinclair, Samuel Private	June 21, 1777, Three Years	First, Morrill	Dec 1777; Jan 1778 on guard; Feb-June 1778.
Siscow/Sisscow, Samuel Private	Feb 17, 1777, Three Years	First, Farwell	Dec 1777-June 1778.
Siscow, William Private	May 1, 1778, Three Years	First, Farwell	June 1778.
Slack, Joseph Private	Nov 14, 1777, Duration of War	Second, Clayes	Dec 1777-March 1778; April 1778 sick in camp; May-June 1778.
Slapp, Edward Private	April 28, 1777, Three Years	First, House	Dec 1777 on furlough by General Gates; Jan 1778 muster roll shows he died on Dec 31, 1777.
Sleeper, Benjamin Private	April 16, 1777, Three Years	Third, Gray	Dec 1777-April 1778; May 1778 sick present; June 1778.
Small, Benjamin Private	Feb 10, 1777, Duration of War	Second, Bell	Dec 1777 on command in Albany Hospital; Jan 1778 on command at Albany; Feb-March 1778 on command; April-May 1778 on command at Albany.

Smart, Caleb Private	April 7, 1777, Three Years	First, Hutchins	Dec 1777; Jan 1778 on command for provisions; Feb 1778; March 1778 sick present; April-May 1778; June 1778 sick Yellow Springs.
Smart, Elijah Private	April 7, 1777, Three Years	First, Hutchins	Dec 1777-Feb 1778; March 1778 on command ye lines; April 1778; May 1778 sick present; June 1778 sick Yellow Springs.
Smart, Moses Private	March 15, 1777, Three Years	Third, Stone	Dec 1777; Jan 1778 sick in camp; Feb 1778 on command; March-April 1778; May 1778 on guard; June 1778.
Smart, Richard Private	March 10, 1777, Three Years	Third, Stone	Dec 1777; Jan 1778 on command [Colos servant]; Feb-April 1778 on command; May 1778 on guard; June 1778.
Smith, Alexander/ Elexander Private	Nov 12, 1776, Duration of War	First, Morrill	Dec 1777-Jan 1778; Feb 1778 on command at the lines; March 1778 sick in camp; April-May 1778; June 1778 sick at Downingtown.
Smith, Benjamin Private	Nov 15, 1776, Duration of War	First, Wait	Dec 1777-March 1778; April 1778 muster roll shows him as missing on April 26; May 1778 muster rolls shows him as "killed or taken" on April 26, 1778.
Smith, Benjamin Private	March 14, 1777, Three Years	First, Emerson	Dec 1777-May 1778 sick at Fishkill; June 1778.
Smith, Benjamin Corporal/Private	Jan 31, 1777, Duration of War	Third, Frye	Dec 1777; Jan 1, 1778 reduced to Private; Jan-March 1778; April-July 1778 sick in General Hospital.
Smith, David Private	March 14, 1777, Three Years	First, Emerson	Dec 1777 wounded and left at Albany; Jan-May 1778 wounded and at Albany; June 1778.
Smith, David Private	April 10, 1777, Three Years	First, Hutchins	Dec 1777-Jan 1778; Feb 1778 sick in camp; March-April 1778; May 1778 sick present; June 1778 sick Yellow Springs.
Smith, Edward Private	April 17, 1777, Three Years	First, Frye	Dec 1777-March 1778; April 1778 on command in country; May-June 1778.
Smith, Edward Corporal	Nov 15, 1776, Duration of War	Second, Blodget	Dec 1777; Jan 4, 1776 [sic] died. Year should be 1778.
Smith, Elisha Private	March 1, 1777, Three Years	Second, Robinson	Dec 1777-May 1778; June 1778 on command commissary.

Smith, Isaac Private	April 9, 1777, Three Years	First, Wait	Dec 1777-April 1778 sick at Fish Kill; May 1778 on his march to camp; June 1778.
Smith, Isaac Private	March 10, 1777, Three Years	Third, Stone	Dec 1777-April 1778; May 1778 sick in camp; June 1778 sick at General Hospital.
Smith, Jeremiah Private	April 20, 1777, Three Years	Third, Gray	Dec 1777-March 1778; April 1778 sick in camp; May-June 1778.
Smith, John Private	April 5, 1777, Duration of War	First, Scott	Dec 1777-May 1778; June 1778 sick at Cranbury.
Smith, John Corporal	Jan 1, 1777, Duration of War	Second, Norris	Dec 1777 in the hospital; Jan-May 1778 sick at Albany; June 1778.
Smith, John Private	March 21, 1778, Three Years	Third, McClary	April 1778 on a weeks command at the lines; May 1778; June 1778 sick at Valley Forge.
Smith, John Private	April 20, 1777, Three Years	Third, Gray	Dec 1777-Feb 1778 sick absent; March 20, 1778 died.
Smith, Johnson Private	April 5, 1777, Duration of War	First, Scott	Dec 1777 sick at Fish Kill; Jan-April 1778; May 1778 sick in camp; June 1778.
Smith, Joseph Private	April 1, 1777, Three Years	Third, Stonr	Dec 1777-June 1778.
Smith, Joseph Private	Three Years	Third, Gray	Dec 1777-Feb 1778 on furlough; March 20, 1778 died.
Smith, Nathaniel Private	April 30, 1777, Three Years	Third, Frye	Dec 1777; Jan 1778 on command; Feb-March 1778; April-May 1778 sick in camp; June-July 1778 sick in General Hospital.
Smith, Oliver Private	Nov 12, 1776, Duration of War	Second, Blodget	Dec 1777 sick in hospital; Jan 1778 sick in hospital Bethlehem; Feb 1778 sick absent; March 1778; April 1778 on guard; May-June 1778.
Smith, Peter Private	April 16, 1777, Three Years	Third, Gray	Dec 1777; Jan 1778 sick in camp; Feb-April 1778; May 1778 sick present; June 1778.
Smith, Samuel Private	Jan 28, 1777, Duration of War	First, Morrill	Dec 1777; Jan 1778 on duty; Feb-March 1778 on the General's guard; March 19, 1778 transferred to the Commander-in-Chief's Guard.
Snow, Henry Private	Feb 6, 1777, Three Years	First, Frye	Dec 1777; Jan 1778 sick out of camp; Feb 1778; March 1778 in General Washington's Guard; March 19, 1778 transferred to the Commander-in-Chief's Guard.

Name	Enlistment	Regiment	Service Record
Snow, Joshua Private	April 13, 1777, Three Years	Third, Gray	Dec 1777-Feb 1778 sick absent; March-June 1778.
Spaford/Spafford, Tyler Private	Feb 17, 1778, Two Years	First, Wait	April-June 1778.
Sparks, Thomas Private	Nov 16, 1777, Duration of War	Second, Blodget	Dec 1777-March 1778; April 1778 on a fortnights command; May-June 1778.
Speed, Thomas Private	Feb 6, 1777, Three Years	Third, McClary	Dec 1777; Jan 1778 sick in camp; Feb-March 1778 sick in General Hospital; April-June 1778 sick in Red Lion Hospital.
Spencer, Asa Private	April 10, 1777, Duration of War	Third, Stone	Dec 1777; Jan-Feb 1778 sick in camp; March 7, 1778 died.
Spencer, Moses Private	Feb 1, 1777, Duration of War	Second, Bell	Dec 1777; Jan 1778 on command; Feb-May 1778.
Spicer, Peter Private	May 1, 1777, Three Years	First, Scott	Dec 1777-Feb 1778 sick at Reading; March 20, 1778 dead.
Spring, John Private	May 11, 1777, Three Years	Second, Robinson	Dec 1777 sick absent; Jan-May 1778; June 1778 sick Valley Forge.
Springer, Henry/Henery Private	Feb 27, 1777, Three Years	Third, Stone	Dec 1777; Jan 1778 on command; Feb 1778; March 1778 on guard. No further record until the July 1778 muster roll which reports "Returned from Captivity Aug. 1."
Sprowse see Prowse			
Stanton, Charles Corporal	Feb 21, 1777, Three Years	Second, Carr	Dec 1777-May 1778; June 1778 on General's guard.
Stark, Caleb Adjutant	Nov 8, 1776	First	Dec 1777; Jan-March 1778 wounded on furlough; April 1778 doing Brigade Major's duty to General Stark; May-June 1778.
Stearns/Sterns, Asa Private	May 1, 1777, Duration of War	First, Scott	Dec 1777; Jan 1778 on command; Feb-May 1778; June 1778 sick at [ ].
Stearns/Sterns, Daniel Private/Corporal	May 1, 1777, Three Years	First, Scott	Dec 1777 sick in camp; Jan 1778 promoted to Corporal; Jan-June 1778.
Steavens/Stevens, Henerey/Henry Private	May 9, 1777, Eight Months	Third, Ellis	Dec 1777; Jan 10, 1778 discharged.
Sterns/Stearns, Isaac Private	Nov 16, 1776, Duration of War	First, Wait	Dec 1777; Jan 1778 on command; Feb-April 1778; May 1778 sick in camp; June 7, 1778 died.

Name	Enlisted	Company	Service Record
Stevens, Bartholemew, Private	Feb 1, 1777, Three Years	First, Frye	Dec 1777; Jan 1778 on command; Feb 1778 sick in camp; March-June 1778.
Stevens/Stephens, Ephraim/Ephriam, Private	Feb 15, 1777, Three Years	First, Scott	Dec 1777-March 1778 sick at Albany; April 1778; May 1778 on his march from N. Hampshire; June 1778.
Stevens/Stephens, Ephraim/Ephram, Private	March 1, 1777, Three Years	First, Morrill	Dec 1777; Jan 1778 on command; Feb-May 1778; June 1778 sick at Brunswick.
Stevens/Stephens, Henery	March 22, 1778, Two Years	First, Wait	June 1778 sick at [ ].
Stevens/Stephens, Jonathan, Private	April 4, 1777, Three Years	First, Hutchins	Dec 1777 sick at Fish Kill; Jan-April 1778; May 1778 on guard; June 1778 sick at Princeton.
Stevens/Stephens, Peter, Private	Nov 15, 1776, Duration of War	First, Morrill	Dec 1777; Jan 1778 on command; Feb-March 1778; April 1778 sick at French Creek; May 1778; on command at Lancaster.
Stevens, Phineas/Phinehas, Private	April 12, 1777, Duration of War	Third, Livermore	Dec 1777; Jan-March 1778 on furlough; April 21, 1778 dead.
Stevens, William, Private	April 1, 1777, Three Years	Third, Weare	April 8, 1777 deserted; June 1778 on command at Portsmouth, New Hampshire.
Stickney, Levi, Private	April 8, 1777, Three Years	Third, Weare	Dec 1777; Jan 1778 on duty; Feb-April 1778; May 1778 sick in camp; June 1778 sick General Hospital.
Stickney/Stickeny, Thomas, Sergeant	Feb 20, 1777, Three Years	First, Frye	Dec 1777 sick absent; Jan-May 1778 on furlough; June 1778.
Stocker/Stecker, Samuel, Musician	Three Years	First, Hutchins	Dec 1777-June 1778.
Stokels/Stocles, Robert, Private	Nov 15, 1776, Duration of War	Second, Drew	Dec 1777 on command; Jan-May 1778 on command Albany.
Stone, Andrew, Private	May 10, 1777, Three Years	Third, Livermore	Dec 1777 nurse in hospital Albany; Jan 1778 nurse in hospital; Feb-March 1778 on furlough; April 1778; May 1778 on command with the sick; June 1778 sick absent.
Stone, Benjamin, Captain	Nov 8, 1776	Third, Stone	Dec 1777-Feb 1778 on furlough; March-June 1778.
Stone, James, Private	April 15, 1778, One Year	Second, Robinson	June 1778.

Name	Enlistment	Company	Service Record
Stone, Samuel Private	Duration of War	First, Farwell	Dec 1777-Jan 1778 sick at Reding; Feb 1, 1778 died.
Straw, Benjamin Private	Jan 10, 1777, Three Years	Third, Beal	Dec 1777-April 1778; May 1778 sick camp; June-Oct 1778 sick Valley Forge. Muster roll for Nov 1778 states "Deserted 20 July from Valley Forge."
Straw, John Private	March 15, 1777, Three Years	Third, Livermore	Dec 1777; Jan 1778 on command; Feb-March 1778; April-May 1778 sick in camp; June 1778.
Straw, John Private	May 7, 1777, Eight Months	Third, Stone	Dec 1777; Jan 10, 1778 discharged.
Sullivan/Sulivan, Daniel Private	Nov 10, 1776, Three Years	Second, Carr	Dec 1777-May 1778; June 1778 on command.
Sullivan, John Major-General	August 6, 1776		Sullivan had commanded the two Maryland brigades which were stationed at Wilmington for the winter. At Valley Forge he was in charge of building a bridge across the Schuylkill River and remained at Valley Forge until mid-March 1778 when he left to take command in Rhode Island.
Swain, Hezekiah Private	May 2, 1777, Three Years	Third, Livermore	Dec 1777; Jan 1778 on command; Feb-March 1778; April 1778 on command at the Lines; May 1778; June 1778 sick absent.
Swan, John Private	Aug 26, 1777	Second, Blodget	Dec 1777 on command at Albany; Jan-March 1778 on furlough; April-May 1778; June 1778 left sick at Valley Forge.
Sweat/Sweatt, Abraham Corporal	April 13, 1777, Three Years	Third, Gray	Dec 1777; Jan 1778 on command; Feb-April 1778; May 1778 sick present; June 1778 sick at Yellow Springs.
Sweet/Sweat, Benjamin Private	April 16, 1777, Three Years	First, Hutchins	Dec 1777; Jan-Feb 1778 on guard; March 1778 on fortnight command; April 1778 sick at French Creek; May 1778 on guard; June 1778.
Sweet/Sweat, John Private	April 16, 1777, Three Years	First, Hutchins	Dec 1777-March 1778; April 1778 sick in hospital at French Creek; May-June 1778.
Sweetser/Swicker, Stephen Private	Jan 21, 1777, Three Years	Third, Beal	Dec 1777-April 1778; May 1778 sick in camp; June-July 1778 sick Valley Forge.

Name	Enlisted	Company	Service
Taggart, James 1st. Lt.	Nov 8, 1776	First, Farwell	Dec 1777; Jan-March 1778; April-June 1778.
Tagggart/Tagart, John Sergeant	Jan 1, 1777, Three Years	Second, Clayes	Dec 1777 muster roll shows him as a prisoner on July 7, 1777, joined Sept 22; Dec 1777-May 1778; June 1778 sick Valley Forge.
Taggart, Joseph Private	Feb 2, 1777, Three Years	Second, Clayes	Dec 1777 shows him as a prisoner on July 7, 1777, joined Oct 20; Dec 1777-March 1778; April 1778 sick in camp; May 1778; June 1778 sick Valley Forge.
Taggart, William Private	Feb 4, 1778, Three Years	First, Farwell	June 1778.
Taggart, William Ensign	Nov 8, 1776	Second, Clayes	Dec 1777-Jan 1778; Feb-May 1778 sick in camp; June 1778.
Tarnan, Hugh Private	March 21, 1778, Three Years	First, Frye	June 1778 joined since last muster, on command with General McDougall.
Tate/Tatee, Mark Private	March 1, 1777	Second, Carr	Dec 1777-March 1778; April 1778 sick in camp; May 15, 1778 died.
Taylor, Benjamin Private	April 17, 1777, Three Years	First, Emerson	Dec 1777-Feb 1778; March 1778 sick in hospital; April 1778 sick at French Creek Hospital; May 1778; June 1778 on guard.
Taylor, Edward Private	April 10, 1777, Three Years	Third, Livermore	Dec 1777 sick absent; Jan-May 1778 on furlough; June 1778.
Taylor, Jacob Private	March 21, 1778, Three Years	First, Scott	June 1778.
Taylor, John Musician	June 15, 1777, Three Years	First, Emerson	June 1778 muster roll reads "Inlisted June 15th 1777 & not Joined till June 1778 By Reason of Sickness."
Taylor, John Private	April 2, 1777, Three Years	Second, Bell	Dec 1777-May 1778.
Taylor, John Private	Feb 10, 1777, Three Years	Third, Weare	Feb 11, 1777 deserted; Jan 22, 1778 joined; Jan-May 1778; June-July 1778 sick at Valley Forge.
Taylor, Medad Private	March 17, 1778	First, House	June 1778 sick at Valley Forge.
Taylor/Tayler, Nathan Private	Feb 27, 1777, Three Years	Second, Clayes	Dec 1777-April 1778; May 1778 sick in camp; June 1778.

Name	Date	Company	Service
Taylor, Oliver Private	April 10, 1777, Three Years	Third, Livermore	Dec 1777; Jan 1778 on command; Feb-April 1778; May 1778 sick in camp; June 1778.
Thatcher/Thacher, Benjamin/ Benjamen Private	May 1, 1777, Three Years	Third, Ellis	Dec 1777; Jan 1778 on command; Feb-June 1778.
Thirsten, Robert Private	March 7, 1778, Three Years	Third, Weare	June 24, 1778 joined; June 1778 on guard.
Thomas, Enoch Fifer	May 2, 1777, Three Years	Third, Gray	Dec 1777-June 1778.
Thompson, Henry Private	Nov 24, 1776, Three Years	First, Hutchins	Dec 1777; Jan 1778 on command with General Greene; Feb 1778 on command with the butchers; March-June 1778.
Thompson, James Private	Nov 14, 1776, Three Years	First, Frye	Dec 1777 missing since Dec 3, 1777; April 1778 joined; April 1778; May 1778 "Returnd deserted through a Mistake and since joind. now sick present;" June 1778 on guard.
Thompson/ Thomson, James Private	Feb 1, 1777	First, Morrill	Dec 1777-March 1778; April 25, 1778 discharged.
Thompson, John Private	May 12, 1778, Three Years	Second, Robinson	June 1778 on guard.
Thompson, Joshua Ensign	Nov 6, 1776	First, Frye	Dec 1777-March 1778; April 1778 on command at the lines; May-June 1778.
Thompson, Lorine/Loring Private	May 1, 1777, Three Years	First, Scott	July 7, 1777 taken prisoner; Dec 1777-March 1778 at home returned from prison; April-June 1778.
Thompson, Prince Private	May 15, 1777, Three Years	First, Frye	Dec 1777-June 1778 on command with General Gates.
Thompson, Samuel Sergeant	May 3, 1777, Three Years	First, Frye	Dec 1777 sick at New England; Jan-Feb 1778 lost his speech by sickness and on furlough; March-May 1778 on furlough; June 1778 sick at Valley Forge.
Thompson, Seth Private	April 18, 1777, Three Years	First, House	Dec 1777-March 1778; April 1778 on guard; May 1778 sick in camp; June 1778 sick at Downingtown.
Thompson, Silas Private	April 17, 1777, Three Years	First, Frye	Dec 1777; Jan 1778 unfit for service; Feb 25, 1778 discharged.

Name	Enlistment	Regiment, Company	Service Record
Thornton, Hugh Private	March 8, 1777, Three Years	First, Morrill	Dec 1777-March 1778 sick at Fish Kill. The April 1778 muster roll shows he died on Feb 10, 1778, but the May 1778 muster roll shows he died March 1 at "Fishkills."
Thornton, Joshua Fifer	May 27, 1777, Three Years	Third, Gray	Dec 1777-Jan 1778; Feb 1778 sick with the smallpox; March-June 1778.
Thurston/Thursten, Abner Private	Jan 16, 1777, Duration of War	First, Farwell	Dec 1777 wounded and at Albany; Jan 1778 wounded at Albany; Feb-June 1778.
Tilton, James Private	May 9, 1777, Eight Months	Third, Ellis	Dec 1777; Jan 10, 1778 discharged.
Todd, Solomon Private	April 28, 1777, Three Years	First, Frye	Dec 1777 sick at Albany; Jan 1778 "left sick at Albany & I hear gone home"; March-May 1778 at N. England; June 1778.
Torr, Vincent/ Vinson Private	Feb 1, 1777, Three Years	Second, Bell	Dec 1777-May 1778.
Torry/Tory, Daniel Private	April 16, 1777, Three Years	Third, Gray	Dec 1777; Jan 1778 sick in quarters; Feb-March 1778; April 1778 sick in camp; May 1778 sick present; June 1778 sick at Valley Forge.
Towle/Tole, Jeremiah Corporal	April 3, 1777, Three Years	First, Emerson	Dec 1777-May 1778 wounded and at Albany; June 1778 sick in Jerseys.
Towle, Joseph Private	June 4, 1778, Three Years	Third, Weare	First appears on the July 1778 muster roll.
Towle/Tole, William Sergeant	March 2, 1777, Three Years	Second, Rowell	April 1778 muster roll shows he deserted on Nov 5, 1777, joined April 24, 1778; April 1778-June 1778.
Tozer/Tozar, Peter Private	April 1, 1777, Three Years	Third, Livermore	Dec 1777; Jan 1778 on command; Feb-March 1778; April-May 1778 sick in camp; June 1778.
Trickey, Samuel Private	Feb 16, 1778	Second, Drew	June 9, 1778 joined; June 1778 sick at Englishtown.
True, Benjamin Private	May 30, 1777, Eight Months	Third, Gray	Dec 1777; Jan 10, 1778 discharged.
True, Henry, Private	April 3, 1777, Three Years	First, Emerson	Dec 1777-Feb 1778; March 1778 sick in camp; April-May 1778; June 1778 sick in Jersey.
Tuck, Jeremiah Private	April 23, 1777, One Year	Third, Weare	Dec 1777-March 1778; April 26, 1778 discharged.

Name	Date	Company	Notes
Tucker, Joseph Private	Feb 3, 1778, Three Years	First, Farwell	June 1778.
Tucker, Nathaniel Private	April 15, 1778, One Year	Second, Robinson	June 1778.
Turner, Ezra Private	May 5, 1777, Three Years	First, Hutchins	Dec 1777; Jan 1778 shoe making in country; Feb 1778 on command making shoes; March 1778 making shoes ye country; April-May 1778; June 1778 sick Valley Forge.
Tuttle/Tutle, Nathan/Nathaniel Private	April 6, 1777, Three Years	First, Wait	Dec 1777 wounded September 19 and on furlough by General Gates; Jan 1778 on furlough; Feb 1778 wounded and on furlough; March 1778 on furlough; April-May 1778 wounded and on furlough; June 1778.
Tuttle, Thomas Private		First, Hutchins	Dec 1777-Jan 1778; Feb 11, 1778 dead.
Twombly, William Sergeant	Nov 15, 1776, Three Years	Second, Rowell	Dec 1777-June 1778.
Tyler, John Private	March 3, 1777, Three Years	Third, Stone	Nov 7, 1777 deserted.
Tylor, James Private	July 3, 1777, Eight Months	First, Hutchins	Dec 1777; Jan 1778 discharged.
Vance, John Private	April 28, 1777, Three Years	First, Frye	Dec 1777-Jan 1778; Feb 1778 sick in camp; March-June 1778.
Van North, Abraham Private	Nov 18, 1776, Three Years	Second, Blodget	Dec 1777 sick at Albany; Jan-Feb 1778 on command at Albany; March 1778; April 17, 1778 discharged.
Varnum see Farnum			
Veazy/Veasy, Eliphalet Corporal/ Sergeant	Sept 1, 1777, Duration of War	Second, Blodget	Dec 1777; Jan 1778 promoted to Sergeant; Jan 1778-March 1778; April 1778 on weeks command; May 1778 on guard; June 1778 on command with [ ].
Vicker, Ambros Private	May 1, 1777, Three Years	Third, McClary	May-June 1778 on command with General Sullivan.
Vorven, Charles Corporal	April 1, 1778	Third, McClary	June 1778.
Wade, Edward Private/Corporal	Nov 13, 1776, Duration of War	Second, Blodget	Dec 1777-Jan 1778 wounded absent; Feb-March 1778 wounded Albany; April 1, 1778 promoted to Corporal; April-May 1778; June 1778 sick in camp.

Name	Enlistment	Company	Service Record
Wadley/Wadleigh, Elijah, Private	April 18, 1777, Three Years	Third, Gray	Dec 1777-Jan 1778 sick absent; Feb-March 1778; April 1778 sick in camp; May-June 1778.
Wadliegh/Wadley, John, Private	Jan 22, 1777, Duration of War	Third, McClary	Dec 1777; Jan-March 1778 on command; April-June 1778 on command at the Adjutant General's.
Wait, Jason, Captain	Nov 8, 1776	First, Wait	Dec 1777-Feb 1778; March 1778 on command; April-June 1778.
Wait/Wate, John, Private	March 12, 1777, Three Years	Third, Beal	Dec 1777 on duty; Jan-March 1778 on command; April 1778 on command General Poors; May-June 1778 General Poor's servant.
Waldron/Waldon, Ebenezer, Corporal	Feb 11, 1777, Three Years	Second, Carr	Dec 1777-June 1778.
Waldron/Woldon, Nathaniel, Private	March 2, 1777, Three Years	Third, Beal	Dec 1777; Jan 1778 on command; Feb-May 1778; June 1778 sick Valley Forge.
Walker, Jonathan, Private	April 18, 1777, Three Years	First, House	Dec 1777-April 1778; May 1778 sick in camp; June 6, 1778 dead.
Walker, William, Private	May 3, 1777, Three Years	First, Frye	Dec 1777-May 1778; June 1778 sick at Valley Forge.
Wallace, John, Private	Three Years	First, Scott	April-June 1778.
Wallice/Waltice, William/Wilaim, Private	March 5, 1777, Three Years	Third, Weare	Dec 1777-June 1778 left wounded at Albany.
Wallis, William, 1st. Lt.	Nov 8, 1776	Second, Drew	Dec 1777-June 1778 on furlough.
Walls see Wells			
Walls/Wall, Francis, Drummer	July 8, 1777, Duration of War	Second, Rowell	Dec 1777-June 1778.
Walton, Rufus, Private	March 10, 1777, Three Years	First, Wait	Dec 1777; Jan 1778 on command; Feb 1778; March 1778 on command; April-June 1778.
Walton, Samuel, Private	April 9, 1777, Three Years	First, Frye	Dec 1777 wounded and absent; Jan-May 1778 wounded and on furlough; June 1778 sick at Albany.
Ward, Edward, Private	June 10, 1777, Three Years	Third, Stone	Jan-Feb 1778 on command; May 1778 sick in camp; June 1778 sick in General Hospital.

Name	Enlisted	Company	Remarks
Ward, James Private	Nov 14, 1776, Duration of War	Second, Blodget	Dec 1777-Feb 1778; March 1778 on command; April 1778 on weeks command; May 1778 on guard; June 1778 left at Valley Forge sick.
Ward, John Private	April 4, 1777, Duration of War	Second, Robinson	Dec 1777-Jan 1778; Feb 1778 sick in camp; March 1778; April 1778 sick in camp; May-June 1778.
Ward, Meltcher, Private	April 29, 1777, Three Years	Second, Robinson	June 8, 1778 joined; June 1778.
Ward, Richard Private	April 7, 1777, Three Years	Third, Beal	Dec 1777-April 1778; May 18, 1778 died.
Ward, Samuel Private	Feb 1, 1777, Duration of War	Second, Bell	Dec 1777 muster roll shows he deserted on July 7, 1777, returned and was pardoned, Dec 1777-May 1778 sick absent.
Ward, Stephen Private	Nov 17, 1776, Duration of War	First, Wait	Dec 1777; Jan 1778 on command; Feb-March 1778; April 1778 sick in camp; May 1778; June 1778 sick in camp.
Waterhous/ Waterhouse, Thomas Private	Nov 14, 1776, Duration of War	Third, Beal	Dec 1777-March 1778; April 1778 on command Reading; May 1778 sick in camp; June 1778 on guard.
Waters, Thomas Private	April 11, 1777, Duration of War	Third, Beal	April 1778 on command Reading; May 1778 sick in camp; June 1778 on guard.
Watson/Watison, Daniel Private	May 2, 1777, Three Years	Second, Carr	Dec 1777 sick in hospital; Jan-May 1778; June 1778 on command General Poor.
Watson/Wattson, David Private	Feb 10, 1778, Three Years	Second, Rowell	May 16, 1778 joined; May-June 1778.
Watson, Gloster Private	May 1, 1777, Three Years	Second, Drew	Dec 1777-May 1778 sick absent; June 1778 sick at Boston.
Watson, Isaac Private	April 20, 1777, Three Years	Second, Bell	Dec 1777-Jan 1778; Feb-March 1778 on command; April-May 1778.
Weare, Nathan Sergeant	April 8, 1777, Duration of War	Third, Weare	Dec 1777-June 1778.
Weare, Richard Captain	Nov 8, 1776	Third, Weare	August 2, 1777 dead.
Webster, Abel/Abell Private	Feb 26, 1777, Duration of War	Third, Stone	Dec 1777; Jan 1778 on command; June 1778 sick at General Hospital; July 4, 1778 died.

Name	Enlisted	Company	Notes
Webster, Jonathan, Private	March 7, 1777, Three Years	First, Hutchins	Dec 1777-Jan 1778; Feb 1778 sick in camp; March 1778 sick present; April-May 1778; June 1778 sick Fish Kill.
Webster, Stephen Private	April 9, 1778	Third, Livermore	June 1778.
Webster, Thomas Private	Feb 14, 1777, Duration of War	Second, Norris	Dec 1777-Feb 1778; March 1778 on command; April 1778; May 1778 on command a baker; June 1778.
Wedgwood, James 1st. Lt.	Nov 8, 1776	Third, Weare	Dec 1777; Jan-June 1778 on furlough.
Weeks, William Paymaster	Nov 8, 1776	Third	Dec 1777-June 1778.
Welch, John Private	April 2, 1777, Three Years	Second, Bell	Dec 1777-May 1778 on furlough.
Welch/Welsh, Siah/Sias Private	Nov 15, 1777, Three Years	Second, Drew	Dec 1777-April 1778; May 1778 sick present; June 1778 sick Yellow Springs.
Wells, Josiah Private	April 1, 1777, Three Years	First, Emerson	Dec 1777-April 1778; May 1778 sick in camp; June 1778 sick in Pennsylvania.
Wells, Peter Private	Nov 20, 1776, Duration of War	First, Morrill	Dec 1777-June 1778.
Wells, Samuel Sergeant	Nov 13, 1776, Duration of War	First, Morrill	Dec 1777; Jan-March 1778 on command foraging; April 1778; May 1778 Forage Master; June 1778 Commissary Forage.
Wells/Walls, Thomas/Thomes Private	March 19, 1777, Three Years	Second, Carr	Dec 1777-April 1778; May 1778 sick in camp; June 1778 sick Valley Forge.
Welsh/Welch, Silas Private	Nov 15, 1776, Duration of War	Second, Drew	Dec 1777-Jan 1778; Feb 1778 on guard; March-April 1778; May 1778 sick present; June 1778 sick Englishtown.
Welsh/Welch, Thomas Private	Nov 14, 1776, Duration of War	Second, Drew	Dec 1777 muster roll shows him as missing on July 7, 1777, returned on Sept 20; Dec 1777-March 1778; April 1778 sick present; May-June 1778.
Wentworth, Daniel Private	Nov 14, 1776, Duration of War	Second, Drew	Dec 1777 wounded; Jan 1778; Feb-March 1778 wounded absent; April-May 1778 wounded and at Albany; June 1778 muster roll shows he died on May 1, 1778.
Wentworth, Phineas Private	Nov 15, 1776	Second, Bell	April-May 1778.

Name	Enlisted	Company	Notes
Weson, Isaac Private	April 1, 1778, One Year	Second, Robinson	June 1778.
West, Daniel Private	March 21, 1778, Three Years	First, Frye	June 1778 joined since last muster, June 1778 on command with General McDougall.
West, Nehemiah Private	April 16. 1777, Three Years	Third, Gray	Dec 1777-April 1778; May 1778 sick present; June 1778 sick at New Hampstead.
Wheeler/Wheler, Libeus/Lebeus Private	April 10, 1777. Three Years	First, House	Dec 1777; Jan 1778 sick in camp; Feb-May 1778; June 1778 sick at Downingtown
Wheeler/Wheelar, Reuben Private	April 1, 1777, Three Years	First, Wait	Dec 1777 sick at Albany; Jan 1778 sick Albany General Hospital; Feb-March 1778 sick at Albany; April 1778 sick at Brookline; May 1778 on his march to camp; June 1778.
Wheelock, Jonathan Private	Feb 15, 1777, Three Years	First, Scott	Dec 1777-May 1778; June 1778 sick at Valley Forge.
Whelock/ Wheelock, Ithermar/Etham Private	Feb 1, 1777, Three Years	First, Farwell	Dec 1777-May 1778 sick on furlough; June 1778 on furlough N. England.
Whilling/ Whiteing, Abel Private	April 1, 1778, Three Years	First, Emerson	June 1778 sick at Brunswick.
Whipple, Daniel Sergeant	May 9, 1777, Eight Months	Third, Ellis	Dec 1777; Jan 10, 1778 discharged.
Whipple, Jabez/Jabis Private	May 9, 1777, Eight Months	Third, Ellis	Dec 1777; Jan 10, 1778 discharged.
White. James Private	Jan 3. 1777, Duration of War	Third, Beal	Dec 1777-April 1778 sick at Fishkill. May 1778 muster roll shows him dead on Jan 20, 1778.
White, William Private	Jan 1. 1777, Three Years	First, Scott	Dec 1777-Feb 1778 sick at Fish Kill; March 1778 sick at Danbury; April-May 1778; June 1778 sick at Princeton.
White, William Private	April 1. 1777, Three Years	First, Emerson	Dec 1777; Jan 1778 on command after provisions; Feb-May 1778; June 1778 sick in Pennsylvania.
Whitemore/ Whittemore, Peletiah/Palatiah 2nd. Lt.	Nov 6, 1776	Second, Carr	Dec 1777 on furlough; Jan-May 1778; June 1778 sick at Valley Forge.

Name	Enlisted	Company	Service
Whitlock, Thomas Private/Fifer	Jan 1, 1777, Duration of War	First, Scott	Dec 1777-Jan 1778; Jan 1778 promoted to Fifer; Feb 1778 on command; March-May 1778; June 1778 sick at Princeton.
Whitten/Whidden, Samuel Corporal	March 8, 1777, Three Years	First, Morrill	Dec 1777-Feb 1778; March 1778 on guard; April-June 1778.
Whittier/Whitcher, Benjamin Private	May 24, 1777, Three Years	Third, Gray	Dec 1777-June 1778.
Whitton/Whitten, John Private	Feb 13, 1777, Duration of War	Third, Stone	Dec 1777 deserted July 7, 1777; June 1778 sick in the General Hospital.
Wier/Wire, Samuel Private	May 18, 1777, Duration of War	First, Scott	Dec 1777-March 1778 sick at Albany; April 1778; May-June 1778 sick at Albany.
Wiggons/Wiggins, Winterup Private	March 2, 1778, Three Years	Second, Rowell	June 1778.
Wilcomb, Nicholas Private		Second, Norris	Dec 1777 never joined.
Wilder, Willard/Williard Private	April 21, 1777, Three Years	First, House	Dec 1777; Jan-Feb 1778 on duty; March 1778 on command; April 1778; May 1778 sick in camp; June 1778 sick at Downingtown.
Wiley/Willey, William Private	Nov 12, 1776, Duration of War	First, Morrill	Dec 1777-March 1778; April 1778 sick in camp; May-June 1778.
Wilkins, Asa Sergeant	May 7, 1777, Three Years	Third, Frye	Dec 1777-Feb 1778 on command; March 1778; April 1778 on command Adjutant General; May 1778; June 1778 sick at Valley Forge.
Wilkins, Robert B. Sergeant	March 28, 1777, Three Years	Third, Frye	Dec 1777-May 1778; June-July 1778 sick at Valley Forge.
Wilkins, Silvester Sergeant	Feb 1, 1777, Three Years	First, Wait	Dec 1777-April 1778; May 1778 sick in camp; June 1778.
Wilkins, William Henry Private	April 11, 1778, Duration of War	First, Scott	June 1778; June 2[3], 1778 died.
Wilkison/ Willkison, James/Joseph Private	April 1, 1777, Three Years	Third, Weare	Dec 1777-April 1778 on furlough; May 1778 sick in camp; June 1778 on guard.
Willard, Jonathan/ Jonathon Ensign	Nov 8, 1776	First, Farwell	Dec 1777 wounded absent on furlough; Jan-March 1778 wounded and on furlough; April-June 1778.

Name	Enlisted	Company	Service Record
Williams, Benjamin Corporal	April 6, 1777, Three Years	First, Hutchins	Dec 1777 "in the Genl. Guard"; Jan 1778 "on General guard"; Feb 1778 "on the Genl Guards"; March 1778 on present duty; April-May 1778; June 1778 sick Valley Forge.
Williams, Benjamin Private	May 9, 1777, Eight Months	Third, Stone	Dec 1777; Jan 10, 1778 discharged.
Williams, Ebenezer Private	March 10, 1778, Three Years	First, Scott	June 1778 sick Valley Forge.
Williams, Peleg 1st. Lt.	Nov 8, 1776	First, Wait	Dec 1777-March 1778 on furlough per General Gates; April 1778; May 11, 1778 discharged.
Williams, Samuel Private/Corporal	Nov 14, 1776, Duration of War	Second, Drew	Dec 1777-Jan 1778; Feb 1778 sick present; March 1778; April 1778 sick present; May-June 1778; June 1778 promoted to Corporal.
Willoughby, Josiah Private	March 12, 1777, Duration of War	Third, Stone	Dec 1777 sick in General Hospital Albany; Jan 1778 muster roll shows him dead on Dec [31], 1777.
Willson/Wilson, Samuel Private	Jan 1, 1777, Duration of War	Second, Robinson	Dec 1777-June 1778.
Wilson/Willson, George/Gorge Private	Feb 3, 1777, Three Years	First, Wait	Dec 1777-Jan 1778 "on Genl. Guard"; Feb 1778 "on the General Guards"; March 1778; April-May 1778 sick in camp; June 1778.
Wilson/Willson, James Private	April 1, 1777, Three Years	First, Frye	Dec 1777 sick at Fish Kill; Jan 1778; Feb 1778 sick in camp; March-June 1778.
Wilson, John Private	Three Years	Third, Stone	June 1778 deserted.
Wilson/Willson, Jonathon Private	Nov 15, 1776, Three Years	First, Farwell	Dec 1777; Jan 1778 on present duty; Feb-May 1778; June 1778 sick at Valley Forge.
Wilson/Willson, Joseph Private	Feb 15, 1777, Duration of War	First, Scott	Dec 1777; Jan 1778 on command; Feb-May 1778; June 1778 sick at Valley Forge.
Wilson, Joshua Private	Nov 12, 1776, Duration of War	Second, Blodget	Dec 1777 wounded absent; Jan-March 1778 on furlough; April 1778; May 1778 sick in camp; June 1778 left at Valley Forge sick.

Name	Enlisted	Company	Service
Wilson/Willson, Robert Private	April 1, 1777, Three Years	First, Frye	Dec 1777-Jan 1778; Feb 1778 sick in camp; March-June 1778.
Wilson/Willson, Thomas Private	Nov 15, 1776, Duration of War	First, Wait	Dec 1777-Jan 1778; Feb 1778 on command at lines; March-April 1778 on command; May 1778; June 1778 sick at Downingtown.
Wingate/Wingit, Daniel Private	May 10, 1777, Three Years	Second, Rowell	Dec 1777 on guard with the A.G.; Jan-May 1778; June 1778 sick Valley Forge.
Wingate, Enoch Private	May 1, 1777, Three Years	Second, Rowell	Dec 1777-Jan 1778 sick in camp; Feb-June 1778.
Winslow/Winston, Elisha Private	March 1, 1777, Duration of War	Third, Weare	Dec 1777-March 1778; April 1778 on a weeks command at the Lines; June 1778.
Winslow/Wissow, Lewis/Luis Private	Nov 14, 1776, Three Years	First, Wait	Dec 1777-April 1778; May 1778 sick in camp; June 1778 sick at Downingtown.
Wisdom, Henry Private	Nov 15, 1776, Three Years	Second, Bell	Dec 1777-Jan 1778; Feb-March 1778 on command; April-May 1778.
Wise, Abner Private	Feb 14, 1777, Three Years	First, Scott	Dec 1777 sick at Whitemarsh; Jan-April 1778; May 1778 on guard; June 1778.
Witherington, Mathew W. Private	Nov 4, 1777, Three Years	Third, Frye	Feb 1778 joined since last muster; Feb-March 1778; April-May 1778 sick in camp; June 1778.
Woley, Jonathan Private	May 9, 1777, Eight Months	Third, Ellis	Dec 1777; Jan 10, 1778 discharged.
Wolley, John Drummer	Feb 28, 1778, Three Years	Third, Ellis	June 1778.
Wood/Woods, Daniel Private	April 17, 1777, Three Years	First, Emerson	Dec 1777-Jan 1778; Feb 1778 sick present; March-April 1778; May 1778 on main guard; June 1778.
Wood, Edward Private	June 10, 1777, Three Years	Third, Stone	Dec 1777; Jan-Feb 1778 on command; March-April 1778; May 1778 sick in camp; June 1778 sick at General Hospital.
Wood, Gideon/Gedion Private	Feb 27, 1777, Three Years	Third, Stone	Dec 1777; Jan 1778 on command; Feb-May 1778; June 1778 sick at Fish Kill.
Wood, Silas/Silus Sergeant	May 12, 1777, Eight Months	Third, Ellis	Dec 1777; Jan 10, 1778 discharged.
Wood, Thomas Private	Feb 27, 1777, Three Years	Third, Stone	Dec 1777-April 1778; May 1778 on command; June 1778 sick at General Hospital.

Name	Date	Company	Notes
Woodall/Woodell, Timothy, Private	Jan 1, 1777, Duration of War	Second, Robinson	Dec 1777-June 1778 sick at Albany.
Woodbery/Woodbury, Luke, Ensign	Nov 6, 1776	Second, Robinson	Dec 1777-June 1778.
Woodbery/Woodbury, William, Private	April 23, 1777, Three Years	Second, Robinson	Dec 1777-Jan 1778; Feb 1778 sick absent; March-May 1778; June 1778 sick at Brunswick.
Woodburry, Israel, Private	April 23, 1777, Three Years	Second, Robinson	June 1778 muster roll shows him as taken on July 7, 1777, joined on June 8, 1778; June 1778.
Woodcock, Jonathan, Private	Feb 10, 1778, Three Years	Third, Ellis	June 1778.
Woodman, Daniel, Private	June 23, 1777, Three Years	Second, Rowell	Dec 1777-June 1778.
Woods, Paul, Fifer	April 1, 1777, Three Years	First, Emerson	Dec 1777-June 1778.
Wooster/Woster, James, Private	Jan 4, 1777, Duration of War	Third, Beal	Dec 1777-Jan 1778; Feb-March 1778 on command; April 1778 on command Gen. Backhouse; May 1778 sick in camp; June-July sick at Valley Forge.
Worthing, Samuel, Private	April 9, 1777, Three Years	Third, Livermore	Nov 4, 1777 deserted; April 24, 1778 joined; April 1778; May 1778 sick in camp; June 1778 sick absent.
Wright, David, Private	March 17, 1778, Three Years	First, House	June 1778.
Wright, Jonathan, Private	April 22, 1777, Three Years	First, House	Dec 1777-Jan 1778; Feb 1778 on duty; March-May 1778; June 1778 sick in camp.
Wright/Right, Joseph, Private	April 1, 1778, Two Years	First, Wait	June 1778.
Wright, Phinehus/Phinehas, Corporal/Private		First, House	Dec 1777 sick at Lebanon; Jan 1778 muster roll shows he joined on Jan 23 and was reduced to Private; Feb 1778 payroll shows he was "Taken prisoner Sept. 1st. 1777 Joined february 28 1778"; Feb-May 1778; June 1778 sick at Downingtown.
Writter/Writer, Daniel, Private	April 17, 1777, Three Years	First, Wait	Dec 1777; Jan 1778 on command at the Lines; Feb-March 1778; April 1778 on guard; May 1778 on a weeks command; June 1778.

Name	Enlistment	Company	Service Record
Wyman/Wiman, Daniel Corporal	April 16, 1777, Three Years	Second, Bell	Dec 1777-May 1778.
Yeoman/Yoman, John Private	June 1, 1777, Three Years	First, Farwell	Dec 1777-May 1778 wounded on furlough; June 1778 muster roll shows he deserted on May 20, 1778.
York, Joseph Private	March 1, 1777, Duration of War	First, Morrill	Dec 1777 on duty; Jan 1778 sick present; Feb 1778; March 1778 sick in camp; April-May 1778; June 1778 on General Lee's guard.
Young, Daniel Private	Jan 27, 1778, Three Years	First, Frye	May 1778 joined; May 1778; June 1778 sick at Valley Forge.
Young, James Private	April 23, 1777, Three Years	Second, Robinson	Dec 1777; Jan 1778 lame in camp; Feb 1778 sick in camp; March-May 1778; June 1778 sick Peekskill.
Young, Joseph Private	Duration of War	Second, Rowell	May 1778 muster roll shows him as a prisoner on July 7, 1777, joined May 16; May-June 1778.
Youngman, John Private	April 20, 1777, Three Years	Third, Frye	Dec 1777; Jan-Feb 1778 on command; March 1778; April 1778 on guard; May 1778; June-Aug 1778 sick at Valley Forge.
Youngman, Thomas Private	April 20, 1777, Three Years	Third, Frye	Dec 1777; Jan 1778 on command; Feb 1778; March-April 1778 sick in camp; May 1778; Jun-Oct 1778 sick at Valley Forge.

Rhode Island

Name/ Rank	Enlistment or Commission Date/Term of Enlistment	Regiment/ Company	Remarks
Aaron, Benedict Private		First, Clarke	Dec 1777 sick absent; Jan 1778; Feb-March 1778 on command; April 1778.
Aaron/Aron, Benedict Private	Three Years	First, Arnold	May 1778; June 1778 absent with leave.
Adams/Addams, Abijah Private	Jan 1, 1777, Three Years	Second, Olney. C.	Dec 1777-March 1778 on command; April 1778; May 1778 on command; June 1778.
Albrow/Albrau, Robert Private	March 1, 1777, Duration of War	Second, Tew	Dec 1777 sick present; Jan 1778; Feb-March 1778 on command; April 1778 on command at Rhode Island; May-June 1778 sick at Rhode Island.
Aldrich/Albrigh, Abel/Abill Private	May 20. 1777, Three Years	Second, Olney. C.	Dec 1777-March 1778 sick absent; April 1778 sick at Lidice; May-June 1778.
Allen, Dick Private	May 1, 1778	First, Dexter	June 1778 on command.
Allen, Jack Private	Three Years	First, Cole	Dec 1777-March 1778; April 1778 sick present.
Allin, Jack Private	Three Years	First, Arnold	May 18, 1778 died.
Allen/Alling, Joseph Private	May 17, 1777 Three Years	First, Talbot	Dec 1777 sick absent; Jan-April 1778 sick present.
Allen, Joseph Private	Three Years	Second, Dexter	May-June 1778.
Allen, Power Private		First, Flagg	Dec 1777-Jan 1778; Feb 26, 1778 died.
Allen, Richard Private		First, Cole	Dec 1777; Jan-Feb 1778 on furlough; March 1778 on command; April 1778 on furlough.
Allen, Robert Private	Feb 15, 1777 Duration of War	First, Lewis	Dec 1777 sick absent; Jan 1778 on 7 days command; March 15, 1778 deserted.
Allen, Walley Private	April 21, 1778 Duration of War	First, Lewis	June 1778.

Name	Date	Company	Notes
Allen, William Captain	Jan 1, 1777	Second, Allen	Dec 1777; Jan-March 1778 on command; May-June 1778. Oath at Valley Forge on May 24, 1778.
Ames, Sylvanus/Silvanus Corporal	Feb 3, 1777 Duration of War	First, Cole	Dec 1777; Jan-Feb 1778 sick present; March-April 1778.
Ames, Silvanus Corporal	Duration of War	Second, Potter	May 16, 1778 died.
Anderson/ Andrus, Thomas Private	May 16, 1777 Three Years	Second, Dexter	Dec 1777; Jan 1778 on command; Feb 1778; March 1778 on command; April 1778; May 1778 making shoes in the country; June 1778.
Andrews, Jonathan Private	May 17, 1777 Three Years	First, Talbot	Dec 1777; Jan 1778 on command; Feb 1778; March-April 1778 sick present.
Andrews/ Andress, Jonathan Private	May 17, 1777 Three Years	Second, Dexter	May-June 1778.
Andrews, Thomas Private		First, Flagg	Dec 1777-Feb 1778 sick absent; April 1778.
Andrews/Andrew, Thomas Private	Jan 1, 1777	Second, Allen	May 1778; June 1778 absent leave.
Angell, Israel Colonel	Jan 12, 1777	Second	Dec 1777 on command; Jan-March 1778; April-May 1778 on furlough; June 1778 absent on court martial.
Angell, Joseph Private	May 22, 1777 Duration of War	Second, Olney, S.	Dec 1777-Jan 1778; Feb 1778 sick in quarters; March 1778 on ye B.G. Commissary Guard; April-June 1778.
Ann, Anthony Private	Duration of War	First, Clarke	Dec 1777; Jan 1778 on command; Feb-March 1778 sick present; April 1778.
Ann, Antony Private		First, Arnold	May-June 1778.
Anthony, Edward Private	Three Years	First, Arnold	May 1778; June 1778 absent with leave.
Anthony, Edward Private	April 17, 1777, Three Years	Second, Hughes	Dec 1777-Jan 1778; Feb 1778 on guard; March 1778 on command; April 1778 on command at Radnor.
Anthony/Antony, Michael Private	Feb 2, 1777, Duration of War	Second, Olney, S.	Dec 1777; Jan 1778 on guard; Feb 1778 on command; March 1778; April 1778 sick in Brigade hospital; May 1778 sick Yellow Springs; June 1778 sick absent.

Name	Date	Company	Notes
Archer, William Private	Jan 4, 1777	First, Wallen	Dec 1777-April 1778.
Archer, William Private		First, Arnold	May 1778 on picket; June 12, 1778 died.
Arnold, Benjamin Ensign	Feb 11, 1777	Second, Dexter	Dec 1777 under arrest; Jan 6, 1778 cashiered.
Arnold, Bristol Private	March 7, 1778, Duration of War	First, Flagg	June 1778.
Arnold, Edward Drummer	May 12, 1777, Three Years	Second, Olney. S.	Dec 1777-June 1778.
Arnold, Joseph 1st. Lt.	Jan 1, 1777	First, Cole	Dec 1777; Jan-Feb 1778 on command recruiting; March 1778 on command; April 1778 on recruiting service; June 1778.
Arnold, Samuel 2nd. Lt.	Feb 11, 1777	First, Dexter/ Arnold	Dec 1777; Jan 1778 on command recruiting; Feb-March 1778 on command; April-June 1778. In May he transferred to Arnold's Company. Oath at Valley Forge on May 14, 1778.
Arnold, Thomas Captain	March 21, 1777	First, Arnold	Dec 1777; Jan-March 1778 on command; April 1778; May 1778 on court martial; June 1778 wounded absent. Oath at Valley Forge on May 14, 1778.
Arrixson/ Arrexson, Samuel Sergeant	Jan 1, 1777 Duration of War	First, Wallen	Dec 1777; Jan-Feb 1778 on command; March 1778; April 1778 sick in camp.
Arrixson/Alixson, Samuel Sergeant	Duration of War	Second, Olney. S.	May 1778 sick at Yellow Springs; June 1778 sick absent.
Babcock, Prince Private	March 12, 1777, Duration of War	First, Lewis	June 1778.
Babcock, William Private	April 15, 1778, Duration of War	First, Dexter	June 1778; Sept 1, 1778 died.
Backett, Jonas Private	March 6, 1777	First, Flagg	Dec 1777; Jan-March 1778 on command; April 1778 on Radnor picket.
Backett, James/ Jonas Private		Second, Allen	May 1778; May 15, 1778 prisoner; June 1778.
Ballou/Bellow, Elisha Private	May 16, 1777, Three Years	Second, Dexter	Dec 1777; Jan 1778 sick present; Feb 1778 sick absent; March 11, 1778 died.
Banister, Cato Private	March 6, 1778, Duration of War	First, Flagg	June 1778.

Name	Enlisted	Company	Notes
Baptist/Baptis, Francis Private	Feb 27, 1777, Duration of War	First, Cole	Dec 1777; Jan-Feb 1778 sick present; March-April 1778.
Baptis/Baptist, Francis Private	Duration of War	Second, Potter	May-June 1778.
Barber, Elleck Private	March 13, 1778, Duration of War	First, Dexter	June 1778.
Barnes, William Private	Aug 20, 1777, Duration of War	First, Wallen	Dec 1777-April 1778.
Barnes, William Private	Duration of War	Second, Olney, S.	May 1778 sick in camp; June 1778.
Barney, Daniel Corporal/Private	Feb 1, 1777, Three Years	Second, Shaw	Dec 1777; Jan 8, 1778 reduced to Private; Jan 1778 on command; Feb-June 1778.
Barney, William Private	May 15, 1777, Three Years	Second, Tew	Dec 1777-April 1778; May 1778 sick at Yellow Springs; June 1778 sick absent.
Barns/Barnes, Mark Private	Jan 1, 1777, Duration of War	First, Lewis	Dec 1777-April 1778.
Barns/Barrns, Mark Private	Duration of War	Second, Olney, C.	May 1778 on guard; June 1778 sick at English Town.
Barr/Bar, Mathew Private	Feb 16, 1777, Duration of War	Second, Olney, C.	Dec 1777; Jan 15, 1778 deserted.
Barrows/Barrus, Peter Private	May 8, 1777, Duration of War	Second, Dexter	Dec 1777; Jan-March 1778 on command; April-June 1778.
Bartlett/Bartlet, Caleb Corporal	Jan 22, 1777, Duration of War	First, Wallen	Dec 1777; Jan 1778 sick present; Feb 1778; March 1778 sick present; April 1778.
Bartlet, Caleb Corporal	Duration of War	Second, Olney, S.	May-June 1778.
Barton, Andrew Sergeant/Private		First, Flagg	Dec 19, 1777 reduced to Private; Jan 1778 on command; Feb 1778 on guard; March 1778 in hospital; April 1778 sick at French Creek.
Barton, Andrew Private		Second, Allen	May 1778 sick at French Creek; June 1778 sick absent.
Barton, Hampton/ Hamton Private	May 29, 1777, Three Years	First, Arnold	Dec 1777; Jan 1778 sick present; Feb-June 1778.
Barton, Simon Private	March 1, 1778, Duration of War	First, Cole	June 1778.
Bates, Benoni Corporal	March 13, 1777, Duration of War	First, Dexter	Dec 1777-April 1778.

Bates/Baits, Benoni Corporal	Duration of War	Second, Shaw	May-June 1778.
Bemus/Beemus, Jotham Private	April 10, 1777, Duration of War	First, Arnold	Dec 1777 sick in hospital; Jan-March 1778 sick absent; April 1778.
Bemus, Jotham Private	Duration of War	Second, Tew	May-June 1778.
Benjamin, William Private	Duration of War	Second, Potter	May 1778; June 1778 deceased.
Benjamins, William Private	June 13, 1777, Duration of War	First, Cole	Dec 1777-April 1778.
Bennet, Assel/Assal Private	Three Years	Second, Olney, C.	May 1778 on guard; June 28, 1778 killed.
Bennet, Benjamin Private	April 26, 1777, Duration of War	First, Talbot	Dec 1777-Feb 1778 sick absent; March-April 1778.
Bennet, Jonas/Jones Private	April 17, 1777, Three Years	First, Arnold	Dec 1777; Jan-March 1778 on command; April 1778.
Bennett, Asel Private	May 10, 1777, Three Years	First, Lewis	Dec 1777; Jan 1778 on 7 days command; Feb-April 1778.
Bennett, Benjamin Private	Duration of War	Second, Dexter	May 1778; June 1778 absent with leave.
Bennett/Bennit, Jonas Private	Three Years	Second, Tew	May-June 1778.
Bennett, Samuel Drummer/Drum Major	May 10, 1777, Duration of War	First	Dec 1777; Jan 1778 on command recruiting; Feb-April 1778; May promoted to Drum Major; May-June 1778.
Bennit/Bennett, William Private	Jan 24, 1777, Duration of War	Second, Tew	Dec 1777-March 1778 sick absent; April-May 1778; June 1778 absent with leave.
Bent, Prince Private	March 10, 1778, Duration of War	First, Lewis	June 1778.
Bentley, John Private	Feb 12, 1777, Duration of War	Second, Olney, C.	Dec 1777; Jan 1778 on command; Feb 1778; March 1778 on command; April-May 1778; June 1778 sick at Yellow Springs.
Beseair/Brosear, Leus/Luies Private	Feb 25, 1777, Duration of War	Second, Olney, C.	Dec 1777; Jan-March 1778 sick absent; April 1778 sick at French Creek; May-June 1778 sick at Yellows Springs.

Name	Enlistment	Regiment/Company	Service Record
Bickford/ Biggford, Benjamin Quartermaster Sergeant/ Sergeant	Oct 1, 1777, Three Years	Second, Potter	Dec 17, 1777, appointed assistant to Brigade Commissary; Dec 1777; Jan 1778 reduced to Sergeant in Potter's Company; Feb-March 1778 on command; April 1778.
Bickford, Benjamin Sergeant	Duration of War	Second, Allen	May-June 1778 on command.
Bidgood, Remington Private	May 31, 1777, Duration of War	Second, Hughes	Dec 1777; Jan 1778 on command; Feb 1778; March 1778 sick present; April-June 1778.
Bidwell, William Private	March 4, 1777, Duration of War	Second, Dexter	Dec 1777-March 1778; April 1778 under guard; May 1778; June 1, 1778 died.
Billes, Lewis Private	April 1, 1777, Duration of War	First, Dexter	Dec 1777 on command; Jan 1778 on command at Bethlehem; Feb 1778 waiter hospital; March 1778 sick absent; April muster roll shows him deceased on Jan 20, 1778.
Billet/Billit, John Private	Jan 1, 1777, Duration of War	First, Dexter	Dec 1777; Jan 1778 on command in row boat; Feb-March 1778 on command.
Billit, John Private	Duration of War	Second, Shaw	May-June 1778.
Billings, Nathan Private	Three Years	First, Clarke	Dec 1777; Jan 1778 sick present; Feb 1778; March 1778 on command; April 1778 command at Rhode Island.
Billings, Nathan Private	April 26, 1777	Second, Hughes	May 1778; June 1778 absent with leave.
Billings, Nathan Private	April 28, 1777, Three Years	Second, Potter	Dec 1777-Jan 1778; Feb 14, 1778 died.
Billington, John Private	April 6, 1777, Duration of War	Second, Potter	Dec 1777; Jan 1778 on command; Feb 1778 on guard; March 1778 on command; April 1778 on command at Radnor; May-June 1778 sick at Yellow Springs.
Billington, Thomas Private	Jan 31, 1777, Three Years	Second, Potter	Dec 1777; Jan 1778 on command; Feb 1778; March 1778 on guard; April 1778 sick present; May 1778; June 1778 absent with leave.
Billit, John Private		Second, Shaw	May-June 1778.

Name/Rank	Date/Term	Company	Service Record
Bills/Bill, Thomas Private	May 2, 1777. Three Years	Second, Potter	Dec 1777-Feb 1778; March 1778 sick absent; April 1778 sick absent at Yellow Springs; May 1778 on command at Yellow Springs hospital; June 1778 on command Yellow Springs.
Bird/Burd, Benjamin Private	Feb 20, 1777. Duration of War	Second, Dexter	Dec 1777; Jan 1778 on command; Feb 1778 on guard; March 1778 on command; April 1778 on command at Radnor; May 1778 on guard; June 1778 absent with leave.
Bishop, Benoni/ Benjamin Private	Feb 20, 1777. Duration of War	Second, Dexter	Dec 1777; Jan 1778 sick present; Feb 1778 sick absent; March-May 1778; June 1778 on guard.
Blanchard, Benjamin Private	May 21, 1777. Three Years	First, Arnold	Dec 1777; Jan-Feb 1778 on command; March 1778; April 1778 duty Radnor.
Blanchard, Benjamin Private	Three Years	Second, Tew	May 1778 sick in camp; June 1778 sick at hospital.
Blanchard, Elias Ensign	Feb 10, 1777	First Arnold	Dec 1777; Jan-March 1778 on command; April 1778 on command Rhode Island.
Blanchard, Elias Ensign		First, Lewis	June 1778.
Blin/Blinn, George Drummer	Jan 13, 1777, Duration of War	Second, Tew	Dec 1777-May 1778; June 1778 absent with leave.
Bond, Thomas Private	Jan 15, 1777, Duration of War	Second, Tew	Dec 1777-Jan 1778; Feb-March 1778 on command; April-June 1778.
Boroughs, Jack Private	March 10, 1778, Duration of War	First, Lewis	June 1778.
Boss, Benjamin Sergeant	June 17, 1777, Duration of War	Second, Hughes	Dec 1777-Feb 1778 sick absent; March-April 1778; May 1778 on command; June 1778.
Boston, Thomas Private		First, Flagg	Dec 1777; Jan-Feb 1778 sick present; March-April 1778; May 2, 1778 died.
Boswell/Boswill, William Private	March 14, 1777, Duration of War	Second, Tew	Dec 1777-March 1778 sick absent; April-June 1778 sick at Lancaster.
Bourn, Frank Private	Feb 20, 1778, Duration of War	First, Flagg	June 1778.
Bourse, Cato Private	March 16, 1778, Duration of War	First, Cole	June 1778.

Name	Enlistment	Company	Service Record
Bowdish/Bowdis, Asa Private	April 24, 1777, Three Years	First, Arnold	Dec 1777; Jan 1778 on command; Feb 1778 on duty; March 1778 on command; April 1778.
Bowdish, Asa Private	Three Years	Second, Tew	May-June 1778 sick at Yellow Springs.
Bowles, John Ensign	June 24, 1777	First, Cole	Dec 27, 1777 discharged.
Boyer, Joseph Private	May 4, 1778, Duration of War	First, Lewis	June 1778.
Bozworth/Bosworth, Joseph Private	June 14, 1777, Duration of War	Second, Olney, S.	Dec 1777-March 1778; April 1778 sick present; May 21, 1778 died.
Bradford/Bratford, George Private	May 15, 1777, Three Years	Second, Dexter	Dec 1777-Jan 1778; Feb 1778 on command; March-May 1778; June 1778 sick at Princetown.
Bragg, Daniel Private	Jan 1, 1777, Three Years	Second, Potter	Dec 1777 sick absent; Jan 1, 1778 died.
Briant, Israel Private	June 17, 1777, Duration of War	Second, Tew	Dec 1777-April 1778 sick absent.
Briggs, Anderson Private		First, Flagg	Dec 1777; Jan-March 1778 on command; April 1778.
Briggs, Anderson Private	April 4, 1777	Second Allen	May 1778; June 1778 wounded and absent.
Briggs, Jacob Private	March 25, 1777, Three Years	First, Cole	Dec 1777-Feb 1778 sick absent; March 1778 sick in hospital; April 1778.
Briggs, Jacob Private	Duration of War	Second, Potter	May 1778 under guard; June 1778 sick at Princetown.
Briggs, Jonathan Private	March 12, 1777, Duration of War	Second, Hughes	Dec 1777-Feb 1778; March 1778 on guard; April 1778; May-June 1778 sick absent at Yellow Springs.
Briggs, Jonathan Private	Dec 18, 1776, Duration of War	Second, Tew	Dec 1777 sick absent; Jan 1778; Feb 1778 on command; March 1778; April 1778 sick present; May 1778 sick in camp; June 1778 sick at hospital.
Briggs, Stephen Ensign	Feb 20, 1777	First, Flagg	Dec 1777; Jan 7, 1778 discharged.
Briggs, Tobias Private	Jan 1, 1777, Duration of War	First, Dexter	Dec 1777-April 1778.
Briggs, Tobias Private	Duration of War	Second, Shaw	May 1778 on guard; June 1778.
Briggs, William Corporal		First, Flagg	Dec 1777-Feb 1778; March-April 1778 sick present.
Briggs, William Corporal	Duration of War	Second, Allen	May 1778; June 1778 absent leave.

Name	Date	Company	Notes
Bristol, Peter Private	June 4, 1777, Duration of War	First, Wallen/ Arnold	Dec 1777 sick present; Jan-Feb 1778; March 1778 on fatigue; April 1778; May 1778 sick in camp; June 6, 1778 died.
Brosear see Beseair			
Brown, Cato Private	Feb 25, 1778, Duration of War	First, Cole	June 1778.
Brown, Davis/ Davice Private	March 24, 1777, Three Years	Second, Dexter	Dec 1777-Jan 1778; Feb 1778 on fatigue; March 1778 on command; April 1, 1778, in His Excellency's Guard.
Brown, Israel Private	May 10, 1777, Three Years	Second, Allen	Dec 1777-March 1778 on command; April 1778 on furlough at Rhode Island; May-June 1778 on furlough.
Brown, Joseph Sergeant	Feb 17, 1777, Duration of War	First, Dexter	Dec 1777; Jan-March 1778 on command; April 1778 recruiting at Rhode Island.
Brown, Joseph Sergeant	May 1, 1778, Duration of War	First, Flagg	June 1778.
Brown, Joseph Private	Jan 1, 1777, Duration of War	Second, Allen	Dec 1777-Feb 1778; March 1778 on guard; April 1778; May 1778 on guard; June 1778.
Brown, Primus Private	March 20, 1778	First, Cole	June 1778.
Brown, Scipio Drummer	March 16, 1778, Duration of War	First, Flagg	June 1778.
Brown, Thomas Drummer	Feb 25, 1778,	First, Lewis	June 1778.
Brown, Zephaniah 2nd. Lt.	Feb 10, 1777	First, Arnold/ Flagg	Dec 1777-March 1778; April 1778 on command Rhode Island. In June 1778 he is listed present in Flagg's Company.
Bryant/Briant, James Drummer/ Private	June 17, 1777, Duration of War	Second, Dexter	Dec 1777-Feb 1778 sick absent; Feb 1, 1777 reduced to Private; March-April 1778; May 1778 on detachment; June 1778 on guard.
Bryant, Mathew Private	March 11, 1777, Two Years	Second, Olney, S.	Dec 1777; Jan 1778 on command; Feb 1778; March 1778 on command; April-May 1778; June 1778 sick absent.
Buck, Aaron Private/ Sergeant		First, Flagg	Dec 1 promoted to Sergeant; Dec 1777 on guard; Jan-Feb 1778; March 1778 in hospital; April 1778 sick at French Creek.
Buck, Aaron Sergeant		Second, Allen	May 1778; June 1778 absent with leave.

Name	Enlisted	Company	Notes
Bucklin, Prince Private	Feb 28, 1778, Duration of War	First, Flagg	June 1778.
Bugee, Abijah Private	Jan 4, 1777, Three Years	Second, Shaw	Dec 1777; Jan 1778 sick in quarters; Feb 1778; March 11, 1778 died.
Bump, Abel Private	Feb 17, 1777, Duration of War	Second, Dexter	Dec 1777-Feb 1778 sick absent; March 1, 1778 dead.
Burke, Africa Private	March 5, 1778, Duration of War	First, Flagg	June 1778.
Burlinggame/ Burllinggame, John Private	March 24, 1777, Three Years	Second, Dexter	Dec 1777-Feb 1778; March 1778 on command; April-June 1778.
Burn/Burne, Peter Private	Duration of War	Second, Potter	May 1778 under guard; June 1778.
Burns/Burne, Peter Private	Feb 15, 1777, Duration of War	First, Cole	Dec 1777-Feb 1778 sick absent; March-April 1778.
Burt, Alexander Private	Jan 4, 1777, Three Years	Second, Shaw	Dec 1777; Jan 18, 1778 deserted.
Burton, Job Private	Feb 28, 1778, Duration of War	First, Flagg	June 1778.
Butrick/Buttrick, Edward/Edwerd Sergeant	Feb 16, 1777, Duration of War	Second, Olney, C.	Dec 1777-May 1778; June 1778 absent with leave.
Button, John Private		First, Flagg	Dec 1777-Jan 1778; Feb 1778 on guard; March 1778; April 1778 sick present.
Button, John Private		Second, Allen	May 1778 sick Yellow Springs; June 1778 sick absent.
Button/Butten, William Private	Dec 25, 1776, Duration of War	Second, Hughes	Dec 1777 sick present; Jan 24, 1778 died.
Butts/Buts, William Private	May 7, 1777, Three Years	First, Talbot	Jan-Feb 1778 on duty; March 1778 on command; April 1778 command Rhode Island.
Butts, William Private	Three Years	Second, Dexter	May-June 1778 sick at Rhode Island.
Capwell, James Private	May 18, 1777, Three Years	First, Lewis	Dec 1777; Jan 1778 on seven days command; Feb-April 1778.
Capwell/Capwel, James Private	May 18, 1777, Three Years	Second, Olney, C.	May 1778; June 1778 absent with leave.
Capwell, Jeremiah Private	May 17, 1777, Three Years	First, Lewis	Dec 1777-April 1778.
Capwell, Jeremiah Private	May 17, 1777, Three Years	Second, Olney, C.	May-June 1778.
Card, Potter Private	Jan 1, 1777, Duration of War	First, Lewis	Dec 1777-April 1778.

Name	Enlisted	Company	Service Record
Card, Pottar Private	Jan 1, 1777, Three Years	Second, Olney, C.	May 1778; June 1778 absent with leave.
Carpenter, Abel 2nd. Lt.	Feb 17, 1777	Second, Potter	Dec 1777; Jan 1778 on command recruiting; Feb-March 1778 on command; April-June 1778.
Carpenter, James Private	Duration of War	First, Arnold	June 1778.
Carpenter, Richard Private	Duration of War	First, Arnold	June 1778 sick Englishtown.
Carr, John Private	June 19, 1777, Duration of War	First, Cole	Dec 1777-Feb 1778; March 1778 on command; April 1778.
Carr, John Private	Duration of War	Second, Potter	May-June 1778; August 17, 1778 died.
Case, Prince Private	Feb 10, 1778, Duration of War	First, Cole	June 1778.
Casey, Gideon 2nd. Lt.	Feb. 20, 1777	First, Flagg	Dec 1777-March 1778 on furlough.
Cass, Robert Private	May 10, 1777, Three Years	Second, Allen	Dec 1777-Jan 1778; Feb 1778 on command; March 1778; April 1778 on command at Radnor; May-June 1778.
Caton/Keaton, Patrick Private	April 3, 1777, Duration of War	Second, Shaw	Jan 1778 sick in quarters; Feb-May 1778; June 28, 1778 killed.
Cays see Coys			
Ceasar/Seaser, Ebenzer Private	Duration of War	First, Arnold	May 1778 sick in camp; June 1778 sick Valley Forge.
Ceazer/Caezar, Ebenezer Private	May 4, 1777, Duration of War	First, Cole	Dec 1777-March 1778; April 1778 on command at hospital.
Chace, Joseph Fifer	Feb 10, 1777	First, Dexter	Dec 1777-Jan 1778; Feb 6, 1778 deserted.
Chace, Joseph Fifer		Second, Shaw	June 1778.
Chadwick, John Private	Jan 13, 1777, Duration of War	Second, Tew	Dec 1777-Feb 1778; March 1778 sick present; April-May 1778; June 1778 sick in hospital.
Chaffee/Cheffie, Noah Private	Feb 24, 1777, Duration of War	Second, Olney, C.	Dec 1777-Feb 1778; March 1778 on command; April 1778 May 1778 sick absent; June 1778 on command with Major Thayer.

Name	Enlistment	Company	Service Record
Chaffee, Shubill/ Shewbill Corporal	Feb 1, 1777, Duration of War	Second, Olney, C.	Dec 1777-Feb 1778; March 1778 on command; April 1778 on command Providence; May 1778 sick absent; June 1778 on command with baggage.
Champlin, Cudjo Private	March 6, 1778, Duration of War	First, Flagg	June 1778.
Champlin, Edward Private		First, Wallen	Dec 1777; Jan-March 1778 on command; April 1778.
Champlin, Edward Private	Jan 1, 1777	Second, Olney, S.	May-June 1778.
Champlin, Jack Private	Feb 18, 1778, Duration of War	First, Cole	June 1778.
Champlin, July Private	June 6, 1778, Duration of War	First, Lewis	June 1778.
Champlin, Newport Private	Feb 19, 1778, Duration of War	First, Flagg	June 1778 on guard.
Champlin, Sharper Private	May 14, 1778, Duration of War	First, Cole	June 1778.
Champlin, William Private	Three Years	First, Clarke	Dec 1777 sick present; Jan 24, 1778 died.
Champlin/ Champlain, William Private	April 10, 1777, Duration of War	First, Lewis	Dec 1777; Jan 1778 on 7 days command; Feb-April 1778.
Champlin, William Private	Duration of War	Second, Olney, C.	May 1778; June 1778 on furlough at Morristown.
Champlin, Yorke Private	March 15, 1778, Duration of War	First, Lewis	June 1778.
Chapman/ Champman, Rufus Private	May 9, 1777, Three Years	Second, Olney, S.	Dec 1777-Jan 1778; Feb 1778 on guard; March 1778 sick in camp; April-May 1778; June 1778 sick absent.
Charles, John/ Jonathan Private	Duration of War	First, Arnold	May 1778; June 1778 sick Princeton.
Charles, John Private	March 24, 1777, Duration of War	Second, Hughes	Dec 1777; Jan 1778 on command; Feb-March 1778; April 1778 sick present.
Charles/Cherles, Thomas/Tomas Private	Jan 1, 1777, Duration of War	Second, Olney, C.	Dec 1777 on guard; Jan-March 1778 on command; April-June 1778.
Chase, Cato Private	March 4, 1778, Duration of War	First, Dexter	June 1778.

Name	Date	Company	Notes
Chenserman/ Cencherman, Aaron Private	Aug 23, 1777, Duration of War	Second, Potter	Dec 1777-March 1778 sick absent.
Childs, Prince Private	April 13, 1777 Duration of War	First, Arnold	Dec 1777-May 1778; June 1778 absent with leave.
Chillson/ Chilson, John Sergeant	May 9, 1777, Duration of War	Second, Olney, S.	Dec 1777-May 1778; June 1778 absent without leave.
Clan/Clann, Robert Private	April 27, 1777	First, Talbot	Dec 1777; Jan-March 1778 on command; April 1778 sick present.
Clan, Robert Private	Duration of War	Second, Dexter	May-June 1778.
Clark, Beriah Private		Second, Dexter	May 1778; June 1778 New Providence, New Jersey.
Clark, Paul Corporal	Duration of War	Second, Shaw	May-June 1778.
Clarke, Beriah Private	April 4, 1777, Duration of War	First, Talbot	Dec 1777-Feb 1778 sick absent; April 1778.
Clarke, George Fifer	June 14, 1777, Duration of War	Second, Hughes	Dec 1777; Jan-Feb 1778 on furlough; March 3, 1778 deserted; April 19, 1778 joined; May 1778; June 1778 absent with leave.
Clarke, James Private	March 2, 1778, Duration of War	First, Lewis	June 1778
Clarke, James Private	Feb 20, 1778, Duration of War	First, Cole	June 1778.
Clarke, Jeremiah Sergeant/ Private	Three Years	First, Clarke	Dec 1777; Jan 4, 1778 reduced to Private; Jan-Feb 1778 sick present; March 1778 tending sick present; April 28, 1778 died.
Clarke, Jonathan Corporal		First, Clarke	Dec 1777-Feb 1778 wounded absent; March 1778 in hospital.
Clarke, Oliver Captain	Feb 11, 1777	First, Clarke	October 22, 1777 taken prisoner; Dec 1777-Feb 1778 prisoner with the enemy.
Clarke, Paul Corporal	Jan 1, 1777, Duration of War	First, Lewis	Dec 1777-April 1778.
Clarke, Thomas Private		First, Flagg	Dec 1777; Jan-Feb 1778 sick present; March 1778 in hospital; April 1778 sick at French Creek.
Clarke/Clark, Thomas Private		Second, Allen	May 1778 sick French Creek; June 1778 absent leave.
Clefford, Francis Private	June 17, 1777, Duration of War	Second, Olney, S.	Dec 1777 sick absent; Jan 22, 1778 discharged.

Name	Enlisted	Company	Service Record
Clinker, Humphrey Private		First, Flagg	Dec 1777-Jan 1778; Feb 1778 sick present; March 21, 1778 died.
Clossen/Classon, Nathan Private	Jan 1, 1777, Duration of War	First, Lewis	Dec 1777-April 1778.
Closson/Classon, Nathan Private	Duration of War	Second, Olney, C.	May 1778; June 1778 absent with leave.
Cobb, John Private	May 10, 1777, Three Years	First, Lewis	Dec 1777; Jan 1778 on guard; Feb-April 1778.
Cobb, John Private	Three Years	Second, Olney, C.	May 1778 on command at the lines; June 1778.
Cobb, Thomas Private	May 21, 1777 Three Years	Second, Olney, S.	Dec 1777-March 1778 sick absent; April-May 1778 sick Lancaster; June 1778.
Coddington, Jack Private	March 7, 1778, Duration of War	First, Flagg	June 1778.
Cole, Ceaser/ Cesar Private	May 18, 1777 Three Years	First, Talbot	Dec 1777 sick in hospital; Jan 23, 1778 died.
Cole, Edward Private	April 8, 1777 Three Years	First, Arnold	Dec 1777-Jan 1778; Feb 1778 on command; March-April 1778.
Cole, Edward Private	Three Years	Second, Tew	May 1778; June 1778 absent with leave.
Cole, Levi Private		First, Arnold	Dec 1777; Jan 1778 on command; Feb 1777; March 1778 on duty; April 1778 sick present.
Cole, Levi/Levey Private	Three Years	Second, Tew	May 1778 sick in camp; June 1778 absent with leave.
Cole, Thomas Captain	Jan 1, 1777	First, Cole	Dec 1777-March 1778; April 1778 on recruiting service; June 1778.
Coleby/Caleby, Abraham Private		Second, Shaw	May-June 1778.
Colegrove, Francis Private	Three Years	First, Clarke	Dec 1777 on guard; Jan-Feb 1778 sick present; March 1778 on guard; April 1778 sick present.
Colegrove, Francis Private	Three Years	Second, Hughes	May-June 1778.
Colegrove, William Fifer		First, Flagg	Dec 1777-Feb 1778 sick absent; March 1778 in hospital; April roll shows he died on March 20, 1778.
Coller/Collar, David Private	Jan 6, 1777, Duration of War	Second, Olney, C.	Dec 1777-June 1778.

Name	Enlistment	Company	Service Record
Collins/Collens, Joseph Private	May 10, 1777, Three Years	Second, Olney, C.	Dec 1777-June 1778.
Comstock, Adam Lt. Col.	Jan 1, 1777	First	Dec 1777-March 1778 on command; April 1778 on command at Rhode Island; May-June 1778.
Congdon, Joseph Private	April 4, 1777, Three Years	Second, Potter	Dec 1777-March 1778; April 1778 on command; May-June 1778 sick absent at Yellow Springs.
Congdon, Robert Private	April 10, 1777, Duration of War	First, Dexter	Dec 1777-Jan 1778 sick absent; Feb 1778 on guard; March-April 1778.
Congdon, Robert Private	Duration of War	Second, Shaw	May 1778 on guard; June 1778.
Cook/Cooke, Ceasar/Ceasor Private	May 5, 1777, Duration of War	Second, Potter	Dec 1777-Jan 1778; Feb 1778 on command; March 1778 sick present; April 30, 1778 died.
Cook/Cooke, John Quartermaster/ 1st. Lt.	March 15, 1777	First, Cole	Dec 1777 sick absent; Jan-March 1778 on command; April 1778 on command at Rhode Island; May-June 1778. On June 1, 1778 he became a First Lieutenant in Cole's Company.
Cook/Cooke, John Private	Feb 8, 1777, Duration of War	Second, Shaw	Jan 1778 on duty; Feb-June 1778.
Cook, Quam Private	May 22, 1777, Three Years	First, Cole	Dec 1777-Jan 1778; Feb 25, 1778 died.
Cooney, Michael Private	Jan 12, 1777, Duration of War	Second, Tew	Dec 1777; Jan 1778 on command; Feb 20, 1778 deserted.
Coopen/Coopon, William Private	March 25, 1777	Second, Hughes	Dec 1777-Jan 1778; Feb 1778 on command; March 1778; April 1778 sick present.
Coopin/Cooping, William Private	Duration of War	First, Arnold	May 1778 on Commissaries Guard; June 1778 sick Corryell's Ferry.
Cordos/Cordoz, Joseph Private	March 8, 1777, Duration of War	Second, Olney, C.	Dec 1777; Jan 1778 on fatigue; Feb 1778; March 16, 1778 deserted.
Corey/Cory, Gideon Private	Feb 28, 1777, Duration of War	First, Dexter	Dec 1777-Jan 1778 sick absent; Feb 1778; March 1778 on fatigue; April 1778 sick in camp. May-June 1778.
Corey/Carey, Gideon Private		Second, Shaw	

Name	Enlisted	Company	Service
Cornelius, Elias Surgeon's Mate	Jan 1, 1777	Second	Aug 22, 1777 taken prisoner; April-May 1778; June 1778 on command Valley Forge.
Cornell, Joseph Ensign	June 20, 1777	First, Wallen	Dec 1777; Jan 1778 on fatigue; Feb 1778 on command; March 1778 sick in camp; April 1778 on command at Rhode Island.
Cornell, Joseph Ensign		First, Dexter	June 1778.
Coys/Coies, Tobey Private	May 20, 1777, Duration of War	Second, Hughes	Dec 1777-Jan 1778; Feb 1778 on guard; March 1778 on command; April 1778.
Coys/Cois, Toby Private	Duration of War	First, Arnold	May 1778; June 1778 on command.
Couzens, Dick Fifer	June 5, 1778	First, Lewis	June 1778.
Crandal/Crandrill, John Private	May 1, 1777 Three Years	First, Arnold	Dec 1777 sick in quarters; Jan-March 1778 on command; April 1778 sick present; May 1778.
Crandall/Crandal, John, Private	Three Years	Second, Tew	May 1778 sick in camp; June 1778 absent with leave.
Crandoll, Chrisopher Private	Duration of War	First, Arnold	May-June 1778.
Crandall/Crandal, Hosea Sergeant		First, Flagg	Dec 1777-March 1778; April 30, 1778 taken prisoner.
Crandol, Hosea Private		Second, Allen	On the June 1778 payroll he is paid from May 1, "taken prisoner" April 30.
Crandrell/Crandrill, Christopher Private	Feb 17, 1777, Duration of War	First, Talbot	Dec 1777-Feb 1778; March 1778 sick present; April 1778.
Cranston, Samuel Corporal	Three Years	First, Talbot	Dec 1777; Jan 1778 sick present; Feb-June 1778.
Creek/Crick, Conrad Private	Duration of War	Second, Potter	May 1778; June 1778 absent with leave.
Creek, Conroid/Conrod Private	April 1, 1777, Duration of War	First, Cole	Dec 1777; Jan-Feb 1778 sick absent; March 1778 sick in hospital; April 1778.
Crosbee/Crosby, Charles/Charls Private	Jan 1, 1777, Three Years	Second, Olney, C.	Dec 1777; Jan 1778 on guard; Feb 1778 on command; March 1778-June 1778.
Cross, James Corporal	Three Years	First, Clarke	Dec 1777; Jan-April 1778 sick present.

Name	Enlisted	Company	Service
Cross, James Corporal	Three Years	Second, Hughes	May 1778; June 28, 1778 killed.
Croucher, John Private	May 21, 1777, Duration of War	Second, Potter	Dec 1777-Jan 1778; Feb 1778 on guard; March-April 1778; May-June 1778 sick absent at Yellow Springs.
Curtis, Bethuel 2nd. Lt.	Feb 11, 1777	Second, Hughes	Dec 1777 on command; Jan 1778 on command recruiting; Feb-March 1778 on command; April 1778; May 3, 1778 discharged.
Curtis, Jonah Sergeant	May 14, 1777, Duration of War	Second, Hughes	Dec 1777-June 1778.
Cushing, Samuel Private	May 1, 1777, Duration of War	Second, Allen	Dec 1777-May 1778; June 28, 1778 killed.
Dailey/Daily, James Private	Jan 1, 1777, Duration of War	First, Dexter	Dec 1777-March 1778; April 1778 on command at Radnor.
Dailey/Daley, Solomon Corporal	June 17, 1777, Duration of War	Second, Hughes	Dec 1777-Feb 1778; March 18, 1778 transferred to his Excellency's guard.
Daley/Dayly, Field/Feild Private	March 1, 1777, Duration of War	First, Cole	Dec 1777-Feb 1778 sick absent; March 1778 sick in hospital; April 1778 sick absent at Rhode Island.
Daley/Dayley, Field Private	Duration of War	Second, Potter	May 1778 sick absent at Rhode Island; June 1778 sick at Rhode Island.
Daley/Darley, James Private	Duration of War	First, Arnold	May-June 1778.
Daley, Peter Private	March 1, 1778, Duration of War	First, Dexter	June 1778.
Daniels, John Private	Duration of War	First, Arnold	May 1778; June 1778 absent with leave.
Daniels/ Danniels, John Private	April 22, 1777, Duration of War	Second, Potter	Dec 1777-March 1778; April 1778 on command at Radnor.
Darby/Darbey, William Private	June 7, 1777, Duration of War	Second, Olney, C.	Dec 1777; Jan-March 1778 on command; April 1778 wounded at Wilmington; May-June 1778 sick at Wilmington.
Davenport, Pomp Private	April 15, 1778, Duration of War	First, Dexter	June 1778.
David, Ebenezer Chaplain	May 10, 1777	Second	Dec 1777 on furlough. He resigned, became a Surgeon's Mate and died at Lancaster, Pennsylvania. See his collected letters in the Bibliography

Name	Enlistment	Company	Service
Davis, Benajah Corporal	Three Years	First, Clarke	Dec 1777 on duty; Jan-March 1778 on command; April 1778 on command Rhode Island.
Davis, Benajor Sergeant	May 1, 1777	First, Cole	June 1778.
Davis, Henry Sergeant	Feb 17, 1777, Duration of War	First, Talbot	Dec 1777-April 1778; March 1778 on command; April 1778.
Davis, Henry Sergeant		Second, Dexter	May-June 1778.
Davis/Davie, John Private	Jan 1, 1777, Duration of War	Second, Shaw	Jan-June 1778.
Davis, Samuel Private		First, Flagg	Dec 1777-Feb 1778; March 1778 on command; April 1778.
Davis, Samuel Private		Second, Allen	May-June 1778.
Davis, Silvester/ Silvenus Private	June 3, 1777 Three Years	Second, Potter	Dec 1777-March 1778 sick absent; April 1778 sick at Providence; May-June 1778 sick at Rhode Island.
Davis, Sylvester/ Silvaster Private	June 3, 1777 Three Years	Second, Dexter	Dec 1777 sick absent; Jan 30, 1778 died.
Davis, William 1st. Lt.	Feb 11, 1777	First, Wallen	Dec 1777-Feb 1778; March 15, 1778 discharged.
Davis, William Drummer	Feb 15, 1777 Duration of War	First, Cole	Dec 1777-April 1778.
Davis, William Fifer	June 3, 1777, Three Years	Second, Potter	Dec 1777-May 1778; June 1778 absent with leave.
Davis, William Drum Major	May 1, 1778	Second	May 1778; June 1778 sick at [Grummich].
Davis, William Private	Feb 3, 1777, Duration of War	Second, Olney, S.	Dec 1777; Jan 1778 on command; Feb 1778; March 11, 1778 deserted.
Dawley/Dowly, Ephraim/ Epharim Private	Feb 1, 1777, Duration of War	Second, Hughes	Dec 1777 sick present; Jan-Feb 1778; March 1778 on command; April 1778; May sick Yellow Springs; June 1778 sick at Yellow Springs or Red Lion.
Debago, Simon Private	Duration of War	First, Clarke	Dec 1777 on guard; Jan 1778 sick present; Feb 1778 on guard; March 1778 absent without leave; April 30, 1778 died.
Demus, Abraham/ Abram Private	May 10, 1777	First, Wallen	Dec 1777; Jan 1778 on command; Feb 1778; March on command; April 1778.
Demus, Abraham Private		First, Arnold	May-June 1778.

Name	Date	Company	Service
Deplumagalt/ Deplomagalt, Mikel/Michael Corporal	August 1, 1777, Duration of War	Second, Olney, C.	Dec 1777-Jan 1778; Feb 1778 sick present; March 1778; April 1778 on command Radnor; May 1778; June 1778 sick at Yellow Springs.
Deruce/Druce, John Private	March 12, 1777, Duration of War	Second, Hughes	Dec 1777; Jan 1778 on command; Feb-March 1778; April 1778 sick present; May-June 1778.
Dexter, David Captain	Feb 11, 1777	Second, Dexter	Dec 1777; Jan 1778 on command; Feb 1778 on command recruiting; March-April 1778 on command; May-June 1778.
Dexter, Eseck/ Esek Sergeant	Jan 9, 1777, Duration of War	Second, Dexter	Dec 1777; Jan-March 1778 on command; April 1778 recruiting Providence; May 1778; June 1778 absent with leave.
Dexter/Dextor, Gideon Private	Jan 29, 1777, Duration of War	Second, Dexter	Dec 1777-Feb 1778 sick absent; March 1, 1778 dead; April 1778 sick at Princeton; May 1778 sick at Yellow Springs; June 1778 sick at Princeton.
Dexter, John Singer Captain	Jan 1, 1777	First, Dexter	Dec 1777; Jan 1778 on command recruiting; Feb-March 1778 on command; April 1778 recruiting at Rhode Island; June 1778 on command.
Dexter, Joseph Fifer	May 12, 1777, Three Years	Second, Olney, S.	Dec 1777-June 1778.
Dexter, Oliver 2nd. Lt.	April 1, 1777	Second, Tew	Dec 1777-Feb 1778 on furlough; March 1778; April 1778 on command going to Morristown; May 1778; June 1778 on command.
Dexter, Thomas Private	May 21, 1777 Three Years	First, Arnold	Dec 1777; Jan 1778 on duty; Feb 1778; March 1778 on command; April 1778 duty Radnor.
Dexter, Thomas Private	Three Years	Second, Tew	May 1778 on guard; June 1778 absent with leave.
Diamond/ Dimond, Ezekiel Private	Feb 27, 1778, Duration of War	First, Cole	June 1778 sick present.
Difdatt, Joseph Private	Jan 27, 1777, Duration of War	Second, Olney, C.	Dec 1777-March 1778 on command.
Dixon/Dickson, Robert Private	Feb 10, 1777, Duration of War	Second, Allen	Dec 1777; Jan-Feb 1778 on command; March 1778 sick absent; April 1778 on guard; May-June 1778.

Name	Enlistment	Company	Service
Dodge, Edward, Corporal	Duration of War	Second, Hughes	Dec 1777 sick absent; Feb 3, 1778 died.
Dodge, John Sergeant/ Private	Jan 18, 1777, Duration of War	Second, Shaw	Jan 10, 1778 reduced to Private; Jan 1778 on General's Guard; Feb-June 1778.
Doharty/Dorrity, Michael Private	Duration of War	First, Olney, S.	May-June 1778.
Doleby/Dolebey, Jonathan Private	June 7, 1777, Three Years	Second, Hughes	Dec 1777-June 1778.
Dorrity/Dorithy, Michael Private	Jan 20, 1777, Duration of War	First, Wallen	Dec 1777 on guard; Jan-Feb 1778 General's Guard; March 1778 on guard; April 1778.
Dove, Henry Private	March 3, 1777, Three Years	Second, Olney, S.	Dec 1777 lame absent; Jan-March 1778 sick absent; April 1, 1778 deserted.
Dow, William Private	Jan 1, 1777, Duration of War	Second, Olney, C.	Dec 1777; Jan 1778 confined; Feb-March 1778 on command; April-May 1778; June 1778 absent with leave.
Drown, Phillip Private	April 7, 1777 Three Years	First, Arnold	Jan-March 1778 on command; April 1778 command Rhode Island; May 1778.
Drown, Philip Sergeant	May 1, 1778	First, Dexter	June 1778.
Drown, Phillip Private	Three Years	Second, Tew	May 1778 on furlough at Rhode Island; June 1778 on furlough; July 1, 1778 transferred to First Rhode Island.
Druce see Deruce			
Dunbar, John Sergeant	Three Years	First, Clarke	Dec 1777-Feb 1778; March 1778 on guard; April 1778.
Dunbar, John Sergeant	Three Years	Second, Hughes	May-June 1778.
Dunivan/ Donovin, Pierce Private	Feb 28, 1777, Duration of War	Second, Shaw	Jan-June 1778.
Dye, Firman/ Fermin Private	Jan 1, 1777, Duration of War	First, Dexter	Dec 1777-Feb 1778; March 1778 sick present; April 1778 sick in camp.
Dye, Firmin Private	Duration of War	Second, Shaw	May-June 1778.
Dyer, Samuel G. Private	Jan 1, 1777, Duration of War	First, Dexter	Dec 1777 on duty; Jan 1778 on command in row boats; Feb-March 1778 on command; April 1778.

Name	Enlistment	Company	Service Record
Dyer/Dryer, Samuel G. Private	Duration of War	Second, Shaw	May 1778 on command; June 1778.
Easterbrooks/ Easterbrook, Edward Private	April 9, 1777, Three Years	First, Arnold	Dec 1777-March 1778; April 1778 duty Radnor.
Easterbrooks, Edward Private	Three Years	Second, Tew	May 1778 sick at Yellow Springs; June 1778.
Eddy/Edy, Caleb Private	April 7, 1777, Three Years	First, Arnold	Dec 1777; Jan 1778 on duty; Feb 1778; March 1778 on command; April 1778.
Eddy, Caleb Private	Three Years	Second, Tew	May 31, 1778 died.
Eddy/Eady, Caleb Private	May 17, 1777, Duration of War	Second, Hughes	Dec 1777; Jan 1778 on command; Feb 1778 sick present; March 1778 sick absent; April 1778; May 1778 on guard; June 1778.
Edmonds/ Edmond, William Private	Duration of War	Second, Shaw	Jan 1778 on command; Feb-April 1778; June 1778.
Edwards, David Private	April 5, 1777, Three Years	First, Lewis	Dec 1777-April 1778.
Edwards, David Private		Second, Olney, C.	May 1778; June 1778 sick at Yellow Springs.
Edwards, James Private	Duration of War	First, Arnold	May 1, 1778 died.
Edwards, James Private	March 29, 1777, Duration of War	Second, Hughes	Dec 1777-March 1778 on command; April 1778 on command at Reading hospital.
Edwards, Perry Sergeant	May 11, 1777, Three Years	Second, Potter	Dec 1777 sick present; Jan-June 1778.
Edwards, William Private	March 29, 1777, Duration of War	Second, Hughes	Dec 1777; Jan 1778 on command; Feb-March 1778; April 1778 sick present; May-June 1778.
Eldred, Jeremey Private	Three Years	First, Clarke	Dec 1777 sick present; Jan-April 1778.
Eldridge, Cesar Private	March 22, 1778, Duration of War	First, Lewis	June 1778; Aug 31, 1778 died.
Eldridge/Eldred, Jeremiah Private	Feb 14, 1777, Three Years	Second, Hughes	May-June 1778.
Elliott/Eliot, John Private	June 7, 1777, Duration of War	Second, Olney, S.	Dec 1777-Feb 1778 sick absent; March 1778 unfit for duty.
Ellis, Daniel Private	Jan 1, 1777, Duration of War	First, Dexter	Dec 1777; Jan 1778 on 7 days command; Feb-April 1778.

Name/Rank	Enlistment	Company	Service
Ellis, Daniel Private	Duration of War	Second, Shaw	May-June 1778.
Ellis, John Private	Feb 17, 1777, Duration of War	First, Dexter	Dec 1777; Jan 1778 on duty; Feb 1778 on guard; March-April 1778.
Ellis/Ellias, John Private	Duration of War	Second, Shaw	May-June 1778.
Everet/Everett, Nicholas Private	Jan 3, 1777, Duration of War	Second, Shaw	Jan 1778 on command; Feb-April 1778; May 1778 sick at Yellow Springs; June 1778 sick absent.
Exceen/Exceene, John Private	Jan 18, 1777, Duration of War	Second, Tew	Dec 1777-Feb 1778; March 1778 on command; April 1778 sick present; May-June 1778.
Fenner, Daniel Private	Jan 16, 1777	Second, Hughes	Dec 1777; Jan 1778 on command; Feb 1778; March 1778 sick present; April-May 1778; June 1778 sick Valley Forge.
Field, John Private	Nov 20, 1777, Duration of War	Second, Olney, S.	Dec 1777-Feb 1778; March 11, 1778 deserted.
Finch, Ceasar Private	March 1, 1778, Duration of War	First, Dexter	June 1778.
Fish, Aaron Private	Feb 26, 1777, Duration of War	First, Cole	Dec 1777 absent without leave; Jan-Feb 1778; March 1778 on command; April 1778 sick present.
Fish, Aaron Private	Duration of War	Second, Potter	May 1778 under guard; June 28, 1778 deceased.
Fisher, John Private	April 27, 1777, Duration of War	Second, Dexter	Dec 1777-March 1778 sick absent; April 1778 Lancaster hospital; May-June 1778.
Fisher, Seth Corporal	Aprl 26, 1777	First, Talbot	Dec 1777-Feb 1778; March 1778 sick absent; April 1778.
Fisher, Seth Corporal		First, Arnold	May-June 1778.
Fisk, Reuben Private	Jan 14, 1777, Duration of War	Second, Tew	Dec 1777; Jan-March 1778 on command; April 1, 1778 deserted.
Flagg, Ebenezer Captain/ Paymaster	Jan 1, 1777	First, Flagg	Dec 1777-April 1778; June 1778; June 1, 1778 appointed Paymaster. Oath at Valley Forge on May 13, 1778.
Fones/Fomes, Daniel Private	April 5, 1777, Three Years	First, Lewis	Dec 1777; Jan 1778 sick present; Feb-April 1778.
Fones, Daniel/Daniell Private	Three Years	Second, Olney, C.	May-June 1778.
Fones, Jack Private	March 2, 1778, Duration of War	First, Dexter	June 1778.

Name	Enlisted	Company	Service
Fones/Fomes, John Private	April 5, 1777, Three Years	First, Lewis	Dec 1777; Jan 1778 sick present; Feb-April 1778.
Fones/Foons, John Private	Three Years	Second, Olney, C.	May 1778; June 1778 absent with leave.
Ford/Foard, Abijah Private	Feb 2, 1777, Duration of War	Second, Shaw	Jan 1778 on command; Feb-April 1778; May 1778 sick at Yellow Springs; June 1778 sick absent.
Foster, Anthony Private	Feb 26, 1777, Duration of War	Second, Allen	Dec 1777 sick in hospital; Jan-March 1778 sick absent; April-June 1778.
Foster, Jack Private	May 20, 1777	First, Talbot	Dec 1777; Jan 22, 1778 died.
Foster/Fostor, Samuel Corporal	May 15, 1777, Three Years	Second, Dexter	Dec 1777-Jan 1778; Feb 1778 on guard; March 1778 on command; April 1778 on command Providence; May-June 1778.
Foster/Forster, William Private	Feb 8, 1777, Duration of War	Second, Shaw	Jan 1778 on command; Feb-April 1778; May 1778 on guard; June 1778.
Fowler/Fowlar, Benjamin Private	March 15, 1777, Duration of War	Second, Dexter	Dec 1777 sick absent; Jan 1778; Feb 1778 on guard; March 1778 on command; April-May 1778; June 1778 sick at Princeton.
Fowlar/Foular, Richard Private	Duration of War	Second, Olney, C.	May 1778 on command Bickar; June 1778.
Fowler, Richard Private	Jan 1, 1777, Duration of War	First, Lewis	Dec 1777; Jan 1778 sick present; Feb-April 1778.
Fraine, Robert Private		First, Flagg	Dec 5, 1777 deserted.
Frank, Benjamin Private		First, Arnold	May 1778 on command at Radnor; June 1778.
Frank, Benjamin Private	May 12, 1777	Second, Hughes	Dec 1777-April 1778.
Frank, Neheme Private	June 21, 1777, Duration of War	First, Lewis	Dec 25, 1777 died.
Frank, William Private	Three Years	First, Arnold	May-June 1778.
Frank, William Private	June 13, 1777, Three Years	Second, Potter	Dec 1777 unfit for duty; Jan-Feb 1778; March 1778 on command; April 1778 on guard.
Franklin, Job Private	March 12, 1777, Duration of War	Second, Hughes	Dec 1777-March 1778; April 1778 on guard; May-June 1778.
Freeman, Salisbury Private	Three Years	First, Clarke	Dec 1777-April 1778.

Name	Date	Company	Notes
Freeman, Salsbury/ Salisbury Private	April 1, 1777, Three Years	Second, Hughes	May-June 1778.
Frink, Amos Fifer	Three Years	First, Clarke	Dec 1777-April 1778.
Frink, Amos Fifer		Second, Tew	May-June 1778.
Fry, Windsor Private		First, Flagg	Dec 1777; Jan-Feb 1778 sick present; April 1778 on scout.
Fry, Winsor/ Winser Private	Duration of War	First, Arnold	May-June 1778.
Furness/Furnis, Emanuel/ Immanuel Private	Jan 1, 1777, Duration of War	Second, Olney, S.	Dec 1777; Jan-Feb 1778 on command; March-June 1778.
Gardiner, Harculis Private	March 5, 1778, Duration of War	First, Cole	June 1778.
Gardiner, Prince Private	Feb 17, 1778, Duration of War	First, Cole	June 1778.
Gardner/ Gardiner, Amos Private	July 3, 1777	First, Wallen	Dec 1777 sick in camp; Feb 16, 1778 deceased.
Gardner, Asa Private	March 23, 1778	First, Dexter	First appears on muster roll for August 1778.
Gardner, Cuff Fifer	March 5, 1778, Duration of War	First, Flagg	June 1778.
Gardner, Joshua Private	March 23, 1778, Duration of War	First, Dexter	June 1778 sick absent.
Gardner, Mintus Private	Feb 25, 1778, Duration of War	First, Flagg	June 1778.
Gardner, Prime Private	March 31, 1778, Duration of War	First, Dexter	June 1778.
Gardner, Rutter Private	March 13, 1778, Duration of War	First, Lewis	June 1778.
Gardner, Sharper Private	Feb 27, 1778, Duration of War	First, Dexter	June 1778.
Garew/Garrew, John Lewis Private	Feb 1, 1777, Duration of War	Second, Potter	Dec 1777-May 1778; June 28, 1778 prisoner.
Garrow/Garrew, Charles Private	April 4, 1777, Duration of War	Second, Olney, C.	Dec 1777-Jan 1778; Feb 1778 on command; March 1778; April 1778 sick present in hospital; May 9, 1778 died.
Gears, Samuel Private		Second, Hughes	May 1778; June 1778 absent with leave.

Name	Enlisted	Company	Notes
Geers, Samuel Private		First, Clarke	Dec 1777 sick absent; Jan-Feb 1778 on command; March-April 1778.
George, Joshua Private	May 5, 1777	First, Wallen	Dec 1777; Jan 1778 on command; Feb 1778 sick in camp; March 1778; April 1778 unfit for service.
Gibbons/Gibbens, John	Jan 15, 1777, Duration of War	Second, Tew	Dec 1777-March 1778 sick absent; April 1, 1778 died
Gilley/Gille, Robert Private	May 19, 1777, Three Years	Second, Dexter	Dec 1777-Jan 1778; Feb 1778 on guard; March-June 1778.
Godfrey, Jonathan Corporal		First, Flagg	Dec 1777; Jan-Feb 1778 sick present; March-April 1778.
Godfrey, Jonathan Corporal	Duration of War	Second, Allen	May-June 1778.
Goodson, William Private	March 14, 1777, Duration of War	Second, Allen	Dec 1777 sick in hospital; Jan-March 1778 sick absent; April-May 1778; June 1778 tender to sick.
Goodwin/Goodwine, Richard Private	June 1, 1777, Duration of War	Second, Shaw	Jan 1778-April 1778; May 1778 on command; June 1778.
Goram, Robert Private	June 1, 1778, Duration of War	First, Dexter	June 1778.
Gorsman, John Fifer	June 1, 1778, Duration of War	First, Dexter	June 1778.
Gorton, Prosper Private	June 7, 1778, Duration of War	First, Flagg	June 1778.
Gould/Goold, Francis Private	Jan 14, 1777	Second, Tew	Dec 1777 on command waggoner; Jan 1778 sick absent; Feb-March 1778 sick present; April 1778.
Gould, Frank Private	Jan 14, 1777 Duration of War	First, Arnold	May 1778; June 1778 on command.
Gould/Gold, John Corporal	Jan 4, 1777, Duration of War	First, Wallen	Dec 1777-April 1778.
Gould, John Corporal	Duration of War	Second, Olney, S.	May 1778 on guard; June 1778.
Grant, Richard Private		First, Flagg	Dec 1777; Jan 1778 on command; Feb-April 1778.
Grant, Richard Private		Second, Allen	May-June 1778.
Grant, Samuel Private	June 20, 1777, Three Years	Second, Olney, C.	Dec 1777; Jan-March 1778 on guard; April-June 1778.

Name	Date	Company	Notes
Graves, Thomas Private	Feb 30, 1777, Duration of War	Second, Potter	Dec 1777 on command; Jan 1778 on Gen. Varnum's guard; Feb 1778 on command; March-April 1778 on furlough; May 1, 1778 deserted.
Gray/Grey, Charles Private	May 7, 1777, Duration of War	Second, Tew	Dec 1777-Jan 1778; Feb 1778 on guard; March-June 1778.
Gray, Ebenezer Private	March 22, 1778, Duration of War	First, Dexter	June 1778.
Greene, Newport Private	Feb 8, 1778, Duration of War	First, Lewis	June 1778.
Greene/Grene, Cato R. Private	March 6, 1778, Duration of War	First, Flagg	June 1778
Greene, Cato W. Private	Feb 17, 1778, Duration of War	First, Flagg	June 1778.
Greene, Christopher Colonel	Jan 1, 1777	First	Dec 1777-March 1778 on command; April 1778 on command at Rhode Island; May-June 1778 on command.
Greene, Cuff Private	Feb 18, 1778, Duration of War	First, Cole	June 1778.
Greene, Daniel Ensign	March 11, 1777	First, Clarke	Nov 1, 1777 taken prisoner; Dec 1777-Jan 1778 prisoner with enemy.
Greene, Griffin Paymaster	July 18, 1777	First	Dec 1777; Jan-March 1778 on command; April 1778 on command at Rhode Island; May 1778 on command.
Greene, Jack Private	Feb 22, 1778, Duration of War	First, Cole	June 1778.
Greene, James Private	Jan 10, 1777, Duration of War	First, Wallen	Dec 1777-March 1778; April 1778 sick in camp.
Greene, James Private	Duration of War	First, Arnold	May-June 1778.
Greene, Jeremiah Private	Feb 22, 1778, Duration of War	First, Flagg	June 1778.
Greene, Oliver Private		First, Flagg	Dec 1777; Jan 22, 1778 died.
Greene, Peroe Private	Feb 22, 1778, Duration of War	First, Cole	June 1778.
Greene, Prince Private	March 23, 1778, Duration of War	First, Lewis	June 1778.
Greene/Green, Wardel/ Wardwell Sergeant	April 28, 1777, Three Years	First, Lewis	Dec 1777-Jan 1778 on furlough; Feb-April 1778; June 1778 muster roll shows he was discharged in May.

Name	Date	Company	Notes
Greene, William Private	March 1, 1778, Duration of War	First, Flagg	June 1778.
Greenman/Grinman, Jeremiah/Jere Sergeant	Feb 23, 1777, Three Years	Second, Shaw	Jan 1778 recruiting; Feb-June 1778.
Griffin/Griffen, Anthony Private	Duration of War	First, Arnold	May-June 1778.
Griffin/Griffen, Anthony Private	Feb 28, 1778	Second, Hughes	Feb 1778; March 1778 on guard; April 1778.
Gudgeon/Gudgen, Robert Private	Jan 1, 1777, Duration of War	Second, Shaw	Jan 1778 on General's guard; Feb-June 1778.
Gulley/Gully, Stephen Private	May 28, 1777, Duration of War	Second, Hughes	Dec 1777-March 1778; April 1778 sick absent; May 1778 sick absent in the country; June 1778 muster roll shows he deserted on May 21, 1778.
Hackmatt/Hickmit, Patrick Private	May 8, 1777, Duration of War	Second, Potter	Dec 1777-Jan 1778; Feb 1778 on guard; March 1778 on command; April 1778 sick present; May 1778; June 1778 sick at Princeton.
Hagley, John Private	May 5, 1777, Duration of War	Second, Olney, S.	Dec 1777; Jan-March 1778 on command; April-June 1778.
Hale/Haile, James Sergeant	March 7, 1777, Duration of War	Second, Potter	Dec 1777; Jan 1778 on furlough; Feb-March 1778 on command; April 1778 recruiting; May-June 1778.
Hall, Ephraim Private	April 5, 1777, Three Years	First, Lewis	Dec 1777; Jan 1778 on 7 days command; Feb-April 1778.
Hall, Ephraim Private	Three Years	Second, Olney, C.	May 1778; June 1778 absent with leave.
Hall, Joseph Private	Jan 1, 1777, Duration of War	First, Lewis	Dec 1777; Jan 1778 sick present; Feb-April 1778.
Hall, Joseph Private	Duration of War	Second, Olney, C.	May-June 1778.
Hall, London Private	June 10, 1778, Duration of War	First, Dexter	June 1778.
Hall, Nathaniel/Nathan Fife Major		First	Dec 1777; Jan-April 1778 on command; April 1778 on command at Rhode Island; May 1778; June 1778 sick absent.
Hammond, Prince Private	March 3, 1778, Duration of War	First, Cole	June 1778.

Name	Enlistment	Company	Remarks
Handley/ Hendley, Charles Private	Feb 28, 1778	Second, Hughes	Feb-April 1778.
Handley, Charles Private	Duration of War	First, Arnold	May-June 1778 sick at Yellow Springs.
Haney/Hany, James Private	March 29, 1778	First, Cole	March-April 1778.
Haney, James Private	Duration of War	Second, Potter	May 1778 on guard; June 1778.
Haney, John Private		First, Dexter	Dec 1777; Jan 1778 on 7 days command; Feb 1778 on fatigue; March 1778; April 1778 on command at Radnor.
Hany/Haney, John Private	Duration of War	Second, Shaw	May-June 1778.
Hardy, Jacob Private	Jan 1, 1777, Duration of War	First, Lewis	Dec 1777; Jan 1778 on 7 days command; Feb-April 1778.
Hardy, Jacob Private	Duration of War	Second, Olney, C.	May 1778; June 1778 left sick on his return from Col. Morgan.
Hardy/Hardey, Robert Private	Jan 27, 1777, Duration of War	Second, Hughes	Dec 1777; Jan-Feb 1778 on command; March-April 1778; May 1778 sick present; June 1778.
Hardy, William Corporal	Feb 17, 1777 Duration of War	First, Talbot	Dec 1777; Jan-Feb 1778 sick present; March-April 1778.
Hardy, William Corporal	Duration of War	Second Dexter	May 1778 on guard; June 1778.
Harrington, Theophilus Private	Three Years	First, Clarke	Dec 1777-Feb 1778 sick absent; April 1778 sick at Rhode Island.
Harris, Ceasor Private	March 18, 1778, Duration of War	First, Cole	June 1778.
Harris/Herris, Ishmael Private	March 16, 1777, Duration of War	Second, Potter	Dec 1777 on duty; Jan-March 1778 sick present; April 1778; May-June 1778 on guard.
Harris/Harries, Nathaniel Corporal	May 7, 1777, Duration of War	Second, Tew	Dec 1777; Jan 1778 on guard; Feb-June 1778.
Harris, Peter Private	March 18, 1778, Duration of War	First, Dexter	June 1778.
Harrison/ Harrenson, Robert Private	May 2, 1777 Three Years	Second, Dexter	Dec 1777-Feb 1778; March 1778 on command; April 1778 on command at the Gulph; May 1778; June 1778 sick Valley Forge.
Harry, Gideon Private	Duration of War	First, Arnold	May-June 1778.

Name	Enlisted	Company	Service
Harry/Harrey, Gideon Private	March 17, 1777, Duration of War	Second, Hughes	Dec 1777 on guard; Jan-March 1778 on command; April 1778 on guard.
Hart, Matthew Private	April 5, 1777, Three Years	First, Lewis	Dec 1777-April 1778.
Hart, Mathew Private		Second, Olney, C.	May 1778; June 1778 absent with leave.
Hart/Heart, Nicholas Private	Jan 1, 1777, Duration of War	First, Dexter	Dec 1777-Feb 1778; March 1778 on command; April 1778.
Hart, Nicholas Private	Duration of War	Second, Shaw	May-June 1778.
Hart, Robert Private	April 5, 1777, Three Years	First, Lewis	Dec 1777-Jan 1778 sick absent; Feb-March 1778; April 1, 1778 died.
Hathaway, Bennoni Private	March 18, 1778, Duration of War	First, Dexter	June 1778.
Hathaway, James Sergeant	Three Years	First, Clarke	Dec 1777-Jan 1778; Feb 1778 on command; March 1778 on guard; April 1778 on furlough Rhode Island.
Hawkins, Elijah Ensign	May 10, 1777	Second, Olney, S.	Dec 1777-Jan 1778; Feb 1778 on command; March 1778; April-May 1778 on furlough; June 1778.
Hawkins/ Hakens, Hazebiah/ Hesebah Private	May 7, 1777, Duration of War	Second, Olney, S.	Dec 1777; Jan 1778 on command; Feb 1778; March 1778 on command; April 1778 on command at Providence; May 1778 sick in camp; June 1778 sick at Yellow Springs.
Hawkins, Uriah Corporal	May 29, 1777, Three Years	Second, Olney, S.	Dec 1777-May 1778; June 1778 on guard.
Hay, William Private	Feb 17, 1777, Duration of War	First, Cole	Dec 1777; Jan-Feb 1778 on 7 days command; March 1778 on command; April 1778 on command at Schuylkill, oarsman.
Hay, William Private	Duration of War	Second, Potter	May 1778 under guard; June 1778 sick at Englishtown.
Hayes/Hase, James Private		Second, Allen	May-June 1778.
Hays, James Private		First, Flagg	Dec 1777 on guard; Jan 1778 on command; Feb 1778 on guard; March 1778 on command; April 1778 14 days command.
Hazard, Dick Private	March 23, 1778, Duration of War	First, Cole	June 1778.

Hazard/Hazzard, Henry Private		First, Arnold	May-June 1778.
Hazard, Jacob Private	March 2, 1778, Duration of War	First, Cole	June 1778.
Hazard, Peter Private	Feb 21, 1778 Duration of War	First, Cole	June 1778 absent with leave.
Hazard, Peter Private	Feb 21, 1778, Duration of War	First, Dexter	June 1778.
Hazard, Pharoe Private	March 1, 1778, Duration of War	First, Cole	June 1778.
Hazard, Stephen F. Private	April 7, 1777, Duration of War	First, Talbot	Dec 1777; Jan 1778 sick present; Feb 1778 sick absent; March-April 1778.
Hazzard, Baucus, Private	March 2, 1778, Duration of War	First, Lewis	June 1778.
Hazzard/Hazard, Henry Private	April 12, 1777, Three Years	Second, Potter	Dec 1777; Jan 1778 on command; Feb-March 1778 sick present; April 1778.
Hazzard/ Haszard, Jacob J. Private	March 2, 1778, Duration of War	First, Flagg	June 1778.
Hazzard/ Haszard, James Private		First, Flagg	March 16, 1778 joined, March 1778 under guard; April 1778 sick present.
Hazzard/Hazard, James Private	Duration of War	First, Arnold	May-June 1778 sick at Yellow Springs.
Hazzard, Pharo/Pharoah Private	March 1, 1777	First, Wallen	Dec 1777 sick in camp; Jan-Feb 1778; March 1778 on fatigue; April 1778.
Hazzard/Hazard, Pharo Private		First, Arnold	May-June 1778.
Hazzard/ Haszard, Sampson Private	March 4, 1778, Duration of War	First, Flagg	June 1778.
Hazzard, Stephen F. Sergeant	Duration of War	Second, Tew	May-June 1778.
Helmes/ Helme, Peleg Sergeant/ Private	May 11, 1777, Three Years	First, Lewis	Dec 1777 on duty; Jan 1778 on generals guard; Feb-March 1778; April 1778; April 19, 1778 reduced to Private.
Hellems/ Hellims, Peleck Private	Three Years	Second, Olney, C.	May 1778; June 1778 on guard.

Name	Date	Company	Service Record
Henley, Charles Private		First, Wallen	May 1778; June 1778 sick at Yellow Springs.
Herenden/ Herrington, Othniel Private	May 24, 1777, Three Years	Second, Olney, S.	Dec 1777; Jan 1778 on fatigue; Feb 1778 on guard; March 1778 on command; April-June 1778.
Herrenden/ Herrendon, Jonathan Private	March 7, 1777 Duration of War	Second, Allen	Dec 1777 sick in hospital; Jan-March 1778 sick absent; April 1, 1778 deserted.
Herrenden/ Harrenden, Thomas Private	Jan 24, 1777, Duration of War	Second, Dexter	Dec 1777; Jan 1778 on command; Feb 1778; March 1778 on command; April-June 1778.
Hervey/Harvey, Edward Private	April 4, 1777, Duration of War	Second, Potter	Dec 1777; Jan-April 1778 sick present; May 1778 sick absent Yellow Springs; June 1778 sick absent.
Hicks, Samuel 1st. Lt.	April 17, 1777	First, Arnold	Dec 1777-Jan 1778; Feb 21, 1778 discharged.
Hight, Jonathan Sergeant	May 7, 1777, Duration of War	Second, Tew	Dec 1777 sick absent; Jan 1778; Feb 1778 sick absent; March 1778 on command; April 1778 shoe making; May 1778 on furlough at Rhode Island; June 1778 on furlough.
Hill, Jonathan Private	April 9, 1777, Three Years	First, Arnold	Dec 1777-April 1778.
Hill, Jonathan Private	Three Years	Second, Tew	May 1778; June 1778 absent with leave.
Hines/Hinds, Pain Private	March 17, 1777, Duration of War	Second, Shaw	Dec 1777; Jan 1778 on command; Feb-June 1778.
Hines/Hinds, Richard Private	Jan 1, 1777, Duration of War	Second, Shaw	Jan 1778 sick absent; Feb-April 1778.
Hogan/Hogen, Dennis Sergeant	March 17, 1777, Duration of War	Second, Potter	Dec 1777-April 1778; May 1778 on guard; June 1778.
Holden, Charles Paymaster	Jan 7, 1777	Second	Dec 1777 on command; Jan-May 1778 on furlough.
Holden, John Adjutant	Jan 1, 1777	First	Dec 1777; Jan-March 1778 on command; April 1778 on command at Rhode Island; May 1778 on command; June 1778 on command acting B. M.

Holstein/ Holston, William Private	March 26, 1777, Three Years	First, Cole	Dec 1777 sick present; Jan-Feb 1778 on 7 days command; March 1778 on command; April 1778 on command at Schuylkill, oarsman.
Holston/Holsten, William Private	Duration of War	Second, Potter	May 1778 on command at camp hospital; June 1778.
Hopkins, Abraham Private	Jan 1, 17777, Duration of War	Second, Shaw	Jan 1778 on command; Feb-April 1778; May 1778 sick at Yellow Springs; June 30, 1778 deceased.
Hopkins, James Sergeant	March 1, 1777, Duration of War	Second, Shaw	Jan 1778 recruiting; Feb-April 1778; May 1778 on command; June 1778.
Hopkins, Richard Private	April 5, 1777, Three Years	First, Lewis	Dec 1777 on duty; Jan 1778 sick present; Feb-April 1778.
Hopkins, Richard Private	Three Years	Second, Olney, C.	May 1778 on guard; June 1778.
Hoswell/ Hoswill, Ephraim Private	May 7, 1777, Duration of War	Second, Allen	Dec 1777-Jan 1778; Feb 1778 guard; March-June 1778.
Howard, Nathan/ Nathaniel Private	May 21, 1777, Three Years	First, Arnold	Dec 1777; Jan-March 1778 on command; April 1778 command Baker.
Howard, Nathan Private	Three Years	Second, Tew	May 1778 baker on command; June 1778 sick at Princeton.
Howden/ Howdin, Alexander Private	Jan 1, 1777, Duration of War	First, Dexter	Dec 1777 on duty; Jan 1778 on 7 days command; Feb-March 1778 on command; April 1778 on command at Radnor.
Howden, Alexander/ Elaxander Private	Duration of War	Second, Shaw	May-June 1778.
Howland, Robin Private		First, Arnold	June 1778.
Hudson, Benoni Private	Jan 1, 1777, Duration of War	First, Dexter	Dec 1777-March 1778; April 1778 on fatigue.
Hudson/Hutson, Benoni Private	Duration of War	Second, Shaw	May 1778 sick present; June 1778.
Hudson, Daniel Fife Major	August 19, 1777 Duration of War	Second	Dec 1777-Jan 1778; Feb-May 1778 on furlough; June 1, 1778 deserted.
Hughes/Hughs, George Private	May 20, 1777, Duration of War	First, Talbot	Dec 1777-Feb 1778; March 1778 on command; April 1778 sick present.
Hughes, George Private		Second, Dexter	May-June 1778.

Name	Date	Company	Notes
Hughes, Thomas Captain	June 23, 1777	Second, Hughes	Dec 1777-Jan 1778; Feb 1778 on guard; March 1778; April 1778 on command; May-June 1778. Oath at Valley Forge on May 13, 1778.
Hull, Elias 1st. Lt.	Feb 11, 1777	First, Lewis	Dec 1777; Jan 1778 on command recruiting; Feb-March 1778; April 25, 1778 discharged.
Humphrey, William 1st. Lt.	Jan 1, 1777	Second, Olney, C./ Shaw	Dec 17, 1777 transferred to Silvanus Shaw's company; Jan 1778 recruiting; Feb-June 1778.
Hunt, Bennoni/Benoni Private	March 2, 1777, Duration of War	First, Talbot	Dec 1777 sick absent; Jan 1778 sick present; Feb-April 1778.
Hunt, Benoni Private	Duration of War	Second, Dexter	May-June 1778.
Hussey, John Private		First, Flagg	Dec 1777; Jan 1778 on command; Feb 1778; March 1778 under guard; April 1778.
Hussey, John Private		Second, Allen	May-June 1778.
Ingraham, Prince Private	Feb 2, 1778, Duration of War	First, Flagg	June 1778.
Ingraham, William Private	Three Years	First, Clarke	Dec 1777-April 1778.
Ingraham, William Private		Second, Hughes	May 1778; June 1778 absent with leave.
Inman/Inmon, Elisha Private	April 4, 1777, Duration of War	Second, Dexter	Dec 1777-Feb 1778; March 1778 sick present; April 1778 sick present in hospital; May 1778 sick Yellow Springs; June 1, 1778 died.
Inman, Stukley Private	March 8, 1777, Duration of War	Second, Olney, S.	Dec 27, 1777, transferred to General Huntington's Brigade.
Isaacks/Isaac, Abraham Private	June 27, 1777	First, Wallen	Dec 1777-Jan 1778; Feb 1778 on command; March-April 1778.
Isaacks, Abraham Private		First, Arnold	May 19, 1778 died.
Jackson, Benjamin Private	Feb 8, 1777, Duration of War	Second, Olney, C.	Dec 1777; Jan-March 1778 on command; April-May 1778 on guard; June 1778.
Jackson, Prince Private		First, Arnold	May 1778; June 11, 1778 deceased.
Jackson, Prince Private	Feb 7, 1777, Duration of War	Second, Olney, C.	Dec 1777-March 1778; April 1778 on command at Radnor.

137

Name	Enlisted	Company	Remarks
Jacobs, Jonathan Private	Feb 7, 1777, Duration of War	Second, Olney, C.	Dec 1777-Feb 1778; March 1778 sick in camp; April 1778 sick in Brigade Hospital; May 1778; June 1778 sick absent.
Jelly/Jelley, William Private	Feb 18, 1777, Duration of War	First, Talbot	Dec 1777-Jan 1778; Feb 1778 sick present; March 20, 1778 died.
Jenckes/Jinckes, Anthony Private	May 24, 1777, Three Years	Second, Olney, C.	Dec 1777-Jan 1778; Feb-March 1778 on command; April 1778 on command at sawmills; May 1778; June 1778 absent with leave.
Jenckes/Jincks, Oliver 1st. Lt.	June 25, 1777	Second Shaw	Jan 1778 recruiting; Feb-June 1778. Oath at Valley Forge on May 24, 1778.
Jenckins/Jenkins, Benjamin Private		Second, Shaw	May-June 1778.
Jenckes/Jencks, Ichabod Private		First, Flagg	Dec 1777; Jan-Feb 1778 on fatigue; March 1778; April 1778 sick present.
Jencks/Jincks, Primus Private	Feb 21, 1778, Duration of War	First, Cole	June 1778.
Jencks, Prince Private	Feb 28, 1778, Duration of War	First, Cole	June 1778 on guard.
Jenkins, Benjamin Private	Feb 7, 1777, Duration of War	First, Dexter	Dec 1777-April 1778.
Jenks/Jencks, Ichabud Private		Second, Allen	May-June 1778.
Jennings/Jennins, Simeon 2nd. Lt.	June 24, 1777	Second, Dexter	Dec 1777 sick absent; Jan-Feb 1778 on command; March 1778; April 21, 1778 died.
Jerauld/Jarauld, Dutee 1st. Lt.	Jan 1, 1777	Second, Potter	Dec 1777; Jan 1778 on command recruiting; Feb-March 1778 on command; April-June 1778.
Johnson/Johnston, Asa Private	Duration of War	Second, Olney, S.	March 6, 1778 "Join'd with a Certificate to draw pay from 1 Jan^y."; March 1778 on command; April 1778 on His Excellency's guard; May 1778 transferred to His Excellency's guard.
Johnson/Johnston, Benjamin Private	March 18, 1777, Duration of War	First, Wallen	Dec 1777-March 1778 on command; April 1778.
Johnson, Benjamin Private	Duration of War	Second, Olney, S.	May 1778; June 1778 sick absent.

Name	Date	Company	Remarks
Johnson, Peleg Private	March 20, 1777, Duration of War	Second, Tew	Dec 1777; Jan 1778 on command; Feb 1778; March 1778 on command; April-May 1778; June 1778 New Providence.
Johnson/Jonson, Ruben Sergeant	March 6, 1777, Duration of War	Second, Olney, C.	Dec 1777; Jan-March 1778 on command; April 1778 on command Providence; May 1, 1778 discharged.
Johnson/Johnston, Stephen Corporal	Jan 6, 1777, Duration of War	Second, Olney, C.	Dec 1777-Feb 1778; March 1778 on command; April-June 1778.
Johnston/Johnson, David 2nd. Lt.	Feb 10, 1777	First, Lewis	Dec 1777-April 1778.
Johnston, David, 2nd. Lt.	Feb 10, 1777	First, Arnold	May-June 1778. Oath at Valley Forge on May 14, 1778.
Jones, Enoch Sergeant	May 17, 1777	First, Talbot	Dec 1777-March 1778 on command; April 1778 on duty.
Jones, Enock Sergeant	Three Years	Second, Olney, C.	May 1778; June 1778 absent with leave.
Jones, John Fifer/Private	April 5, 1777, Three Years	First, Lewis	Dec 1777; Jan 1778 on guard; Jan 12, 1778 reduced to Private; Feb-April 1778.
Jones, John Private	Three Years	Second, Olney, C.	May-June 1778.
Jones, Uriah Private	March 11, 1777, Duration of War	Second, Dexter	Dec 1777-Jan 1778; Feb-March 1778 on command; April-June 1778.
Jordan/Jorden, Samuel Private	May 21, 1777, Three Years	First, Arnold	Dec 1777-April 1778.
Jordan, Samuel Private	Three Years	Second, Tew	May-June 1778.
Justice/Justis, Phillip Corporal	Jan 7, 1777, Duration of War	Second, Tew	Dec 1777-June 1778.
Keaton see Caton			
Keney/Keeny, Samuel Private	Jan 1, 1777, Duration of War	First, Lewis	Dec 1777 on command; Jan 1778 on command Peekskill; Feb-April 1778.
Keriker/Kerker Frederick Private	Jan 30, 1777, Duration of War	Second, Allen	Dec 1777 sick in hospital; Feb 1, 1778 died.
King, Benjamin Private	March 12, 1777, Duration of War	Second, Allen	Dec 1777-March 1778; April 1778 on furlough Rhode Island; May 1778 on furlough; June 1778.

Name	Enlistment	Company	Remarks
King, Daniel Private	Three Years	First, Clarke	Dec 1777-Feb 1778 sick absent; March 1778 sick in hospital; April 20, 1778 died.
King, James Private	Jan 30, 1777, Duration of War	Second, Olney, S.	Dec 1777; Jan 1778 on command; Feb-April 1778; May 1778 sick in camp; June 1778.
Kinne/Kinne, Samuel Private	Duration of War	Second, Olney, C.	May 1778 on guard; June 1778 absent with leave.
Kinyon, Joseph Sergeant	March 5, 1777, Duration of War	Second, Hughes	Dec 1777-Feb 1778 sick absent; March-May 1778; June 28, 1778 killed.
Kipp, William Sergeant	Feb 15, 1777, Duration of War	First, Cole	Dec 1777-March 1778; April 1778 sick present.
Kipp, William Sergeant	Duration of War	First, Arnold	May 1778; June 1778 sick Valley Forge.
Knight/Night, David Private	May 10, 1777, Three Years	Second, Olney, C.	Dec 1777-Feb 1778; March 1778 on command; April-June 1778.
Ladd, Joseph Private		First, Flagg	Dec 1777; Jan 14, 1778 died.
Lane, William Private	Jan 1, 1777, Duration of War	First, Lewis	Dec 1777; Jan 1778 on command in Rowboats; Feb-March 1778; April 1, 1778 deserted.
Langworthy/ Lanworthy, Southcot Private	Jan [ ], 1777 Duration of War	Second, Olney, S.	Dec 1777-March 1778 on command; April-June 1778.
Larkin/Larkins, Covil/Covel Corporal/Private	April 2, 1777, Duration of War	Second, Potter	Dec 1777-Jan 1778; Jan 7, 1778 reduced to Private; Feb-March 1778 sick present; April-June 1778.
Law, John Private	March 10, 1777, Duration of War	First, Wallen	Dec 1777-Jan 1778 sick absent; Feb-April 1778.
Law, John Private	Duration of War	Second, Olney, S.	May 1778 on guard; June 1778.
Lawrence, Daniel Ensign	June 12, 1777	Second, Olney, C.	Dec 1777; Jan-Feb 1778 on command recruiting; March-April 1778 on command; May 1778 absent without leave.
Lawrence, John Corporal/Private	Dec 26, 1776, Duration of War	Second, Allen	Dec 1777; Jan-Feb 1778 sick absent; March-May 1778; June 9, 1778 reduced to Private; June 1778 sick absent.
Leach, Jabez Private	June 22, 1777, Duration of War	Second, Dexter	Dec 1777-Feb 1778 sick absent; March 1778 dead.
Leavet, Peter Private	Feb 18, 1778, Duration of War	First, Lewis	June 1778.

Name	Enlistment	Company	Notes
Lefavour, Thomas, Private	Feb 20, 1778, Duration of War	First, Lewis	June 1778 on command.
Leroach, Benjamin, Private	March 10, 1777, Duration of War	Second, Olney, C.	Dec 1777-June 1778.
Leveck, Joseph, Private	Jan 26, 1777, Duration of War	Second, Olney, C.	Dec 1777-March 1778 on command.
Lewis, Asa, Sergeant	April 10, 1777, Duration of War	First, Arnold	Dec 1777 sick in hospital; Jan-June 1778.
Lewis, Elijah, Captain	Jan 1, 1777	First, Lewis	Dec 1777; Jan 1778 on command recruiting; Feb-April 1778; June 1778.
Lewis, Obadiah, Private		First, Flagg	Dec 1777 on guard; Jan 1778 on command; March 1778 in hospital; April 1, 1778 died.
Limbrook/Limbrok, Christopher, Private/Drummer	June 6, 1777, Duration of War	Second, Dexter	Dec 1777-Jan 1778; Feb 1, 1778 promoted to Drummer; Feb-June 1778.
Limus, Prince, Private	March 16, 1778, Duration of War	First, Cole	June 1778.
Lippett, Prince, Private	May 16, 1777, Duration of War	Second, Shaw	Jan-April 1778.
Little, Clarke, Private	March 25, 1777, Duration of War	First, Cole	Dec 1777-April 1778.
Little/Littel, Clark, Private	Duration of War	Second, Potter	May 1778; June 1778 absent with leave.
Littlefield, William, 2nd. Lt.	Jan 1, 1777	Second, Hughes	Feb 1778 on guard; March-April 1778 on command; May 1778 on command Rhode Island by order of General Greene; June 1778 absent with leave.
Lobb/Lob, James, Private	Jan 2, 1777, Duration of War	Second, Dexter	Dec 1777; Jan-March 1778 on command; April-May 1778; June 1778 absent with leave.
Loring, Samuel, Private	Three Years	Second, Tew	May 1778; June 1778 on guard.
Love, Alexander, Drummer	April 10, 1777, Duration of War	First, Arnold	Dec 1777-June 1778.
Lovet, Peter, Private		First, Lewis	June 1778.
Low, Charles, Private	April 5, 1777, Three Years	First, Lewis	Dec 1777; Jan 1778 on 7 days command; Feb-April 1778.
Low, Charles, Private	Three Years	Second, Olney, C.	May 1778 on guard; June 1778.

Name	Enlisted	Company	Service Record
Lowen/Loring, William Private	May 19, 1777, Three Years	Second, Dexter	Dec 1777 on command; Jan 1778; Feb 1778 on fatigue; March 1778 on command; April 1778 sick in camp; May 1778; June 1778 on command Valley Forge.
Lowrey/Lawrey, James Private	Jan 6, 1777, Duration of War	Second, Tew	Dec 1777 on command a waggoner; Jan 7, 1778 discharged.
Lowring/Loring, Samuel Private	April 30, 1777, Three Years	First, Arnold	Dec 1777; Jan-Feb 1778 on command; March 1778; April 1778 duty Radnor.
Luther/Luthar, John Private	May 2, 1777, Three Years	Second, Allen	Dec 1777 sick present; Jan 9, 1778 died.
Macomber, Ebenezer 1st. Lt.	Feb 17, 1777	Second, Tew	Dec 1777-March 1778; April-May 1778 on furlough Rhode Island; June 1778.
Macomber, John Sergeant	Dec 18, 1776, Three Years	Second, Tew	Dec 1777-Feb 1778; March 1778 on guard; April-June 1778.
Macomber, Reuben Private	Jan 13, 1777, Duration of War	Second, Tew	Dec 1777; Jan 1778 on command; Feb 1778 on fatigue; March-April 1778; May 1778 on guard; June 1778 absent with leave.
Manchester/ Manchister, John Private	May 9, 1777, Three Years	Second, Potter	Dec 1777 sick present; Jan-April 1778 on furlough.
Manchester, Joseph Private	May 17, 1777	First, Talbot	Dec 1777; Jan 1778 on command; Feb 1778; March 1778 on duty; April 1778.
Manchester, Joseph Private	Three Years	Second, Dexter	May 1778 on detachment; June 1778.
Manning, Joseph Private	May 12, 1777, Duration of War	Second, Allen	Dec 1777-March 1778 on command; April 1778 on command with the commissary; May 1778 transferred to the Commissary Department.
Martin/Marten, John Private	Dec 25, 1776, Duration of War	Second, Olney, C.	Dec 1777-March 1778 sick absent.
Mason, Warren Private	April 29, 1778, Duration of War	First, Cole	June 1778.
Masury/ Massury, Joseph Sergeant	Jan 28, 1777, Duration of War	Second, Allen	Dec 1777-May 1778; June 1778 absent leave.
Mathews, Joseph Private		Second, Shaw	May 1778 sick present; June 1778.

Name	Enlistment	Company	Remarks
Mathews, Joseph Jr. Private	Duration of War	Second, Shaw	May 1778 sick present; June 1778.
Matthews/Mathews, Joseph Private	Jan 1, 1777, Three Years	First, Dexter	Dec 1777-Jan 1778; Feb 1778 on guard; March 1778 on fatigue; April 1778 sick in camp.
Matthews/Mathews, Joseph Jr. Private	Jan 1, 1777, Duration of War	First, Dexter	Dec 1777; Jan 1778 on duty; Feb 1778 on guard; March 1778 on command; April 1778.
Matthewson/Mathewson, Joseph Private	May 26, 1777, Three Years	First, Lewis	Dec 1777-April 1778.
Mattison, Joseph Private	Three Years	Second, Olney, C.	May-June 1778.
Mauney, Silas/Sias Private	March 9, 1778, Duration of War	First, Dexter	June 1778.
Maxfield, Daniel Private	April 3, 1777, Three Years	First, Arnold	Dec 1777; Jan 1778 on command; Feb-March 1778; April 1778 sick present.
Maxfield, Daniel Private	Three Years	Second, Tew	May-June 1778 sick at Yellow Springs.
McAfferty, Charles Private	Jan 15, 1777, Duration of War	First, Wallen	Dec 1777; Jan 1778 sick present; Feb-March 1778 sick in camp; April 1778.
McAfferty, Charles Private	Duration of War	Second, Olney, S.	May 1778; June 1778 on guard.
McAllen, William Corporal	Jan 19, 1777, Duration of War	Second, Shaw	Jan-June 1778.
McCoy, William Quartermaster Sergeant		First	Dec 1777; Jan-April 1778 on command; May-June 1778.
McDarmit/McDermitt, Barnabas Corporal	May 9, 1777, Duration of War	Second, Potter	Dec 1777-March 1778; April 1778 on command, May 1778; June 1778 on command.
McDougall/McDougal, Hugh Private	April 5, 1777, Duration of War	Second, Shaw	Jan 1778 sick in quarters; Feb-April 1778; May 1778 at Yellow Springs; June 1778 sick absent.
McIntiar, Samuel Private	June 15, 1777, Three Years	Second, Olney, C.	Dec 23, 1777 deserted.
McLagin/McLaggin, Charles, Private	May 7, 1777, Duration of War	Second, Tew	Dec 1777-March 1778 on command; April 1, 1778 deserted.

Name	Enlistment	Company	Service Notes
Meigs, George Private	Duration of War	Second, Dexter	May 1778.
Meligan/Milligan, Micajah Private	Feb 28, 1777, Duration of War	First, Allen	Dec 1777-Jan 1778; Feb 1778 on guard; March 18, 1778 dead.
Mercey/Marcy, Jacques Private	March 28, 1777, Duration of War	Second, Shaw	Jan 1778 on command; Feb-April 1778; May 1778 sick at Dunkers Town; June 1778 sick absent.
Merethew/Merithew, Samuel Corporal	Feb 22, 1777, Three Years	First, Cole	Dec 1777-April 1778.
Merithew, Samuel Corporal	Three Years	Second, Potter	May 1778; June 1778 sick absent.
Millard, Elias Private	Three Years	First, Clarke	Dec 30, 1777 died.
Millard/Millerd, William Sergeant	Feb 12, 1777, Duration of War	First, Cole	Dec 1777-Feb 1778 sick absent; March-April 1778.
Milleman/Millimon, George Private	April 10, 1777, Three Years	First, Arnold	Dec 1777-Jan 1778; Feb 1778 on duty; March-April 1778.
Miller/Millar, Daniel Private	Dec 11, 1776, Duration of War	Second, Dexter	Dec 1777; Jan 1778 on command; Feb-March 1778; April 1778 sick in camp; May-June 1778.
Miller, William Sergeant	Duration of War	Second, Potter	May 1778; June 1778 on command.
Millet, Zebulon Private	Jan 20, 1777, Three Years	First, Cole	Dec 1777-Feb 1778 on generals guard; March 1778 on command; April 1778 on guard.
Millet/Millit, Zebulon Private	Three Years	Second, Potter	May 1778 on guard; June 1778 absent with leave.
Milliman/Millerman, George Private	Three Years	Second, Tew	May 1778; June 1778 sick at hospital.
Minthon, Jack Private	March 2, 1778, Duration of War	First, Dexter	June 1778.
Mitchell, James Private	Feb 2, 1777, Three Years	Second, Shaw	Jan 1778 sick in quarters; Feb-June 1778; July 15, 1778 died.
Mitchell/Michel, Thomas Fifer	May 22, 1777, Three Years	Second, Dexter	Dec 1777-April 1778; May-June 1778 sick at Yellow Springs.
Monks/Moncks, Daniel Private	April 4, 1777, Duration of War	First, Wallen	Dec 1777 sick in camp; Jan 1778 sick present; Feb 1778 sick in camp; March-April 1778.
Moncks Daniel Private	Duration of War	Second, Olney, S.	May-June 1778.

Name	Enlistment	Company	Service Record
Moore/Moor, Christopher Private	Jan 1, 1777, Duration of War	Second, Shaw	Jan-June 1778.
Morse/Morss, James Private/Corporal	May 21, 1777, Three Years	First, Arnold	Dec 1777; Jan 1778 promoted to Corporal; Jan-April 1778; May 1778 on Commissaries guard; June 1778.
Mowrey/Mowry, Cain Private	Jan 27, 1777, Duration of War	Second, Olney, S.	Dec 1777 on command; Jan-Feb 1778 on Generals guard; March 1778 on General Varnum's guard; April 1778 on command at the lines; March 1778; June 1778 on guard.
Mowry, Pero Private	March 7, 1778, Duration of War	First, Flagg	June 1778.
Mumford, Ebenezer Private	Feb 20, 1778, Duration of War	First, Cole	June 1778.
Nason, James Sergeant Major		First	Dec 1777; Jan-April 1778 on command; May-June 1778.
Nice, Magnus Private	Jan 13, 17777, Duration of War	Second, Tew	Dec 1777-Jan 1778; Feb-March 1778 on command; April 1778; May 1778 sick in camp; June 1778 on guard.
Nichols, Thomas Private	March 10, 1778, Duration of War	First, Cole	June 1778.
Nichols, William Private	May 24, 1777, Three Years	First, Arnold	Dec 1777 on command; Jan 1778 leave of absence; Feb 1778 sick present; March 1778 sick absent; April 1778.
Nichols, William Private	Three Years	Second, Tew	May-June 1778.
Niles, George Private	March 15, 1777, Duration of War	Second, Potter	Dec 1777; Jan 1778 sick present; Feb 1778; March 1778 tending the sick; April 30, 1778 died.
Niles, Simeon Private	March 1, 1777, Duration of War	Second, Hughes	Dec 31, 1777 died.
Nocake, Joseph Private	March 16, 1777, Duration of War	Second, Hughes	Dec 1777-April 1778 sick absent.
Nocake, Joseph Private	Duration of War	First, Arnold	May 1778 sick at Reading; June 1778 sick at Princeton.
Nokeheg/ Nokekig, Robert Private	Three Years	First, Clarke	Dec 1777-Jan 1778; Feb 4, 1778 died.
Northup, Ichabod Private	March 1, 1778, Duration of War	First, Lewis	June 1778.
Northup, James Fifer	March 2, 1778	First, Lewis	June 1778.

Name	Enlistment	Company	Service Record
Novander, Hans Private	Duration of War	Second, Olney, S.	Dec 1777-Feb 1778 sick absent; March 1778; April 1778 on command at the Lines; May 1778 on guard; June 1778.
Noyce, Nathaniel Sergeant	May 13, 1777, Duration of War	First, Dexter	Dec 1777; Jan-March 1778 on command; April 1778 on command recruiting at Rhode Island.
Noyce, Timothy Private	Jan 1, 1777, Three Years	First, Dexter	Dec 1777-Jan 1778 sick absent; Feb roll shows he died on January 24, 1778.
Noyes, Nathanial Sergeant		First, Lewis	June 1778.
Oakman/ Oachman, Samuel Private	Jan 1, 1777, Duration of War	Second, Shaw	Jan 1778 on command; Feb-June 1778.
O'Briant, William Private	March 1, 1777, Duration of War	Second, Tew	Dec 1777-Feb 1778; March-April 1778 sick present; May-June 1778.
Ogg, James Private	May 5, 1777, Duration of War	Second, Olney, C.	Dec 1777-Feb 1778; March 1778 on furlough; April-June 1778.
Okey, John Private	Jan 10, 1777, Duration of War	Second, Tew	Dec 1777-March 1778 sick absent; April 1778 transferred to the Invalid Corps.
Olney, Coggeshall Captain	Jan 1, 1777	Second, Olney, C.	Dec 1777-March 1778; April 1778 on furlough; May-June 1778 on furlough at Providence.
Olney, Jermiah Lt. Col.	Jan 13, 1777	Second	Dec 1777; Jan-March 1778 on command; April-June 1778. Oath at Valley Forge on May 13, 1778.
Olney, Stephen Captain	Feb 11, 1777	Second, Olney, S.	Dec 1777-March 1778; April-May 1778 on furlough; June 1778.
Ormsbe/Ormsbie, Thomas Private	Three Years	Second, Tew	May-June 1778 sick at Yellow Springs; July 1, 1778 died.
Ormsby/Ormby, Thomas Private	April 9, 1777, Three Years	First, Arnold	Dec 1777; Jan 1778 on command; Feb 1778; March 1778 on command; April 1778.
Owen, Richard Private	May 7, 1777, Duration of War	Second, Dexter	Dec 1777 on command.
Pain/Paine, Edward Corporal	Duration of War	Second, Hughes	Dec 1777-Feb 1778; March-April 1778 sick present; May-June 1778.
Paine/Pain, Joseph Private	Feb 20, 1777, Duration of War	Second, Allen	Dec 1777; Jan 1778 on guard; Feb-June 1778.

Name	Enlistment	Company	Service Record
Pallaseure/ Paluseor, James Surgeon's Mate	April 1, 1777	First	Dec 1777; January muster roll shows he was discharged on Feb 1, 1778.
Palmer/Parmer, Allen Private	April 20, 1777, Three Years	First, Cole	Dec 1777-Feb 1778 sick absent; March 1778 sick in hospital; April 1778 sick absent in Rhode Island.
Palmer, Job Corporal/ Private	Jan 1, 1777, Duration of War	Second, Allen	Dec 1777-May 1778; June 9, 1778 reduced to Private; June 1778.
Parker, Robert Private	Jan 6, 1777, Duration of War	Second, Dexter	Dec 1777-March 1778 sick absent; April 1778 sick at Lidice; May-June 1778.
Parker, William Sergeant	Three Years	First, Clarke	Dec 1777; Jan-March 1778 on command; April 1778 on command at Rhode Island.
Parker, William, Sr. Private	Jan 27, 1777, Duration of War	Second, Tew	Dec 1777 on command; Jan-Feb 1778 sick present; March 1778 on command; April 1778 sick present; May 1778 sick in camp; June 1778 tender at Hospital.
Parker, William, Jr. Private	May 10, 1777, Three Years	Second, Tew	Dec 1777; Jan 1778 on command; Feb-June 1778.
Parkes, William Sergeant	May 1, 1778, Three Years	First, Flagg	June 1778.
Parmer, Allen Private	Three Years	Second, Potter	May 1778 sick absent at Rhode Island; June 1778 sick at Rhode Island.
Parrish/Parish, John Surgeon's Mate	Aug 27, 1777	Second/ First	Dec 1777-March 1778; March 31, 1778 transferred to Col. Greene's Regiment; April 1778 on command at Rhode Island; May-June 1778.
Patrick/Partrick, James Private	Jan 12, 1777, Three Years	First, Cole	Dec 1777; Jan 1778 on fatigue; Feb 1778 on 4 days command; March 1778; April 1778 on guard.
Patrick, James Private	Three Years	Second, Potter	May 1778 sick present; June 1778.
Patterson/ Paterson, John Private	Jan 11, 1777, Duration of War	Second, Shaw	Jan 1778 on command; Feb-April 1778; May 1778 on command at Peekskill; June 1778.
Pearce/Peirce, Abraham Private	April 15, 1777, Three Years	First, Arnold	Dec 1777; Jan-March 1778 on command; April-March 1778; June 1778 sick Yellow Springs.

Name	Enlistment	Company	Service Record
Pearce/Pierce, David Private		Second, Allen	May-June 1778.
Pearce/Peirce, Ezekiel Private	May 15, 1777	First, Talbot	Dec 1777-March 1778; April 1778 duty picket.
Pearce/Perce, Ezekiel Private	Three Years	Second, Dexter	May-June 1778.
Pearce/Peirce, John 2nd. Lt.	Feb 17, 1777	First, Talbot	Dec 1777; Jan-March 1778 on command; April 1778 command Rhode Island.
Pearce, John 2nd. Lt.		First, Dexter	June 1778 on furlough.
Pearce/Pierce, John Private	May 10, 1777, Three Years	Second, Allen	Dec 1777 sick in hospital; Jan-March 1778 sick absent; April 1778 sick at Rhode Island; May-June 1778 on furlough.
Pearce/Peirce, Jonathan Private	May 24, 1777, Three Years	First, Arnold	Dec 1777 sick in hospital; Jan-Feb 1778 sick absent; March 1778 on duty; April 1778.
Pearce/Pearse, Jonathan Private	Three Years	Second, Tew	May 1778 sick in camp; June 1778 absent with leave.
Pearce, Richard Private		First, Wallen	April 1778 muster roll shows he was taken prisoner on December 7, 1776; April payroll shows he was taken prisoner on Jan 1, 1777; April 12, 1778 joined; April 1778.
Pearce, Richard Private		Second, Olney, S.	May-June 1778.
Peck, Gius/Gaius Private	Feb 24, 1777, Duration of War	Second, Olney, C.	Dec 1777-March 1778; April-May 1778 on command at Providence; June 1778 on furlough with Col. Angell.
Peck, Ichobod/Ickbod Private	May 16, 1777, Three Years	Second, Dexter	Dec 1777 sick absent; Jan 30, 1778 dead.
Peckham, Benjamin L. Ensign	Feb 11, 1777	Second, Hughes	Dec 1777; Jan-March 1778 acting as Quartermaster; April-May 1778 on furlough; June 1778.
Peckham, Cuff Private	March 15, 1777, Duration of War	Second, Hughes	Feb 1778 on guard; March 1778 on command; April 1778 sick present.
Peckham/Peckum, Cuff Private	Duration of War	First, Arnold	May-June 1778.

Name	Enlisted	Company	Notes
Penagar/Penigan, Edmond, Private	Feb 28, 1777, Duration of War	Second, Allen	May 1778 sick present; June 1778 sick absent.
Pendell/Pendall, Thomas Corporal	June 12, 1777, Duration of War	Second, Dexter	Dec 1777; Jan-March 1778 on furlough; April 30, 1778 deserted.
Perkins, Francis Private	April 11, 1777, Three Years	First, Arnold	Dec 1777-March 1778 sick absent; April 8, 1778 deserted.
Perkins, Moses Private	March 2, 1777, Duration of War	Second, Hughes	Dec 1777 on duty; Jan-Feb 1778; March 1778 on command; April 1778 on guard; May-June 1778.
Perkins/Parkins, William Private	Jan 13, 1777, Duration of War	Second, Tew	Dec 1777-March 1778; April 1778 on command at Radnor; May-June 1778.
Perry, Ganset Private	March 15, 1778, Duration of War	First, Arnold	June 1778.
Perry, John Private		First, Flagg	Dec 1777 on guard; Jan 1778 on command; Feb-March 1778 sick present; April 8, 1778 died.
Phillips, Daniel Private	April 8, 1777, Three Years	Second, Allen	Dec 1777 waggoner; Jan 7, 1778 discharged.
Phillips, James Private	Jan 12, 1777, Duration of War	First, Cole	Dec 1777; Jan 1778 sick present; Feb 1778; March 1778 on guard; April 1778 on command at Artificers.
Phillips, James Private	Duration of War	Second, Potter	May 1778 sick at Yellow Springs; June 1778 sick on the road.
Phillips, John Private	May 15, 1777, Three Years	Second, Olney, S	Dec 1777 on fatigue; Jan 1778 on duty; Feb 1778 on guard; March 1778 on command; April 1778 on command with Gen. Sullivan's baggage; May 1778 on command Rhode Island; June 1778 on command.
Phillips, Stephen Private	Feb 26, 1777, Duration of War	Second, Allen	Dec 1777-May 1778; June 1778 absent with leave.
Phillips, Toney Private	May 20, 1778, Duration of War	First, Flagg	June 1778.
Phillips, William Drummer	Three Years	First, Clarke	Dec 1777 sick absent; Jan 1778 sick present; Feb-March 1778; April 1778 sick present.
Phillips, William Drummer	Duration of War	Second, Hughes	May 13, 1778 died.
Phillops, Philo Private	March 15, 1778, Duration of War	First, Lewis	June 1778.

Name	Date	Company	Notes
Pierce, Charles Ensign	Feb 11, 1777	First, Dexter	Dec 1777; Jan 1778 on command recruiting; Feb-March 1778 on command; April 1778 recruiting at Rhode Island.
Pierce, Charles Ensign		First, Flagg	June 1778 absent by leave.
Pierce, Daniel 1st. Lt.	Feb 11, 1777	First, Clarke	Dec 1777; Jan-April 1778 on command; June 1778.
Pierce, Daniel/ David Private		First, Flagg	Dec 1777-Feb 1778 on command; March 1778 sick present; April 1778 on guard. On the March and April rolls he appears as David.
Pierce, Titus Private	Feb 26, 1778, Duration of War	First, Flagg	June 1778.
Pillar/Piller, John Private	Jan 13, 1777, Duration of War	First, Wallen	Dec 1777; Jan-March 1778 on command; April 1778.
Pillar/Piller, John Private		Second, Olney, S.	May-June 1778.
Piper, Robert Private	Jan 13, 1777, Duration of War	Second, Dexter	Dec 1777; Jan-March 1778 on command; April-May 1778; June 1778 absent with leave.
Pisquish, Henery Private	May 24, 1777	First, Wallen	Dec 1777; Jan 3, 1778 died.
Pollard/Pollert, Abiather/Abithar Private	Jan 1, 1777, Three Years	Second, Olney, C.	Dec 1777; Jan 1778 on command; Feb 1778 on guard; March 1778 on command; April 1778 on command up Schuylkill in boats; May 1778 on command at the lines; June 1778 sick at Brunswick.
Pollard, James Private	May 10, 1777, Duration of War	Second, Olney, S.	Dec 1777; Jan 1778 on command; Feb 1778 on guard; March-June 1778.
Polluck/Polock, Asher Private	April 16, 1777, Duration of War	Second, Allen	Dec 1777 tender in hospital; Jan-March 1778 on command; April 1778 on command at hospital; May on command at Yellow Springs; June 1778 tender to sick.
Pomp, Jakes Private		First, Arnold	May 1778 on commissaries guard; June 1778.
Pomp, Jehu Private	Three Years	First, Clarke	Dec 1777-Jan 1778; Feb 1778 on command; March 1778 sick present; April 1778 tending sick present.
Pomp, Richard Private	March 12, 1777, Duration of War	Second, Hughes	Dec 1777-Jan 1778; Feb 1778 sick present; March 1778; April 1778 sick present.

Name	Enlistment	Company	Service
Pomp, Richard Private	Duration of War	First, Arnold	May 13, 1778 deceased.
Popple, George Sergeant	April 1, 1777, Three Years	First, Dexter	Dec 1777-Jan 1778 wounded absent; Feb-March 1778 sick absent; April 1778.
Popple, George Sergeant	Three Years	Second, Shaw	May-June 1778.
Potter, David Private	May 7, 1778, Duration of War	First, Lewis	June 1778.
Potter, George Private	March 18, 1777, Three Years	First, Lewis	Dec 1777; Jan 1778 sick present; Feb-April 1778; June 1778.
Pottar, Gorg/ George Private	Three Years	Second, Olney, C.	May 1778 on command tending the sick; June 1778 attending the sick at Yellow Springs.
Potter/Pottar, John Private	Feb 1, 1777	First, Wallen	Dec 1777 sick absent; Jan 1778; Feb-March 1778 sick in camp; April 1778.
Potter, John Private		Second, Olney, S.	May 1778 sick in camp; June 1778 sick absent.
Potter/Pottar, Richard Private	May 2, 1777	First, Wallen	Dec 1777-Jan 1778; Feb 1778 on command; March 1778 on fatigue; April 1778.
Potter, Richard Private		First, Arnold	May 1778 sick in camp; June 1778 sick Valley Forge.
Potter, William Private	May 10, 1777, Duration of War	First, Talbot	Dec 1777; Jan-Feb 1778 sick present; March 1778 on duty; April 1778.
Potter, William Captain	Feb 11, 1777	Second Potter	Dec 1777; Jan 1778 on command recruiting; Feb-March 1778 on command; April 1778 recruiting; May 1778 recruiting at Rhode Island; June 1778.
Potter, William Private	Duration of War	Second, Dexter	May 1778 on guard; June 1778 absent with leave.
Powell, William Private	Duration of War	Second, Potter	June 1778 left sick on the road.
Pratt, Jabez Private	Feb 24, 1777, Duration of War	Second, Potter	Dec 1777; Jan 1778 on command; Feb 1778 on guard; March-May 1778; June 1778 sick at Princeton.
Pratt, William Sergeant	Feb 22, 1777 Three Years	Second, Tew	Dec 1777-June 1778.
Preston, Samuel Private	Jan 1, 1777, Duration of War	Second, Shaw	Jan-June 1778.
Prichard/ Pritchard, Richard Private	Jan 1, 1777, Duration of War	Second, Shaw	Jan 1778 General's waiter absent; Feb-April 1778; May 1778 waiter to General Varnum; June 1778.

151

Name	Date	Company	Notes
Procter/Proctor, William Sergeant Major	June 12, 1777. Duration of War	Second	Dec 1777-June 1778.
Quaco, James Private		First, Clarke	Dec 1777 on duty; Jan 1778 on command; Feb 1778 sick present; March 5, 1778 died.
Radford, John Private	June 3, 1777, Three Years	Second, Potter	Dec 1777 sick absent; Jan 1778 discharged for a waggoner.
Ragen, John Corporal	Feb 3, 1777, Duration of War	Second, Olney, C.	Dec 1777 sick absent; Feb 13, 1778 deserted.
Ralph, John Private/ Corporal/Private	March 10, 1777, Duration of War	First, Wallen	Dec 1777; Jan 1778 on guard; Feb 1778 on fatigue; March-April 1778 sick in camp; April 27, 1778 reduced to Private. He appears as promoted to Corporal in January, but all payrolls show him paid as a Private.
Ralph/Relph, John Private	Duration of War	Second, Olney, S.	May 1778 sick in camp; June 1778 absent with leave.
Randall/Randol, John Private	Feb 12, 1777, Duration of War	First, Cole	Dec 1777-Feb 1778; March 1778 on guard; April 1778.
Randel/Randall, John Private	Duration of War	Second, Potter	May 1778 under guard; June 1778.
Randall, Prince Private	March 2, 1778, Duration of War	First, Lewis	June 1778.
Rankin, John Private	March 13, 1778	Second, Hughes	March 18, 1778 deserted.
Remington, Acro Private	April 15, 1778, Duration of War	First, Dexter	June 1778.
Remington, Jabin Private	March 3, 1778, Duration of War	First, Dexter	June 1778.
Reynald, Sampson Private	June 4, 1778, Duration of War	First, Cole	June 1778.
Reynolds, Mingo Private	June 4, 1778, Duration of War	First, Lewis	June 1778.
Reynolds, Thomas Private	April 17, 1777, Duration of War	First, Arnold	Dec 1777; Jan-Feb 1778 sick present; April-June 1778.
Rhodes, Bristol Private	Feb 26, 1778, Duration of War	First, Dexter	June 1778.
Rhodes/Rodes, John Private	Jan 2, 1777, Duration of War	Second, Allen	Dec 1777; Jan-Feb 1778 on command; March-April 1778; May-June 1778 on guard.
Rhodes, Prince Private	Feb 22, 1778, Duration of War	First, Flagg	June 1778.
Rhodes, Richard Private	Feb 20, 1778 Duration of War	First, Wallen	June 1778 sick Englishtown.

Name	Enlistment	Company	Notes
Rhodes, Samuel Private	Feb 22, 1778, Duration of War	First, Lewis	June 1778.
Richards, Ebenezer Private	March 18, 1778, Duration of War	First, Flagg	May 1, 1778 died.
Richards, Joseph A. Private	March 9, 1777, Duration of War	Second, Olney. C.	Dec 1777; Jan 1778 sick present; Feb 1778; March 1778 sick present; April-June 1778.
Richmond, Sigby Private	March 25, 1778, Duration of War	First, Lewis	June 1778.
Riley, John	May 19, 1777, Three Years	First, Talbot	Dec 1777 on duty; Jan 1778 sick present; Feb 1778; March 15, 1778 deserted.
Robellard, James Fifer	Duration of War	Second, Shaw	May 1778 sick present.
Roberson/ Robinson, John Private	Feb 5, 1777, Duration of War	Second, Olney. S.	Dec 1777; Jan 1778 absent without leave; Feb 1778; March 1778 tender to the sick; April 1778 sick present; May 1778; June 1778 sick absent.
Roberts, Cuff Private	March 18, 1778, Duration of War	First, Dexter	June 1778.
Roberts, John Private	Jan 1, 1777, Duration of War	First, Dexter	Dec 1777; Jan 1778 on command row boats; Feb-March 1778 on command; April 8, 1778 deserted.
Roberts, John Sergeant	April 5, 1777, Three Years	First, Lewis	Dec 1777; Jan 1778 recruiting; Feb-April 1778.
Roberts, Reuben Private	Feb 20, 1778, Duration of War	First, Dexter	June 1778.
Robertson, Mingo Private	March 7, 1778, Duration of War	First, Flagg	June 1778.
Robillard, James Fifer	April 28, 1777	First, Talbot	Dec 1777-April 1778.
Robillard, James Fifer		First, Arnold	June 1778 absent without leave.
Robinson, William Private	Three Years	First, Clarke	Dec 1777-April 1778.
Robinson/ Robberson, William Private	Three Years	Second, Hughes	May-June 1778.
Rodman, Isaac Private	Feb 25, 1778, Duration of War	First, Lewis	June 1778.
Rodman, Mingo Musician	Feb 25, 1778, Duration of War	First, Dexter	June 1778.
Rodman, Prince Private	March 25, 1778, Duration of War	First, Dexter	June 1778 on guard.

Name	Enlistment	Company	Service Record
Rogers, George Private		First, Flagg	Dec 1777; Jan 1778 sick present; Feb 1778; March 1778 on command; April 1778 on scout.
Rogers, George Private	Duration of War	First, Arnold	May-June 1778.
Rogers, John Private	Feb 5, 1777, Duration of War	First, Wallen	Dec 1777-April 1778.
Rogers, John Sergeant	March 6, 1778, Duration of War	Second, Olney, S.	Dec 1777-April 1778.
Rogers, John Private	Duration of War	Second, Olney, S.	May 1778; June 1778 absent with leave.
Rogers/Rodgers, John Sergeant	Three Years	Second, Shaw	May-June 1778.
Rogers, Robert 1st. Lt.	Feb 19, 1777	First, Cole	Dec 1777-Feb 1778; March-April 1778 on furlough; June 1778.
Rose, Abraham Private	Jan 30, 1777, Duration of War	Second, Tew	Dec 1777; Jan 1778 on command; Feb 1778; March-April 1778 sick present; May 1778 sick at Yellow Springs; June 1778 absent with leave.
Rose, Ceaser Private	March 16, 1778, Duration of War	First, Dexter	June 1778.
Rose, Daniel Private	Three Years	First, Clarke	Dec 1777 on duty; Jan 25, 1778 died.
Rose, Ned/ Edward Private	March 2, 1778, Duration of War	First, Dexter	June 1778.
Rose, Toney Private	March 21, 1778, Duration of War	First, Lewis	June 1778.
Ross, Joshua Private	Jan 1, 1777, Duration of War	First, Lewis	Dec 1777-April 1778.
Ross, Joshway/ Johuay Private	Duration of War	Second, Olney, C.	May 1778; June 1778 absent with leave.
Rossy, Solomon Private	April 5, 1777, Three Years	First, Talbot	Dec 1777-April 1778.
Rounds, Isaac Sergeant	March 10, 1777, Duration of War	First, Wallen	Dec 1777; Jan-Feb 1778 on command; March 1778; April 1, 1778 deserted.
Ruffie/Roffee, Solomon Private	Three Years	Second, Olney, C.	May-June 1778.
Russell/Russel, Simeon Corporal/Private	April 5, 1777, Three Years	First, Lewis	Dec 1777 on duty; Jan 12, 1778 reduced to Private; Feb-April 1778.
Russell, Simion Private		Second, Olney, C.	May 1778; June 1778 absent with leave.

Russell/Russall, William Private	March 19, 1777, Duration of War	Second, Dexter	Dec 1777-Feb 1778; March 1778 sick present; April 1, 1778 died in hospital.
Rutter/Rotter, Jacob Private	Jan 14, 1777, Duration of War	Second, Olney, S.	Dec 1777; Jan-Feb 1778 on command; March 1778 on furlough; April-May 1778; June 1778 acting as waggoner.
Sabens/Sabin, Thomas Sergeant	May 16, 1777, Duration of War	Second, Olney, S.	Dec 1777-Feb 1778; March 1778 on command; April 1778; May 1778 sick at Yellow Springs; June 20, 1778 died.
Sabins, Ceaser, Private	May 20, 1777	First, Talbot	Dec 1777-March 1778 on command; April 1778 command Rhode Island.
Sabins, Ceaser Private	May 1, 1778, Duration of War	First, Dexter	June 1778 on guard.
Sailes, Fortune Private	May 25, 1777, Duration of War	Second, Hughes	Dec 1777-March 1778 sick absent.
Sales, Prince Private	May 24, 1778, Duration of War	First, Flagg	June 1778.
Salisbury, Benjamin Private	Three Years	First, Clarke	Dec 1777-Jan 1778; Feb-April 1778 sick present.
Salisbury/ Salsbury, William Private	April 3, 1777, Three Years	First, Arnold	Dec 1777; Jan 1778 on duty; Feb 1778; March 1778 on command; April 1778.
Salisbury/ Salsbury, William	Three Years	Second, Tew	May 1778; June 1778 on guard.
Salsbury/ Salsbery, Anthony/ Anthoney Corporal/ Private	Feb 25, 1777, Duration of War	Second, Shaw	Jan-June 1778; June 1778 reduced to Private.
Salsbury, Benjamin Private		Second, Hughes	May 1778; June 1778 on guard.
Saltonstall, Briton Private	March 18, 1778, Duration of War	First, Flagg	June 1778.
Sambo, George Private		First, Flagg	Dec 1777; Jan-March 1778 on command; April 1778.
Sambo, George Private	Duration of War	First, Arnold	May 1778 on command at Gen. Greene; June 1778 on command.
Sanders, Samson Private	March 3, 1778, Duration of War	First, Dexter	June 1778 on guard.
Sarles, Primus Private	May 24	First, Flagg	June 1778.

155

Name	Enlistment	Company	Service Record
Saunders/Sanders, John Private	May 12, 1777, Three Years	Second, Allen	Dec 1777; Jan 1778 on guard; Feb-May 1778; June 1778 on guard.
Sawyer/Sawer, John Private	Three Years	Second, Dexter	May-June 1778.
Sayer/Sayor, John Private	May 15, 1777	First, Talbot	Jan-Feb 1778 sick present; March 1778; April 1778 duty Radnor.
Sayles/Sarles, David 1st. Lt.	June 12, 1777	Second, Dexter	Dec 1777-March 1778; April 1778 on command; March 1778 on furlough; May-June 1778.
Schyrms/ Scarmes, John Private	Duration of War	Second, Shaw	Jan 1778 sick in quarters; Feb-June 1778.
Scrivens, Zebulon Private	Three Years	First, Clarke	Dec 1777; Jan 1778 on guard; Feb-April 1778.
Scriveons/ Scribbens, Zebulon Private	Three Years	Second, Hughes	May-June 1778.
Searles/Searls, Thomas Private	Feb 17, 1777, Duration of War	First, Cole	Dec 1777-April 1778.
Searles/Sairls, Thomas Private	Duration of War	Second, Potter	May 1778 under guard; June 1778 absent with leave.
Seaser—see Ceaser			
Sephton/Septon, Richard Private	Feb 20, 1777, Duration of War	Second, Allen	Dec 1777 sick in hospital; Jan-March 1778 sick absent; April-June 1778.
Shearman/ Shareman, Elisha Sergeant	April 29, 1777, Three Years	First, Lewis	Dec 1777 on duty; Jan 1778 sick present; Feb-March 1778; April 8, 1778 died.
Shelding, Cesar Private	March 12, 1778, Duration of War	First, Lewis	June 1778.
Sheldon, Job Sergeant	June 25, 1777, Duration of War	Second, Allen	Dec 1777-June 1778.
Sheldon/Shelden, Jonathan Private	May 24, 1777, Duration of War	Second, Hughes	Dec 1777 on guard; Jan-Feb 1778 sick present; March 1778 on command; April 1778; May 1778 sick Yellow Springs; June 1778.
Shippey/Shippy, Solomon Private	Feb 7, 1777, Duration of War	Second, Hughes	Dec 1777; Jan 1778 on command; Feb 1778; March 1778 sick present; April 8, 1778 died in camp.

Name	Enlisted	Company	Notes
Simmons/Simons, Benjamin Sergeant	May 5, 1777, Duration of War	Second, Dexter	Dec 1777; Jan 1778 on guard; Feb-March 1778 on command; April 1778 on command Schuylkill; May 1778; June 1778 absent with leave.
Simmons, John Private	Three Years	First, Clarke	Dec 1777; Jan 1778 on command; Feb 1778; March 1778 on guard; April 1778.
Simmons, John/Jonathan Private	Three Years	Second, Hughes	May-June 1778.
Siscoe/Sischo, Noah Private	April 27, 1777, Duration of War	Second, Potter	Dec 1777; Jan 3, 1778 deserted.
Sisson, Caleb Private	April 22, 1777, Three Years	First, Arnold	Dec 3, 1777 died.
Sisson, George Sergeant	April 7, 1777, Three Years	First, Arnold	Dec 1777; Jan 1778 on command; Feb 1778 absent with leave, March 1778; April 1778 on picket; May 1778; June 1778 sick Princeton.
Sisson, Jack/Jak Private	March 16, 1778, Duration of War	First, Cole	June 1778 absent with leave.
Slew/Slue, Phillip Fifer	May 1, 1777, Duration of War	Second, Shaw	Jan-June 1778.
Slocum, Ebenezer Drummer	Feb 15, 1777, Duration of War	First, Wallen	Dec 1777 sick absent; Jan-Feb 1778; March 1778 sick absent; April 1778.
Slocum, Ebeneser Drummer	Duration of War	First, Arnold	May-June 1778.
Slocum/Slocom, Edward 1st. Lt.	Jan 1, 1777	First, Talbot	Dec 1777; Jan 1778; Feb-March 1778; April 1778 command Rhode Island.
Slocum, John Private	May 7, 1777, Duration of War	Second, Tew	Dec 1777-Feb 1778; March 1778 on command; March 18, 1778 transferred to His Excellency's Guard.
Smith, Abram/Abraham Private	March 6, 1777, Duration of War	Second, Allen	Dec 1777-Jan 1778; Feb 1778 on guard; March 1778 on command; April 1778 on command at Radnor; May-June 1778.
Smith, Arthur Corporal	Jan 7, 1777, Duration of War	Second, Tew	Dec 1777-March 1778 sick absent; April 1778 sick absent at Lancaster May 1778; The June 1778 muster roll shows him missing on June 28. The June 1778 payroll shows him killed on June 28.

Name	Enlisted	Company	Service Record
Smith, Benjamin Private	Jan 27, 1777, Duration of War	Second, Dexter	Dec 1777; Jan 1778 on command; Feb 1778; March 1778 on guard; April 1778 sick in camp; May 1778 sick Yellow Springs; June 1778.
Smith, Job Corporal	April 1, 1777, Duration of War	Second, Shaw	Jan 1778 sick absent; Feb-March 1778; April 1, 1778 deserted.
Smith, John Sergeant	May 1, 1777, Three Years	First, Arnold	Dec 1777; Jan-March 1778 on command; April 1778 on command Rhode Island.
Smith, John Sergeant		First, Lewis	June 1778 on command.
Smith, John Private	March 7, 1777, Duration of War	Second, Potter	Dec 1777 sick absent; Feb 1778 transferred to the Invalids.
Smith, Joshua Private	Three Years	First, Clarke	Dec 1777; Jan-April 1778 sick present.
Smith, Joshua Private		Second, Hughes	May 1778; June 1778 sick Princeton.
Smith, Juba Private	April 1, 1778, Duration of War	First, Dexter	June 1778.
Smith, Randall Corporal	Jan 1, 1777, Duration of War	Second, Olney, S.	Dec 1777-Feb 1778 sick absent; March-June 1778.
Smith, Reuben/Rubin Corporal	Jan 23, 1777, Duration of War	Second, Dexter	Dec 1777-April 1778.
Smith, Ruebin Corporal	Duration of War	Second, Tew	May-June 1778.
Smith, Samuel Drummer	July 3, 1777, Three Years	Second, Potter	Dec 1777-May 1778; June 1778 absent with leave.
Smith, Simion/Simeon Ensign	May 7, 1777	First, Talbot	Dec 1777; Jan 5, 1778 discharged.
Smith, Stephen Fifer	June 12, 1777, Duration of War	Second, Olney. C.	Dec 1777; Jan-Feb 1778 sick present; March-May 1778; June 1778 absent with leave.
Smith, Thomas Private	May 18, 1777, Duration of War	First, Talbot	Dec 1777-April 1778.
Smith, Thomas Private	Duration of War	First, Arnold	May-June 1778.
Smith, William Private		First, Flagg	Dec 31, 1777 deserted; March 27, 1778 joined; March 1778 sick present; April 20, 1778 died.
Snow, Aaron Corporal	April 1, 1778	First, Flagg	June 1778.
Sole, Josiah Private	March 12, 1777	First, Wallen	Dec 1777-Jan 1778; Feb 1778 on command; March-April 1778.

Name	Term	Company	Notes
Sole/Soles, Josiah/Joshiah Private		First, Arnold	May-June 1778.
Solomon, John Private	March 30, 1778, Duration of War	First, Flagg	June 1778.
Sotton/Satton, Thomas Private	Duration of War	Second, Olney, C.	May-June 1778.
Southward, Olding/Holden Sergeant	May 15, 1777	First, Talbot	Dec 1777-March 1778 sick absent; April 1778.
Southworth, Alding Sergeant	Three Years	Second, Dexter	May 1778 on guard; June 1778.
Sparks/Sparkes, John Private	Jan 1, 1777, Duration of War	First, Dexter	Dec 1777; Jan 1778 on 7 days command; Feb 1778; March 1778 on command; April 1778.
Sparks/Sparkes, John Private		Second, Shaw	May-June 1778.
Spears, Johnson/Johnston Private	Jan 11, 1777, Duration of War	First, Wallen	Dec 1777; Jan-March 1778 on command; April 1778.
Spears, Johnson Private	Duration of War	Second, Olney, S	May 1778; June 1778 sick in camp.
Spencer, Thomas Private		First, Flagg	Dec 1777-Feb 1778; March 1778 in hospital; April 1778.
Spencer, Thomas Private		First, Arnold	May 1778 sick in camp; June 1778.
Spink, Eldridge Private	May 10, 1777	First, Talbot	Dec 1777-April 1778.
Spink, Eldridge Private		First, Arnold	May-June 1778.
Spink, Nicholas Corporal	May 10, 1777, Duration of War	First, Lewis	Dec 1777 on duty; Jan 1778 on general guard; Feb-April 1778.
Spink, Nicholas Corporal	Duration of War	First, Arnold	May-June 1778.
Sprague, Benjamin Private	Jan 1, 1777, Duration of War	First, Dexter	Dec 1777; Jan 1778 on duty; Feb 1778; March 1778 on command; April 1778.
Sprague, Benjamin Private	Duration of War	Second, Shaw	May-June 1778.
Sprague, Wiliam Private	March 20, 1777, Duration of War	First, Dexter	Dec 1777-Jan 1778 sick absent; Feb 1778 on guard; March 1778 on command; April 1778 sick in camp.
Sprague, William Private	Duration of War	Second, Shaw	May-June 1778.

Name	Enlisted	Regiment	Service
Springer, Durfee/Durphey Private	Jan 3, 1777, Duration of War	Second, Allen	Dec 1777-June 1778.
Stafford, John Private	Jan 7, 1777, Three Years	First, Cole	Dec 1777-April 1778.
Stafford, John Private	Three Years	Second, Potter	May-June 1778.
Stafford, Michael Private	May 21, 1777, Three Years	First, Arnold	Dec 1777 on guard; Jan-Feb 1778 sick present; March-April 1778.
Stafford, Michael Private	Three Years	Second, Tew	May-June 1778.
Stafford, Thomas Drummer		First, Flagg	Dec 1777; Jan 1778 absent without leave; Feb 1778 sick present; March-April 1778.
Stafford, Thomas Drummer	Duration of War	First, Arnold	May-June 1778.
Stafford, William Private	June 27, 1777, Duration of War	Second, Olney, S.	Dec 1777; Jan-March 1778 on command; April 1778; May 1778 sick Yellow Springs; June 1778 sick absent.
Stalcott, John Private	May 10, 1777, Duration of War	Second, Allen	Dec 1777 waggoner; Jan 7, 1778 discharged.
Stanton, Enoch 2nd. Lt.	Feb 20, 1777	First, Wallen	Dec 1777-Feb 1778; March 1778 on command; April 1778 on command at Rhode Island.
Stanton, Enoch 2nd. Lt.		First, Cole	June 1778.
Stedman, Amos/Amoss Private	March 17, 1777, Duration of War	Second, Hughes	Dec 1777-Jan 1778; Feb 1778 sick present; March 1778; April 1778 on guard.
Stedmon, Amos Private	Duration of War	First, Arnold	May 1778; June 13, 1778 died.
Straight/Strait, Reuben Private	Jan 1, 1777, Duration of War	First, Dexter	Dec 1777-Jan 1778; Feb 1778 on command; March 1778 sick present; April 1778 on command commissary.
Straight/Stright, Reuben Private	Duration of War	Second, Shaw	May-June 1778.
Strange/Streng, John Drummer	June 6, 1777, Duration of War	Second, Olney, C.	Dec 1777-Feb 1778 sick absent; March-May 1778; June 1778 absent with leave.
Stratton, Anthony Private	Three Years	First, Clarke	Dec 1777; Jan 1778 sick present; Feb 1778 sick absent; March 1778 sick in hospital; April 1778 sick at French Creek.

Name	Enlistment	Company	Service Record
Stratton/Straton, Anthony Private		Second, Hughes	May 15, 1778 died.
Stuart/Stewart, Alexander/Elexander Sergeant	March 9, 1777, Duration of War	Second, Olney, C.	Dec 1777; Jan-Feb 1778 recruiting; March 1778 on command; April 1778 on command Providence; May-June 1778.
Stutson, Stephen Private	March 5, 1777, Duration of War	Second, Hughes	Dec 22, 1777 died.
Sutton, Thomas Private	Jan 1, 1777, Duration of War	First, Lewis	Dec 1777; Jan 1778 on 7 days command; Feb-April 1778.
Sweet, Benjamin Private	May 10, 1777, Three Years	First, Lewis	Dec 1777-April 1778.
Sweet, Benjamin Private	Three Years	Second, Olney. C.	May 1778; June 1778 on guard.
Sweet, Daniel Corporal	April 4, 1777, Duration of War	First, Talbot	Dec 1777-April 1778.
Sweet, Daniel Corporal	Duration of War	Second, Dexter	May-June 1778.
Sweet, William Private		First, Flagg	Dec 1777 sick absent; Jan 8, 1778 died.
Sweeting, Jerry Private	Feb 28, 1778, Duration of War	First, Lewis	June 1778.
Sweetser, Thomas Private	March 17, 1777, Duration of War	Second, Olney. S.	Dec 1777 on command; Jan 1778; Feb-March 1778 acting as waggoner; April 1778 foraging in the country; May 1778 on command; June 1778 acting as assistant forage master.
Taber, Noel Private	March 12, 1777, Duration of War	First, Talbot	Dec 1777 on duty; Jan-March 1778 on command; April 1778 general guard.
Tabor/Tabour, John Private	Feb 25, 1777, Duration of War	Second, Shaw	Jan-April 1778; May 1778 sick at Yellow Springs; June 1778 sick absent.
Tabor/Tabour, Noel Private	Duration of War	Second, Dexter	May-June 1778.
Talbot, Silas Captain/Major	Jan 1, 1777	First, Talbot	Dec 24, 1777 promoted to Major, retroactive to September 1, 1777. However both Rhode Island regiments were already had Majors, and Talbot does not appear on later muster rolls
Talbut/Tolbut, Ebenezer Sergeant	April 28, 1777	First, Talbot	Dec 1777-March 1778 on command; April 1778 on furlough Rhode Island.

Name	Enlisted	Company	Service
Talpey, Richard Private	May 13, 1777, Duration of War	Second, Shaw	Jan 1778 sick absent; Feb-March 1778.
Tanner, Joseph Corporal	March 6, 1777	Second, Hughes	Dec 1777-June 1778.
Tanner, Quam Private	March 8, 1778, Duration of War	First, Lewis	June 1778 on guard.
Tanner, William Corporal	April 15, 1777, Three Years	First, Lewis	Dec 1777-April 1778.
Tannar, William Corporal	Three Years	Second, Olney, C.	May-June 1778 on His Excellency's Guard.
Taylor, Bennoni Private	May 10, 1777, Three Years	First, Talbot	Dec 1777-Feb 1778 sick absent; March-April 1778.
Taylor, Benoni Private	Three Years	Second, Dexter	May-June 1778.
Taylor, John Private	Feb 10, 1777, Three Years	First, Cole	Dec 1777-March 1778; April 26, 1778 died.
Taylor, John Private	March 10, 1777, Duration of War	First, Wallen	Dec 1777; Jan 1778 sick present; Feb 1778 sick in camp; March-April 1778.
Taylor, John Private	Duration of War	Second, Olney, S.	May-June 1778.
Taylor/Taylar, John H. Private	May 16, 1777, Duration of War	Second, Dexter	Dec 1777-March 1778 on command; April 1778 on command at Bethlehem; May-June 1778 on command at Lancaster
Taylor, Nathaniel Private		First, Flagg	Dec 1777-Jan 1778; Feb 1778 on fatigue; March 1778; April 1778 sick present.
Taylor, Nathaniel Private		Second, Allen	May 1778 sick at Yellow Springs; June 1778 sick absent.
Taylor, Thomas Private	Jan 7, 1777, Three Years	First, Cole	Dec 1777-March 1778; April 1778 sick present.
Taylor, Thomas Corporal	Three Years	Second, Potter	May-June 1778.
Taylor, William Sergeant	Feb 10, 1777, Three Years	First, Cole	Dec 1777 Col. Greene's orderly; Jan 1778 on command recruiting; Feb-March 1778 on command; April 1778 on command at Rhode Island; June 1778.
Tennant/Tenent, Franklin Private	Jan 1, 1777, Duration of War	Second, Allen	Dec 1777 sick in hospital; Jan-Feb 1778; March 1778 on command; April 1778 on command at Radnor; May 1778; June 1778 on guard.
Tenny, Samuel Surgeon	Jan 1, 1777	Second	Dec 1777-May 1778; June 1778 absent Morristown. Oath at Valley Forge on May 13, 1778.

Name	Date	Regiment	Notes
Tew, Benedict 2nd. Lt.	Jan 1, 1777	Second, Allen	Dec 1777; Jan 1778 on command; Feb-March 1778; April 1778 on furlough at Rhode Island; May 1778 on furlough; June 1778.
Tew, William Captain	April 1, 1777	Second, Tew	Dec 1777; Jan-March 1778 on command; April-June 1778. Oath at Valley Forge on May 30, 1778.
Thayer, Simeon Major	Jan 1, 1777	Second	Dec 1777-Jan 1778 on duty; Feb 1778; March 1778 on furlough; April-May 1778; June 1778 sick Morristown. Oath at Valley Forge on May 13, 1778.
Thomas, John Corporal	May 10, 1777, Duration of War	First, Talbot	Dec 1777-March 1778 on command; April 1778.
Thomas, John Corporal	Duration of War	Second, Dexter	May-June 1778.
Thomas, William Private	Feb 27, 1777, Duration of War	First, Cole	Dec 1777 sick present; Jan-April 1778.
Thomas, William Private	Duration of War	Second, Potter	May-June 1778.
Thompson, Charles Chaplain	March 17, 1777	First	Dec 1777-Jan 1778 on furlough; Feb 1778; March 1778 absent with leave; April 1778 on furlough; May 1778 prisoner with the enemy
Thompson, Elias 2nd. Lt.	Feb 19, 1777	First, Clarke	Dec 1777-April 1778.
Thompson, Elias 2nd. Lt.		First, Lewis	June 1778.
Thompson, Enoch Sergeant/ Private	May 7, 1777, Three Years	First, Wallen	Dec 1777 sick absent; Jan 1778; Feb 1778 on guard; March 1778; April 27, 1778 reduced to Private; April 1778 sick in camp.
Thompson, Enoch Private	Three Years	Second, Olney, S.	May 1778; June 1778 sick absent.
Thompson, Lowden/Louden Private	Three Years	First, Arnold	Dec 1777-Feb 1778; March-April 1778 sick present.
Thompson, Lowden Private	Three Years	First, Arnold	May-June 1778.
Thompson, Reuben Private	Jan 13, 1777, Duration of War	Second, Tew	Dec 1777-April 1778; May-June 1778 sick at Yellow Springs.
Thompson, Samuel Private		First, Flagg	Dec 1777-Jan 1778; Feb 1778 on guard; March 1778 on command; April 1778 on command Radnor picket.

Name	Enlisted	Company	Notes
Thompson, Samuel Private		Second, Allen	May 1778 sick at Yellow Springs; June 1778 sick absent.
Thorn, Henry Private	Feb 17, 1777, Duration of War	First, Talbot	Dec 1777-April 1778.
Thorn, Henry Private	Duration of War	Second, Dexter	May 1778 on guard; June 1778.
Thorps, Reuben Sergeant	March 20, 1777, Duration of War	Second, Dexter	Dec 1777; Jan 7, 1778 discharged.
Thorrington/ Torington, Thomas Private	March 5, 1777, Duration of War	Second, Hughes	Dec 1777-Jan 1778; Feb 1778 sick present; March 1778 tending sick; April 1778; May 1778 on guard; June 1778.
Thrasher, Joseph Private	April 30, 1777, Duration of War	First, Arnold	Dec 1777-April 1778.
Thrasher, Joseph Private	Duration of War	Second, Tew	May 1778; June 1778 sick in hospital.
Thurber, Amos Private	Jan 13, 1777, Duration of War	Second, Tew	Dec 1777 sick present; Jan 1778 on command; Feb 1778; March 1778 on command; April-May 1778; June 1778 Yellow Springs.
Thurber, Darius Fifer/Private	Jan 13, 1777, Duration of War	Second, Tew	Dec 1777 sick present; Jan-Feb 1778; March 1778 on fatigue; March 18, 1778 reduced to Private; April-June 1778.
Tibbits, Benjamin Private	May 31, 1777, Three Years	First, Arnold	Dec 1777 on command; Feb 15, 1778 deserted.
Tifft, Francis Private	Duration of War	First, Arnold	June 1, 1778 died.
Tift, Francis Private	May 29, 1777, Duration of War	Second, Potter	Dec 1777-Jan 1778; Feb 1778 on command; March-April 1778 sick present.
Tillinghast, Cuff Private	Feb 20, 1778, Duration of War	First, Flagg	June 1778.
Tillinghast, Daniel Ensign	Feb 11, 1777	First, Lewis	Dec 1777; Jan 1778 on command recruiting; Feb-April 1778.
Tillinghast, Daniel C. Ensign	Feb 11, 1777	First, Arnold	May 1778; June 1778 on guard. Oath at Valley Forge on May 14, 1778.
Talbot, Ebenezer Sergeant	May 1, 1778	First, Dexter	June 1778.
Tomkins/ Thomkins, George Private	Duration of War	First, Arnold	May-June 1778.
Tompkins, George Private	Duration of War	First, Clarke	Dec 1777 on duty; Jan 1778 sick present; Feb 1778 on command; March-April 1778 sick present.

Name/Rank	Enlistment	Company	Remarks
Tompkins/Tomkins, James Private	March 6, 1777, Three Years	Second, Shaw	Jan-March 1778; May 1778 sick at Yellow Springs; June 1778 sick absent.
Trim, Benjamin Private	Feb 27, 1777, Duration of War	First, Cole	Dec 1777-April 1778 on command at Peekskill.
Tripp, Joshua Private	Feb 18, 1777, Duration of War	First, Dexter	Dec 1777; Jan 1778 on 7 day command; Feb 1778 sick in camp; March 1778; April 1778 on command at Radnor.
Tripp, Joshua Private	Duration of War	Second, Shaw	May-June 1778.
Tucker, Robert Private	May 14, 1777, Three Years	Second, Olney, S.	Dec 1777; Jan 1778 on guard; Feb 1778 on command; March-April 1778; May 1778 sick in camp; June 1778.
Tuley/Teuley, John Private	Feb 16, 1777, Duration of War	Second, Shaw	Jan-June 1778.
Turner, Henry Private	Three Years	First, Clarke	Dec 1777 sick present; Jan-Feb 1778; March 1778 sick present; April 1778.
Turner, Henry Private/Drummer	Three Years	Second, Hughes	May 1778; May 13, 1778 promoted to Drummer; June 1778 absent with leave.
Turner, Joseph Private	Jan 11, 1777, Duration of War	Second, Shaw	Jan-March 1778; April 31, 1778 deceased.
Turner, Peter Surgeon	March 15, 1777	Second	Dec 1777; Jan-March 1778 on command; April 1778 on command at Rhode Island; May 1778 on furlough; June 1778.
Twitchell/Twichell, Benjamin Private	May 15, 1777, Three Years	Second, Allen	Dec 1777-May 1778; June 1778 sick absent.
Tyler, Nathaniel Private		Second, Allen	June 1778 sick absent.
Tyler, Nicholas Drummer	Feb 12, 1777	First, Dexter	Dec 1777; Feb 6, 1778 deserted.
Updike, Ceaser Private	March 15, 1778, Duration of War	First, Cole	June 1778.
Updike, Moses Private	March 3, 1778, Duration of War	First, Cole	June 1778.
Usher, John Private	March 18, 1777, Duration of War	Second, Tew	Dec 1777 on command; Jan-Feb 1778; March 1778 on command; April 1778 on command at Rhode Island; May-June 1778.
Van Doorn, Plato Private	Feb 20, 1777, Duration of War	First, Lewis	June 1778.

Name	Enlistment	Company	Service Record
Vangover/Vangober, Derrick Private	May 4, 1777, Duration of War	First, Cole	Dec 1777-March 1778; April 1778 sick present.
Vanzover, Derick Private	Three Years	First, Arnold	May-June 1778 sick at Yellow Springs.
Varnum/Vernum, Cato Private	Duration of War	First, Arnold	May-June 1778.
Varnum, James Mitchell Brigadier General	Feb 21, 1777		Brigadier General Varnum commanded a brigade composed of the First and Second Rhode Island and the Fourth and Eighth Connecticut Regiments. He left for Rhode Island shortly after June 7, 1778. Oath of Allegiance at Valley Forge.
Varnum, Samuel Private		First, Dexter	Dec 1777; Jan 1778 on fatigue; Feb 1778; March 1778 sick present; April 1778.
Varnum, Samuel Private		Second, Allen	May 1778; June 1778 tender to sick.
Vaughn, Prince Private	Feb 25, 1778, Duration of War	First, Cole	June 1778.
Vernon, Cato Private		First, Flagg	April 1778.
Vibut/Vibet, Isaac Private	April 9, 1777, Three Years	Second, Potter	Dec 1777; Jan 1778 sick present; Feb 23, 1778 died.
Viol, John Ensign	June 24, 1777	Second, Shaw	Dec 1777; Jan 1778 recruiting; Feb-June 1778. Oath at Valley Forge on May 14, 1778.
Vorse/Vose, Henry Private	Three Years	First, Clarke	Dec 1777-Jan 1778 sick present; Feb 1778 sick absent; March 1778 sick present; April 1778 command at Radnor.
Vose/Voce, Henry Private		Second, Hughes	May 1778 under guard; June 30, 1778 deserted.
Waily, Thomas Private	Jan 1, 1777, Duration of War	First, Lewis	Dec 1777-April 1778.
Wait, Joseph Private	March 8, 1777, Duration of War	Second, Olney, S.	Dec 1777-March 1778 sick absent; April-May 1778 sick at Bethlehem; June 1778.
Walker, Alexander/Elexander Private	June 1, 1777, Duration of War	Second, Potter	Dec 1777; Jan 1778 on command; Feb 1778; March 1778 on command; April-May 1778; June 1778 on guard.

Name	Date	Regiment	Notes
Wallen/Wallnin, Jonathan, Captain	Jan 1, 1777	First, Wallen	Dec 1777; Jan 1778 on command; Feb 1778 on guard; March-April 1778; May-June 1778. Oath at Valley Forge on May 24, 1778.
Wanton, Solomon, Private	April 26, 1777, Duration of War	First, Talbot	Dec 1777-Feb 1778 sick absent; March-April 1778.
Wanton/Wonton, Solomon, Private	Duration of War	Second, Arnold	May 1778; June 1778 absent with leave.
Ward, Edward, Private	April 6, 1777, Three Years	First, Lewis	Dec 1777; Jan 1778 sick present; Feb-April 1778.
Ward, Edward, Private	Three Years	Second, Olney, C.	May 1778 on guard; June 28, 1778 missing.
Ward, Ephraim, Private		First, Flagg	Dec 1777-Feb 1778 sick absent; March-April 1778 sick at Rhode Island.
Ward, Epheram, Private		Second, Allen	May-June 1778 sick at Rhode Island.
Ward, Jack, Private	July 3, 1777	First, Talbot	Dec 1777 on duty; Jan 1778 sick present; Feb 20, 1778 died.
Ward, Lawrence G., Private	May 1, 1777, Duration of War	Second, Allen	Dec 1777-March 1778 on command; April 1, 1778 deserted.
Ward, Samuel, Major	Jan 12, 1777	First	Dec 1777; Jan-March 1778 on command; April-June 1778.
Washburn, Oliver, Private	Feb 1, 1777, Duration of War	Second, Shaw	Jan 1778 on command; Feb 1778; March 20, 1778 died.
Waterman, John, Quartermaster	March 1, 1777	Second	Dec 17, 1777 appointed Brigade Commissary; April 23, 1778 died.
Waterman, Olney, Sergeant	April 10, 1777, Three Years	Second, Olney, S.	Dec 1777-June 1778.
Waterman, Thomas, Adjutant	August 10, 1777	Second	Dec 1777 sick absent; Jan-Feb 1778; March-May 1778 on furlough; June 1778.
Waterman, Thomas, Ensign/2nd. Lt.	Jan 1, 1777	Second, Allen	Dec 1777 sick absent; Jan-March 1778 on command; April 1778 on command Rhode Island; May 1778; June 11, 1778 promoted to 2nd. Lt.; June 1778 sick absent.
Watson/Waston, Charles, Private	Feb 1, 1777, Duration of War	Second, Olney, S.	Dec 1777-Jan 1778; Feb-March 1778 on command; April 1778 on command at the Lines; May 1778; June 1778 on General Lee's Guard.
Watson, Forting, Private	Feb 21, 1778, Duration of War	First, Cole	June 1778.
Watson, Guy, Private	Feb 19, 1778, Duration of War	First, Lewis	June 1778.

Name	Date	Company	Service
Watson, Jack Private	March 5, 1778, Duration of War	First, Lewis	June 1778.
Watson, Pomp/Pompy Private	May 22, 1777, Three Years	First, Cole	Dec 1777-Jan 1778; Feb 1778 on fatigue; March 1778 on command; April 1778.
Watson, Pomp Private	Three Years	First, Arnold	May-June 1778.
Watson, Prince Private	Duration of War	First, Arnold	May-June 1778.
Weaver, Abial Private	May 31, 1777, Duration of War	First, Arnold	Dec 1777; Jan 1778 sick present; Feb-April 1778.
Weaver, Abial Private	Three Years	Second, Tew	May-June 1778 sick at Yellow Springs.
Weaver, Stephen Private		First, Flagg	Dec 1777-Feb 1778 sick absent; March-April 1778.
Weaver, Stephen Private		Second, Allen	May 1778 sick at Yellow Springs; June 1778 sick absent.
Weaver, William Private	Duration of War	First, Clarke	Dec 1777-Jan 1778; Feb 1778 lame present; March 1778 on guard; April 1778.
Weaver, William Private		Second, Hughes	May 1778 sick Yellow Springs; June 1778 sick Yellow Springs or Red Lion.
Webster, James Private		First, Flagg	Dec 1777-Feb 1778 sick absent; March 1778 in hospital; April 1778.
Webster, James Private		Second, Allen	May 1778 sick at Yellow Springs; June 1778 sick absent.
Weeks/Weekes, Moses Private	Feb 7, 1777	Second, Dexter	Dec 1777-Jan 1778; Feb-March 1778 on command; April 1778 on picket guard.
Weeks, Moses Private	Duration of War	First, Arnold	May 1778 on picket; June 1778 sick at Princeton.
Weeks, Nathan 2nd. Lt.	Feb 17, 1777	Second, Olney. C.	Dec 1777-Feb 1778 on furlough; March-May 1778; June 28, 1778 killed. Oath at Valley Forge on May 24, 1778.
Weicks, Nathaniel Private	March 2, 1778, Duration of War	First, Flagg	June 1778.
Weicks, Saul Private	June 1, 1778, Duration of War	First. Flagg	June 1778.
Welch, William Private	March 10, 1777, Duration of War	Second, Olney, C.	Dec 1777; Jan 1778 sick present; Feb 1778 on guard; March 1778 transferred to Colonel Marshall's Regiment.
Wells. Cesar Private	March 8, 1778, Duration of War	First, Lewis	June 1778.

Name	Enlisted	Company	Service
Wescott/Wescutt, Charles Private	March 18, 1777, Duration of War	Second, Dexter	Dec 1777-May 1778; June 1778 sick Valley Forge.
West, Ebenezer 1st. Lt.	Jan 1, 1777	Second, Allen	Dec 1777 on guard; Jan-March 1778 on command; April-June 1778. Oath at Valley Forge on May 14, 1778. July 9, 1778 cashiered.
West, John Private	March 30, 1777, Duration of War	First, Cole	Dec 1777; Jan 1778 on 7 days command; Feb 1778; March 1778 on command; April 1778 on command at Radnor.
West, John Private	Duration of War	Second, Potter	May-June 1778.
West, Nathan Fifer	Feb 1, 1777, Duration of War	Second, Allen	Dec 1777-May 1778; June 1778 absent with leave.
West, Samuel Corporal	Jan 30, 1777, Three Years	First, Cole	Dec 1777-April 1778.
West, Samuel Corporal	Three Years	Second, Potter	May-June 1778.
West, William Private	Jan 15, 1777, Duration of War	First, Wallen	Dec 1777 on command with the general; Jan-March 1778 general's waiter; April 1778.
West, William Private	Duration of War	Second, Olney, S.	May-June 1778.
Wheaton, Cesar Private	June 1, 1778, Duration of War	First, Lewis	June 1778 on command.
Wheeler/Wheelar, Joseph Private	Jan 1, 1777, Duration of War	First, Dexter	Dec 1777; Jan 1778 on command in row boats; Feb-March 1778 on command; April 1778.
Wheeler, Joseph Private	Duration of War	Second, Shaw	May 1778 on guard; June 1778.
Whipple, John Private	April 28, 1777, Three Years	Second, Olney, S.	Dec 1777 sick absent; Jan-June 1778.
Whipple/Whipples, Samuel 2nd. Lt.	Feb 11, 1777	Second, Olney, S.	Dec 1777 sick absent; Jan 18, 1778 discharged.
Whitaker/Whiteker, Ebenezer Private	Feb 22, 1777, Duration of War	Second, Dexter	Dec 1777 sick absent; Jan 1778; Feb-March 1778 on furlough; April 1778 on furlough at Providence, May 1, 1778 discharged.
White, Simion Private	May 24, 1777, Duration of War	First, Talbot	Dec 1777-Feb 1778 sick absent; March-April 1778.
White, Simeon Private	Duration of War	Second, Dexter	May-June 1778.

Name	Enlisted	Regiment	Service Record
White, William, Private	Jan 10, 1777, Duration of War	Second, Dexter	Dec 1777; Jan 1778 on command; Feb 1778; March 1778 on command; April 1778 sick in camp; May 1778; June 1778 sick Princeton.
Whitford, David, Private	Feb 28, 1777, Duration of War	Second, Hughes	Dec 1777; Jan 1778 on command; Feb 1778 on guard; March 1778 on command; April 1778 on command at Rhode Island; May-June 1778.
Whitman, David, Private	May 9, 1777, Duration of War	Second, Hughes	Dec 1777 sick present; Jan 1778 on command; Feb 1778; March-April 1778 sick absent; May 1778 sick French Creek; June 1778.
Whitmarsh, Joseph 1st. Lt.	Jan 1, 1777	First, Dexter	Dec 1777-Jan 1778; Feb 1778 on guard; March 8, 1778 discharged.
Whitmarsh, Micah 1st. Lt.	Feb 14, 1777	First, Flagg	Dec 1777-March 1778 recruiting; April 25, 1778 discharged.
Whittesey/Whittiesey, James Drummer/Private	March 2, 1777, Three Years	Second, Hughes	Dec 1777-Feb 1778 sick absent; March-May 1778; May 13, 1778 reduced to Private; June 28, 1778 killed.
Whittlelsey/Whittelsy, Nathan Sergeant/Quartermaster Sergeant		Second	Dec 17, 1777 appointed Quartermaster Sergeant; Dec-April 1778; May-June 1778 doing duty of Quartermaster.
Wiggins, Henry Private	April 12, 1777, Three Years	First, Arnold	Dec 1777 sick in hospital; Jan 15, 1778 died.
Wilber/Wilbour, Asa Drummer	Duration of War	Second, Shaw	Jan 1778 recruiting; Feb-June 1778.
Wilber/Wilbour, George Private	Three Years	Second, Dexter	May 1778; June 1778 sick at Princeton.
Wilber, Uriel/Urial Sergeant	Jan 1, 1777, Duration of War	Second, Allen	Dec 1777; Jan-Feb 1778 on command; Feb 30 [sic], 1778 dead. On the June 1778 payroll he received pay back to March 1 with the notation "taken prisoner 28th February."
Wilbour/Wilbur, George Private	May 15, 1777	First, Talbot	Dec 1777-March 1778 on command; April 1778 on duty Radnor.
Wilbourn, Boston Private	March 12, 1778, Duration of War	First, Flagg	June 1778.

Name	Enlistment	Regiment, Company	Service Record
Wilcox/Willcocks, Josiah Private	Jan 2, 1777, Duration of War	Second, Allen	Dec 1777; Jan 1778 on fatigue; Feb-March 1778 on command; April-June 1778.
Wilkey/Wilkee, Jeremiah Private	Jan 10, 1777, Three Years	Second, Potter	Dec 1777-Feb 1778; March 1778 sick present; April 1778 unfit for the service.
Williams, Reuben Private	Jan 10, 1777, Duration of War	Second, Tew	Dec 1777 sick absent; Jan 1778 died.
Williams, William Private	Three Years	Second, Potter	May 1778; June 1778 on command waggoner.
Willie/Wellie, Thomas Private	Duration of War	Second, Olney, C.	May 1778 on guard; June 1778.
Willing/Willings, Aaron Private	Three Years	First, Clarke	Dec 1777; Jan-Feb 1778 sick present; March 1778 on guard; April 1778 sick present.
Willing/Willings, Aaron Private		Second, Hughes	May 1778; June 1778 absent with leave.
Willis/Wyllis, Jesse Private	Jan 1, 1777, Duration of War	First, Dexter	Dec 1777; Jan 1778 on seven day command; Feb 1778; March 1778 on command; April 1778.
Willis, Jesse Private		First, Arnold	May 1778; June 1778 absent with leave.
Wilson/Willson, Nicholas/Nicholls Private	Feb 28, 1777, Duration of War	Second, Allen	Dec 1777 sick in hospital; Jan-Feb 1778 sick absent; March 1778; April 1778 on command Radnor; May-June 1778.
Winman, Charles Private		First, Flagg	Dec 1777-March 1778 sick present; April 6, 1778 died.
Winslow/Windslow, Church Private		Second, Allen	Jan-March 1778 on command May 1778 sick present; June 1778.
Wise, John Drum Major		First	Dec 1777-March 1778 on command; April 1778 on command at Peekskill.
Woggs/Waggs, Elijah Private	May 1, 1777, Three Years	First, Lewis	Dec 1777 waggoner; Jan-April 1778.
Woggs, Elijah Private	Three	First, Arnold	May 1778; June 1778 on command.
Wood, John Private	May 9, 1777, Three Years	Second, Olney. S.	Dec 1777; Jan-Feb 1778 on guard; March 1778; April 1778 on command at the lines; May-June 1778.

Woodard/ Woodward, Joshua Private	May 27, 1777, Three Years	Second, Potter	Dec 1777-Jan 1778; Feb-March 1778 on command; April 1778 sick present; May-June 1778 sick absent at Yellow Springs.
Woodman, Sylvester Private	May 15, 1777	First, Talbot	Dec 1777-Jan 1778 sick absent; Feb-March 1778; April 1778 on duty picket.
Woodman, Sylvester Private	Three Years	Second, Dexter	May-June 1778.
Woodrow/ Woodro, Richard Private	Duration of War	Second, Shaw	Jan 1778 on command; Feb-April 1778.
Young, Enoch Private	Jan 1, 1777, Three Years	Second, Olney, C.	Dec 1777; Jan 15, 1778 deserted.
York, John Private	Jan 1, 1777, Duration of War	Second, Hughes	Dec 1777-June 1778.

BIBLIOGRAPHY

The following publications were not used in compiling the above lists. However they can provide additional information for researchers on the Valley Forge Encampment and New Hampshire and Rhode Island men in the Revolutionary War.

Aldrich, Edgar. "The Affair of the Cedars and the Service of Col. Timothy Bedel in the War of the Revolution." *New Hampshire Historical Society Proceedings*, 3 (December 1891), 194-231.

Amory, Thomas C. *The Military Services and Public Life of Major-General John Sullivan of the American Revolutionary Army.* Boston: Wiggin and Lunt, 1868.

_____. "General John Sullivan." *Pennsylvania Magazine of History and Biography*, 2 (1878), 196-210.

_____. "A Justification of General Sullivan." *Magazine of American History*, 3 (September 1879), 550-554.

Angell, Israel. *Diary of Colonel Israel Angell, Commanding the Second Rhode Island Continental Regiment during the American Revolution, 1778-1781; Transcribed from the Original Manuscript, Together with a Biographical Sketch of the Author and Illustrative Notes.* ed. Edward Field. Providence, 1899; reprint, New York: Arno Press, 1971.

____. "The Israel Angell Diary, 1 October 1777-28 February 1778," *Rhode Island History*, ed. Joseph Lee Boyle. 58 (November 2000), 106-138.

Archambault, Alan H. "The Second Rhode Island Regiment of the Continental Line 1775-1777." *Military Collector and Historian*, 28 (Fall 1976), 133.

_____. and Marko Zlatich. "Rhode Island Regiment, 1781-1783." *Military Collector and Historian*, 36 (Summer 1984), 77.

Arnold, James N. *Vital Records of Rhode Island, 1636-1850.... vol. 12, Revolutionary Rolls & Newspapers*, 1901; reprint, Salem, Ma.: Higginson Book Co., 1994.

Baker, Henry M. "General Enoch Poor." *Journal of American History*, 15 (April 1921), 117-132.

Bartlett, John Russell, ed. *Records of the Colony of Rhode Island and Providence Plantations, in New England, 1636-1792*. (Providence: Greene, 10 vols, 1856-65; reprint New York: AMS Press, 1968. Volume 7 covers 1770-1776, volume 8 1776-1779, and volume 9 1780-1783.

Beane, Samuel Collins. "General Enoch Poor." *Proceedings of the New Hampshire Historical Society*, 3 (1895-1899), 435-472.

Benninghoff, Herman O. III. *Valley Forge: A Genesis for Command and Control*. Gettysburg, Pa: Thomas Publications, 2001.

Bicknell, T. W. *Barrington Soldiers in the War of the Revolution, the Dorr War and the War of the Rebellion*. 1898.

Bingham, Hiram Jr., *Five Straws Gathered from Revolutionary Fields*. Cambridge: Harvard University Press, 1901. Letters by Paymaster William Weeks of the Third New Hampshire.

Bockstruck, Lloyd DeWitt. *Revolutionary War Bounty Land Grants Awarded by State Governments*. Baltimore: Genealogical Publishing Co., 1996.

Bodle, Wayne K. The *Valley Forge Winter: Civilians and Soldiers in War*. University Park, Pa: Penn State University Press, 2002.

_____. "The Vortex of Small Fortunes: The Continental Army at Valley Forge, 1777-1778." Ph. D. Dissertation, University of Pennsylvania, 1987.

Bouton, Nathaniel, et al., eds. *Documents and Records Relating to the Towns and State of New Hampshire*. 40 vols. Concord, Nashua and Manchester: Various publishers, 1867-1943.

Brown, Ann S. K. "Rhode Island Uniforms in the Revolution." *Military Collection and Historian,* 10 (Spring 1958): 1-10.

Brown, John Elliot. *Some Rhode Island Veterans of the American Revolution*. New Ipswich, N.H.: 1928.

Burton, Jonathan. *Diary and Orderly Book of Sergeant Jonathan Burton of Wilton, N.H., While in Service in the Army on Winter Hill, December 10, 177-January 26, 1776, and...While in the Canada Expedition at Mount Independence...1776*. ed. by Isaac W. Hammond. Concord: Republican Press Association, 1885.

Carlson, Paul C., "James Mitchell Varnum and the American Revolution," unpublished M. A. essay, Wesleyan University, May 1, 1965.

Chamberlain, Mildred M. *The Rhode Island 1777 Military Census.* Baltimore: Genealogical Publishing Co., 1985. Originally published in installments in *Rhode Island Roots* between December 1981 and September 1984.

Clark, Murtie June. *The Pension Lists of 1792-1795, With Other Revolutionary War Pension Records.* 1991; reprint, Baltimore: Genealogical Publishing Co., 1996.

Clough, William O. "Colonel Alexander Scammell." *Granite Monthly,* 14 (September 1892), 262-275.

"Conduct of the Black Regiment in the Action of August 29th, 1778, on Rhode Island, as Given by the Orderly Books of the Army," *Rhode Island Historical Tracts,* 6 Providence: Sidney S. Rider, 1878.

Conlon, Noel P. "Rhode Island Negroes in the Revolution: A Bibliography." *Rhode Island History,* 29 (February-May 1970), 52-53.

Cook, Frederick ed, *Journals of the Military Expedition of Major General John Sullivan Against the Six Nations of Indians in 1779 with Records of Centennial Celebrations.* Auburn, N.Y.: Knapp, Peck & Thomson, 1887. This contains journals kept by a number of New Hampshire soldiers.

Cornelius, Elias. *Journal of Dr. Elias Cornelius, a Revolutionary Surgeon: A Graphic Description of His Sufferings While a Prisoner in Provost Jail, New York, 1777 and 1778, with Biographical Sketch.* Washington, D.C.: privately printed, 1903.

Cowell, Benjamin. *Spirit of '76 in Rhode Island: or Sketches of the Efforts of the Government and People in the War of the Revolution.* 1850; reprint, Salem, Ma.: Higginson Book Co., 1996.

David, Ebenezer. *A Rhode Island Chaplain in the Revolution: Letters of Ebenezer David to Nicholas Brown 1775-1778.* ed. by Jeannette D. Black and William Greene Roelker. Providence: Rhode Island Society of the Cincinnati, 1949.

Dearborn, Henry, *Revolutionary War Journals of Henry Dearborn 1775-1783.* ed. by Lloyd A. Brown and Howard H. Peckham. Chicago: The Caxton Club, 1939; reprint, N.Y.: Da Capo Press, 1971.

Field, Edward. *Revolutionary Defences in Rhode Island; an Historical Account of the Fortifications and Beacons Erected during the American Revolution; with Muster Rolls of the Companies Stationed along the Shores of Narragansett Bay.* Providence: Preston and Rounds, 1896.

Fletcher, Ebenezer. *The Narrative of Ebenezer Fletcher, a Soldier of the Revolution, Written by Himself.* ed. by Charles I. Bushnell. New York: Privately printed, 1866.

Fogg, Jeremiah. *Orderly Book Kept by Jeremiah Fogg, Adjutant Colonel Enoch Poor's Second New Hampshire Regiment on Winter Hill, During the Siege of Boston, October 28, 1775, to January 12, 1776.* ed. by Albert A. Folsom. Exeter: *Exeter News-Letter*, 1903.

Foster, John. "The Story of a Private Soldier in the Revolution." *Manchester Historic Association Collections*, 3 (July-September 1902), 86-96.

Fuller, Oliver P. *The History of Warwick, Rhode Island.* Warwick, R.I.: Angell, Burlingame and Co., 1875.

Gardiner, Asa Bird. "General James M. Varnum of the Continental Army," *Magazine of American History* 18, no. 3 (September 1887), 184-93.

Gardiner, Asa B. *The Rhode Island Line in the Continental Army and Its Society of Cincinnati.* Providence: Providence Press Co., 1878.

Giller, Sayde. *Corrections to the Index of Revolutionary War Pension Applications in the National Archives.* Baltimore: Genealogical Publishing Co., 1965.

Gilmore, George C. *Roll of New Hampshire Soldiers at the Battle of Bennington, August 16, 1777.* Manchester, N.H.: John B. Clarke, 1951.

Godfrey, Carlos E. *The Commander-in-Chief's Guard: Revolutionary War* Washington, D.C.: Stevenson-Smith Co., 1904; reprint, Baltimore: Genealogical Publishing Co., 1972.

Goodwin, William F., ed. "Colonel Alexander Scammell and His Letters, From 1768 to 1781, Including His 'Love Letters' to Miss Nabby Bishop." *Historical Magazine*, 2d ser., 8 (1870), 129-46.

_____. ed. "Revolutionary Officers of New Hampshire Regiments." *Historical Magazine*, 2d. ser., 4 (1868): 199-201.

Greene, Christopher. "Orderly Book October 11, 1777, to November 20, 1777." *New Jersey Society of Pennsylvania Yearbook*: 1928.

Greene, Lorenzo J. "Some Observations on the Black Regiment of Rhode Island in the American Revolution." *Journal of Negro History* 37, (1952), 142-72.

Greene, Mary A. "Christopher Greene, the Hero of Red Bank." *American Monthly Magazine*, 2 (May 1893), 521-26.

Greenman, Jeremiah. *Diary of a Common Soldier in the American Revolution, 1775-1783; An Annotated Edition of the Military Journal of Jeremiah Greenman*. ed. by Robert C. Bray and Paul E. Bushnell. DeKalb: Northern Illinois University Press, 1978.

Hadley, Amos. "Poor's brigade." *Granite Monthly*, 3 (1879-80), 60-64.

Hammond, Isaac W., ed. *State Papers: Documents and Records Relating to the Province, Towns and State of New Hampshire*, Vols. 14-17, "Revolutionary Rolls," 5 vols. (Concord and Manchester: The State of New Hampshire, 1885-1889; reprint, New York: AMS Press, 1973.

Hammond, Otis G, ed.. *Letters and Papers of Major-General John Sullivan, Continental Army*, 3 vols. Concord: New Hampshire Historical Society, 1930-1939. (Collections of the New Hampshire Historical Society, Vols. 13, 14, 15).

Heitman, Francis. *Historical Register of Officers of the Continental Army during the War of the Revolution, April 1777 to December 1783*. Washington, D.C: Rare Book Shop Publishing Co.; reprint, Baltimore: Genealogical Publishing Co., 1969.

Hitchcock, Enos. "Diary of Enos Hitchcock, D.D.: A Chaplain in the Revolutionary Army." ed. William B. Weeden. *Publications of the Rhode Island Historical Society*, n. s. 7 (1899-1900), 87-134, 147-194, 207-231.

Hitchcock, Dan. "So Few the Brave (The Second Rhode Island 1777-1781)." *Military Collector and Historian* 30 (1978), 18-22.

Humphrey, William. "A Journal Kept by William Humphrey of Capt. Thayer's Company, on a March to Quebec...1775-1776." *Magazine of History*, extra no. 166.

Huntington, Rev. E.B. *Stanford Soldiers Memorial*. Stanford, R.I.: 1869.

Index of Revolutionary War Pensions. Washington, D.C.: National Genealogical Society, 1966.

Jackson John W. *Valley Forge: Pinnacle of Courage*. Gettysburg, Pa: Thomas Publications, 1992.

Kidder, Frederick. *History of the First New Hampshire Regiment in the War of the Revolution*. Albany: Joel Munsell, 1868.

Knoblock, Glenn A. *"Strong and Brave Fellows": New Hampshire's Black Soldiers and Sailors of the American Revolution, 1775-1784*. Jefferson, N.H.: McFarland & Co., 2003.

Livermore, Daniel. "Orderly Book of Capt. Daniel Livermore's Company, Continental Army." ed. Isaac C. Hammond. *New Hampshire Historical Society Collections*, 9 (1889): 200-244.

Livermore, George. *An Historical Research Respecting the Opinions of the Founders of the Republic on Negroes as Slave, as Citizens, and as Soldiers*. Boston: A. Williams, 1863.

Lovell, Louise Lewis. *Israel Angell, Colonel of the 2nd Rhode Island Regiment*. New York: Knickerbocker Press, 1921.

McMullin, Phillip W. ed. *Grassroots of America*. Salt Lake City: Gendex Corp., 1972. This indexes the 38 volumes of the American State Papers.

Maslowski, Pete. "National Policy Toward the Use of Black Troops in the Revolution," *South Carolina Historical Review*, 73 (January 1972), 1-17.

Metcalfe, Bryce. *Original Members and Other Officers Eligible to the Society of the Cincinnati, 1783-1938*. The Society of the Cincinnati.

Minority Military Service, Rhode Island, 1775-1783. Washington, D.C.: National Society, Daughters of the American Revolution, 1988.

Moore, Howard Parker. *A Life of General John Stark of New Hampshire*. New York: Privately printed, 1949.

Murray, Thomas H. Irish *Rhode Islanders in the American Revolution with Some Mention of Those Serving in the Regiments of Elliott, Lippitt, Topham,*

Crary, Angell, Olney, Greene, and Other Noted Commanders. Providence: American-Irish Historical Society, 1903.

Neagles, James C. and Lila L. Neagles. *Locating Your Revolutionary War Ancestor: A Guide to the Military Records.* Logan, Ut.: The Everton Publishers, 1983.

Neimeyer, Charles P. *America Goes to War: A Social History of the Continental Army.* NY: New York University Press, 1996.

_____. "No Meat, No Soldier: Race, Class, and Ethnicity in the Continental Army." Ph. D. Dissertation, Georgetown University, 1993.

Nell, William Cooper, *The Colored Patriots of the American Revolution....* Boston: F. Walcutt, 1855.

New Hampshire American Revolution Bicentennial Commission. *New Hampshire's Role in the American Revolution, 1763-1789: A Bibliography.* Concord: New Hampshire State Library, 1974.

Newman, Debra S. *List of Black Servicemen, Compiled from the War Department Collections of Revolutionary War Records.* National Archives Special List No. 36 Washington, D.C.: National Archives, 1974.

Peterson, Clarence S. *Known Military Dead during the Revolutionary War.* Baltimore, 1959; reprint, Baltimore: Genealogical Publishing Co., 1967.

Pierce's Register. *Register of the Certificates Issued by John Pierce, Esquire, Paymaster General and Commissioner of Army Accounts for the United States, to Officers and Soldiers of the Continental Army Under Act of July 4, 1783.* 1915; reprint, Baltimore: Genealogical Publishing Co., 1987.

Pillsbury, Hobart. "New Hampshire's Memorial at Valley Forge." *Granite Monthly*, 51 (1919), 283-86.

Potter, Chandler Eastman. Military *History of New Hampshire, From Its Settlement, in 1623, to the Year 1861.* 2 vols. Concord: Adjutant General's Office, 1866-68.

Potter, Israel. *Life and Remarkable Adventures of Israel R. Potter,...Who was a Soldier in the American Revolution...after Which He Was Taken Prisoner by the British, Conveyed to England, Where for Thirty Years He Obtained a Livelihood for Himself and Family*. Providence, 1824; reprint, *Magazine of History*, extra no. 16.

Preston, Howard Willis. *The Battle of Rhode Island: August 29th, 1778*. Providence: State of Rhode Island and Providence Plantations, Office of the Secretary of State, State Bureau of Information. 1928.

Providence, City of. *Names of Officers, Soldiers and Seamen in Rhode Island Regiments*. Providence: Providence Press Co., 1869.

Quarles, Benjamin. *The Negro in the American Revolution*. Chapel Hill, N.C.: 1961.

Reed, Silvanus. "Orderly Book of Adjutant Silvanus Reed." ed. Isaac W. Hammond. *New Hampshire Historical Society Collections*, 9 (1889), 264-414.

Resch, John P. "The Continentals of Peterborough, New Hampshire: Pension Records as a Source for Local History." *Prologue*, 16 (Fall 1984), 169-83.

Revolutionary Correspondence From 1775 to 1782. Rhode Island Historical Society Collections, vol 6, part 2. Providence Rhode Island Historical Society, 1867.

Revolutionary War Records and Biographical Sketches of the Ancestors of Rhode Island Daughters of the American Revolution 3 vols. State Society, Daughters of the American Revolution.

Rider, Sidney S. *An Historical Inquiry Concerning the Attempt to Raise a Regiment of Slaves by Rhode Island during the War of the Revolution*. Rhode Island Historical Tracts, no. 10, Providence: Sidney S. Rider, 1880.

Scammell, Alexander. "Two Letters of Col. Alexander Scammell." *Magazine of American History*, 10 (August 1883), 151-55.

_____. "Colonel Alexander Scammell and His Letters, From 1768 to 1781, Including His 'Love Letters' to Miss Nabby Bishop." *Historical Magazine*, 2d Ser., 8 (September 1870), 129-46.

Smith, John. "Sergeant John Smith's Diary of 1776." ed. Louise Rau. *Mississippi Valley Historical Review*, 20 (1933): 247-70.

Smith, Jonathan Peterborough, *New Hampshire, in the American Revolution* 1913; reprint, Earlysville, Va.: Old Books Publishing, 1996.

Smith, Jonathan "How New Hampshire Raised Her Armies for the Revolution," *The Granite Monthly: New Hampshire State Magazine*, 54 (1922), 7-18.

Smith, Joseph J. *Civil and Military List of Rhode Island, 1647-1800*. 2 vols. Providence: Preston and Rounds, 1901.

Smith, Samuel. *Memoirs of Samuel Smith, a Soldier of the Revolution, 1776-1786. Written by Himself.* ed. Charles I. Bushnell. New York: Privately printed, 1860. (originally published Middleborough, Mass.: Privately printed, 1853).

Spoffard, Charles B., comp. *Soldiers of the Revolution Who Enlisted from; or Afterwards Lived in Claremont, New Hampshire With a List of the Pensioners Living in Sullivan County Under Act of June 7, 1832 and a Muster Roll of Captain Joseph Taylor's Company*. Claremont, N.H.: Nathan W. Fay, 1894.

Stark, Caleb, *Memoir and Official Correspondence of Gen. John Stark, With Notice of Several Other Officers of the Revolution....* Concord: G. Parker Lyon, 1860.

State of Rhode Island...In General Assembly, February 14, 1778. "Bill permitting Slaves to inlist into the Continental Battalions." Attleborough: Printed by S. Southwick, (1778), 14-18, 21, 23.

State of Rhode Island...In General Assembly, May 1778. "No Slave to inlist after the 10th of June next." Providence: Printed by John Carter, (1778), 15.

Stewart, Mrs. Frank Ross. *Black Soldiers in the American Revolutionary War.* Centre, Ala.: Stewart University Press, 1978.

Sullivan, John. *Letters and Papers of Major-General John Sullivan, Continental Army.* ed. by Otis G. Hammond. 3 vols. Concord: New Hampshire Historical Society, 1930-1939.

Thayer, Simeon. "A Journal of the Indefatigable March of Col. Benedict Arnold...in the Years 1775-1776." In Edwin Martin Stone, ed., *The Invasion of Canada in 1775*, 1-45. *Collections of the Rhode Island Historical Society*, vol. 6. Providence, 1867. Also in Kenneth Roberts, ed. *March to Quebec*. New York: Doubleday, Doran & Co., 1938, 247-94.

Topham, John. "Journal of the Quebec Expedition." *Magazine of History*, extra no. 50.

Tuckerman, Henry T. *The Life of Silas Talbot, a Commodore in the Navy of the United States*. New York: J. C. Riker, 1850,

U. S. Congress, Walter Lowrie and Walter S. Franklin, eds. *American State Papers; Documents, Legislative and Executive, on the Congress of the United States, from the First Session of the First to the Second Session of the Seventeenth Congress, inclusive; Commencing March 4, 1789, and Ending March 8, 1823. Class IX Claims*. Washington, D.C.: 1834. Contains much information on thousands of Revolutionary War service claims filed in Congress. See McMullin, Phillip W. Grassroots of America, for a thorough index.

U. S. Congress. *Digested Summary and Alphabetical List of Private Claims, Which Have Been Presented to the House of Representatives from the First to the Thirty-first Congress*. 3 vols. House. Misc. Doc.; reprint, Baltimore: Genealogical Publishing Co., 1970.

U. S. Department of the Interior. *Report of the Secretary of the Interior, with a Statement of Rejected or Suspended Applications for Revolutionary War Pensions, 1852*. Sen. Exec. Doc. 37; reprint, Baltimore: Genealogical Publishing Co., 1969.

U. S. House of Representatives. *Resolutions, Laws, and Ordinances, Relating to the Pay, Half Pay, Commutation of Half Pay, Bounty Lands...Officers and Soldiers of the Revolution...and to Funding Revolutionary Debt*. 1838; reprint, Baltimore: Genealogical Publishing Co., 1998.

U. S. War Department. *Letter from the Secretary of War, Communicating a Transcript of the Pension List of the United States - June 1, 1813*. Washington, D.C., 1813; reprinted as *Revolutionary Pensioners; a Transcript of the Pension List of 1813*. Baltimore: Genealogical Publishing Co., 1959.

U.S. War Department. *Letter from the Secretary of War, Transmitting a Report of the Names, Rank and Line of Every Person Placed on the Pension List, in Pursuance of the Act of 18th March 1818*. Washington, D.C., 1820; reprint, Baltimore: Genealogical Publishing Co., 1955.

U. S. War Department. *Message from the Presidents of the United States, Transmitting a Report of the Secretary of War in Compliance "A list of the pensioners of the United States, the sum annually paid to each, and the state or territories in which the said pensioners reside*. Washington, D.C., 1818; reprinted as *Revolutionary Pensioners of 1818*. Baltimore: Southern Book Co., 1959.

U.S. War Department. *Letter From the Secretary of War, Transmitting a List of the Names of Pensioners Under the Act of 18th of March, 1818, Whose Names Were Struck Off the List by Act of 1st May, 1820, and Subsequently Restored.* Washington, D.C.: 1836; reprinted as *Pensioners of Revolutionary War—Struck Off the Roll.* Baltimore: Genealogical Publishing Co., 1969.

U.S. War Department. *Report from the Secretary of War...in Relation to the Pension Establishment of the United States*, 3 vols. 1834, Sen. Doc. 514, reprinted as *The Pension Roll of 1835.* Baltimore: Genealogical Publishing Co., 1968.

U. S. War Department. *Revolutionary Pensioners: A Transcript of the Pension list for the United States for 1813.* 1813; reprint, Baltimore: Clearfield Co., 1997.

Varnum, James Mitchell. *A Sketch of the Life and Public Services of James Mitchell Varnum of Rhode Island.* Boston: D. Clapp & Son, 1906.

Waldenmaier, Nellie Protsman. *Some of the Earliest Oaths of Allegiance in the United States of America.* Lancaster, Pa.: Privately printed, 1944.

Walker, Anthony. *So Few the Brave: Rhode Island Continentals, 1775-1783.* Newport, R.I.: Seafield Press, 1981.

Ward, John. *A Memoir of Lieut.-Col. Samuel Ward, First Rhode Island Regiment, Army of the American Revolution; with a Genealogy of the Ward Family.* New York: Privately printed, 1875. Reprinted from *New York Genealogical and Biographical Record*, 6 (July 1875), 113-28.

Washington, George. *The Writings of George Washington from the Original Manuscript Sources, 1745-1799.* 39 vols. ed. John C. Fitzpatrick. Washington, D.C.: Library of Congress, 1931-1944.

Watson, Elkanah. *Men and Times of the Revolution; or, Memoirs of Elkanah Watson, Including Journals of Travels in Europe and America, from 1777 to 1842, with His Correspondence with Public Men and Reminiscences and Incidents of the Revolution.* ed. Winslow C. Watson. New York: 1856.

Wheeler, Bennett. "Extract from the Diary of Major Bennett Wheeler: The British in Rhode Island." *Publications of the Rhode Island Historical Society*, n. s. 6 (1898): 91.

Whittemore, Charles P. *A General of the Revolution: John Sullivan of New Hampshire.* New York: Columbia University Press, 1961.

Williams, Catherine R. *Biography of Revolutionary Heroes; Containing the Life of Brigadier Gen. William Barton, and Also, of Captain Stephen Olney.* New York: Wiley & Putnam, 1839.

Witcher, William F. *The Relation of New Hampshire Men to the Siege of Boston.* Concord: Rumford Printing Co., 1904.

Worthen, Samuel Copp. "Colonel Pierse Long's Regiment: Portsmouth Man's Exploits Shed Lustre on Military Annals of State During Revolution." *Granite Monthly,* 57 (1925): 262-66.

www.ingramcontent.com/pod-product-compliance
Lightning Source LLC
Chambersburg PA
CBHW070259230426
43664CB00014B/2583